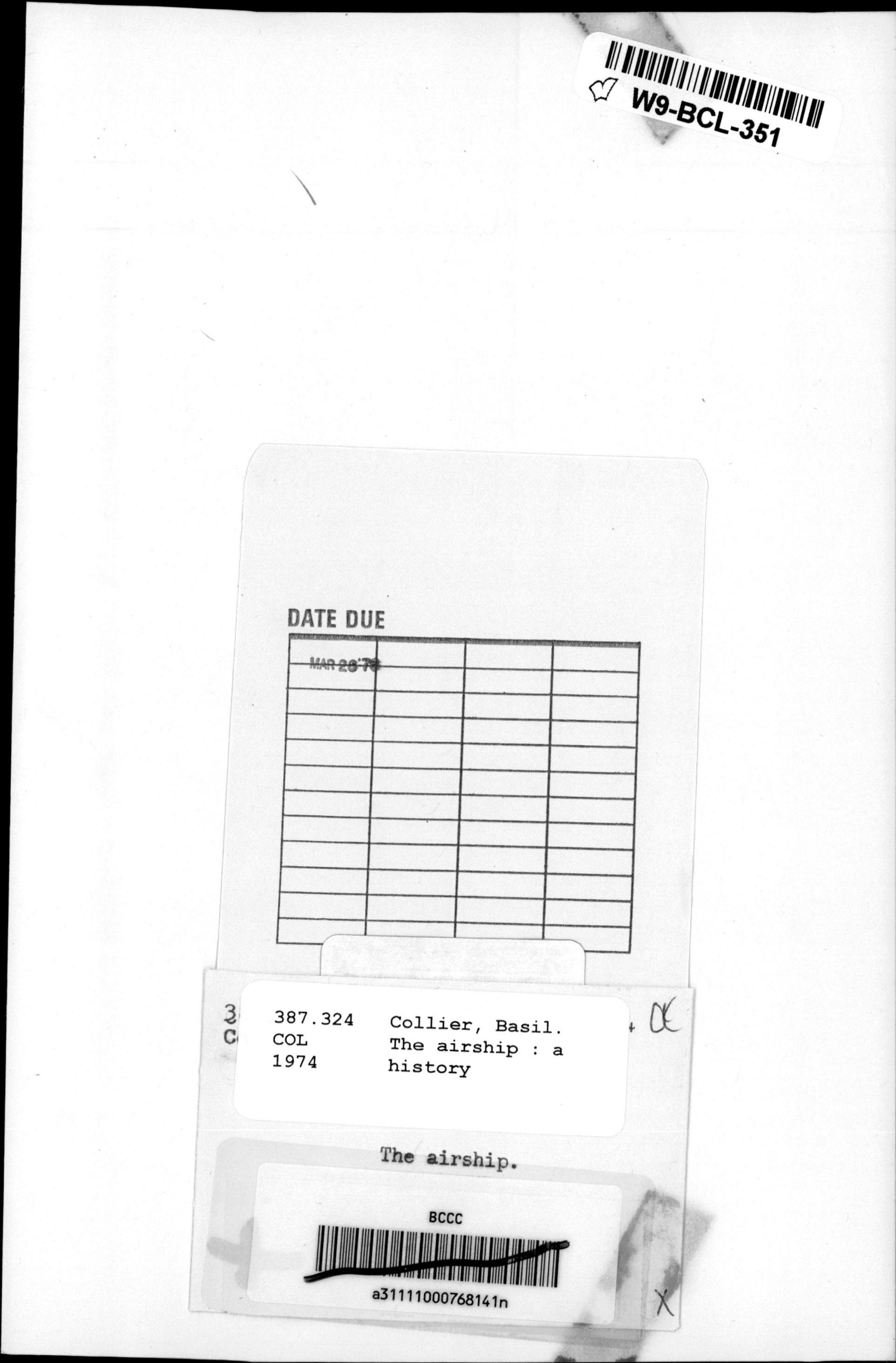

The Airship

Also by Basil Collier

The Defence of the United Kingdom
The Battle of Britain
The Battle of the V-Weapons, 1944–1945
A Short History of the Second World War
The War in the Far East, 1941–1945
The Lion and the Eagle:
British and Anglo-American Strategy, 1900–1950
A History of Air Power

Basil Collier

The Airship

A History

FOUNDED 1838
GPPS

G. P. Putnam's Sons, New York

FIRST AMERICAN EDITION 1974

SBN: 399-11430-0
Library of Congress Catalog Card Number: 74-14386

PRINTED IN THE UNITED STATES OF AMERICA

Contents

Acknowledgements 7
Author's preface 9

1 Beginnings 15
2 The airship flies 28
3 The rigid airship: 1895–1914 52
4 Airships in World War I: 1914–15 68
5 Airships in World War I: 1916 85
6 Airships in World War I: 1917–18 114
7 The post-War Years 148
8 New Horizons 161
9 The intercontinental airship: 1928–30 181
10 The intercontinental airship: 1930–37 196
11 Yesterday and tomorrow 218

Appendices
1 German rigid airships completed before the First World War *240*
2 German naval airships, 1914–18 *242*
3 German military airships, 1914–18 *243*
4 United States naval airships, 1916–64 *244*

Bibliography 247
Notes 250

Tables
1 German airship raids on Britain, 1915: Phase One *255*
2 German airship raids on Britain, 1915: Phase Two *256*
3 German airship raids on Britain, 1916: Phase One *257*
4 German airship raids on Britain, 1916: Phase Two *258*
5 German airship raids on Britain, 1917 *259*
6 German airship raids on Britain, 1918 *260*
7 Ship's company of airship *Italia*, 23 May 1928 *261*

Index 262

Acknowledgements

The photographs and illustrations in this book are reproduced by kind permission of the following. Those on pages 8, 17, 19, 23, 27, 33, 41, 44, 157, 166, 194 The Science Museum; pages 21, 29, 30, 31, 59 Musée de l'Air; pages 50, 130, 158, 209, 210, 226, 229 Goodyear; page 32 National Air Space Museum – Smithsonian Institution; pages 34, 39, 65, 76, 153, 162, 170, 205, 206 Radio Times Hulton Picture Library; pages 35, 105 Deutsches Museum – München; page 37 Contemporary Engraving; pages 42, 50, 138, 150, 214, 225 Flight International; the title page and pages 43, 45, 46, 47, 48, 49, 59, 63, 66, 69, 102, 123, 128, 131, 149, 150, 154, 167, 170, 183, 184, 185, 189, 197, 213, 220, 222, 225 The Royal Aeronautical Society; pages 48, 70, 71, 75, 94, 99, 112, 115, 116, 127, 132, 136, 141, 145, 147, 164, 167 The Imperial War Museum; pages 53 and 65 The Department of Prints and Drawings – British Museum; pages 57, 119, 120, 124, 162, 168, 169, 191, 195 Vickers Limited; page 193 Luftschiffbau Zeppelin; page 215 United Press International; pages 216 and 217 The Zeppelin Museum; page 231 The Aereon Corporation, Princeton, New Jersey, USA; pages 232 and 233 Airfloat Transport Limited, London; page 235 Aerospace Development Corporation; page 239 Cargo Airships Limited; Illustration Research supplied the pictures.

Cayley's navigable balloon.

Author's preface

The airship, long regarded by all save a few enthusiasts as an outmoded form of transport or at best a picturesque survival, has begun in recent years to figure in the calculations of sober economists as a possible key to problems of distribution which, if left unsolved, might become a serious obstacle to human progress. I therefore conclude this history of the airship with an account of some current projects for the development of a new generation of large rigid airships intended primarily as freighters.

I think most readers, irrespective of their views about the future, will agree that in the past the potentialities of lighter-than-air machines have, for various reasons, been less fully exploited than they might have been.

One reason is that for many years airships relied for their lift on highly inflammable hydrogen. Helium, which is almost as buoyant as hydrogen and does not burn, did not become available in commercial quantities until some seventy years after the introduction of the airship, and even then it was for some years almost unobtainable outside the United States. Although many more accidents to airships have been due to human errors than to the lethal properties of hydrogen, the destruction by fire of a number of airships in circumstances which attracted wide publicity gave hydrogen-filled airships a bad name. Even today the word 'airship' tends to evoke memories of the loss of the R.101 and the *Hindenburg* and the shooting down of Zeppelins in flames.

Another factor which hampered the development of the airship was the introduction of powered man-carrying aeroplanes at a moment when airships were beginning to be accepted as a reliable means of transport. Henri Giffard, whose name is almost forgotten by the general public, made in an airship as long ago as 1852 the first powered flight ever made by man. But his aerial steamer was too slow to be manoeuvrable in anything but a dead calm or light airs, and he lacked the means of building a bigger and faster ship. The first airship truly dirigible in a twenty-mile-an-hour wind did not appear until fifty years later. Soon afterwards the brothers Wilbur and Orville Wright, of Dayton, Ohio, showed that powered aeroplanes could be controlled in the air and were capable of sustained flight. The machines they devised in the light of experiments with gliders were inherently unstable and difficult to fly, but their efforts stimulated an interest in aviation which soon led to the creation of an aircraft industry devoted to the manufacture of heavier-than-air machines. One consequence was that the airship and the aeroplane, instead of developing along divergent lines as alternative modes of transport, came to be regarded as rivals.

The deleterious effects of this rivalry were aggravated by the outbreak of the First World War. At the beginning of the war the naval and military airships manufactured in Germany by the firms of Zeppelin and Schütte-Lanz could outclimb most contemporary aeroplanes, but the British and the French soon provided themselves with aeroplanes with faster rates of climb and higher ceilings. In an attempt to maintain their lead, the Germans then built airships in which comfort, safety and even speed were sacrificed to the capacity to reach altitudes of 20,000 feet and more. From the point of view of the long-term development of the large rigid airship as a passenger aircraft or freighter, this was a retrograde step, since airships do not give their best performance at such altitudes.

When peace returned, the directors of the Zeppelin organization wished to revert to the commercial airships with which they had made a good beginning before the war, but they were hampered by restrictions imposed by the victorious Allies on the size of the airships they were allowed to build, and by lack of accommodation. The restrictions were removed by the time the successful *Graf Zeppelin* was built, but her dimensions were governed by the size of the shed in which she was constructed. In consequence she was both smaller and slimmer than her designers would have liked to make her, and her performance and payload were correspondingly reduced. Despite her remarkable achievements, she was not quite fast enough or large enough to serve as a perfect example of the revenue-producing commercial airship.

It was left to the British to produce, in the R.100, the first large rigid airship with a true streamlined shape. With a maximum speed in excess of eighty miles an hour, the R.100 was fast by the standards of her day, but her payload was little more than a tenth of that envisaged for the cargo airships of the future. The government's decision to scrap her on grounds of economy after her unsuccessful rival, the R.101, had come to grief left the Germans with a clear field so far as the construction and operation of large commercial airships were concerned. The *Akron* and the *Macon*, completed by the Goodyear-Zeppelin Corporation in the United States in 1931 and 1933 respectively, were essentially naval airships, intended for maritime reconnaissance at long ranges and as airborne aircraft carriers. Both used helium instead of hydrogen, as did all American airships then in service. The Goodyear-Zeppelin Corporation could have built similar airships for commercial purposes

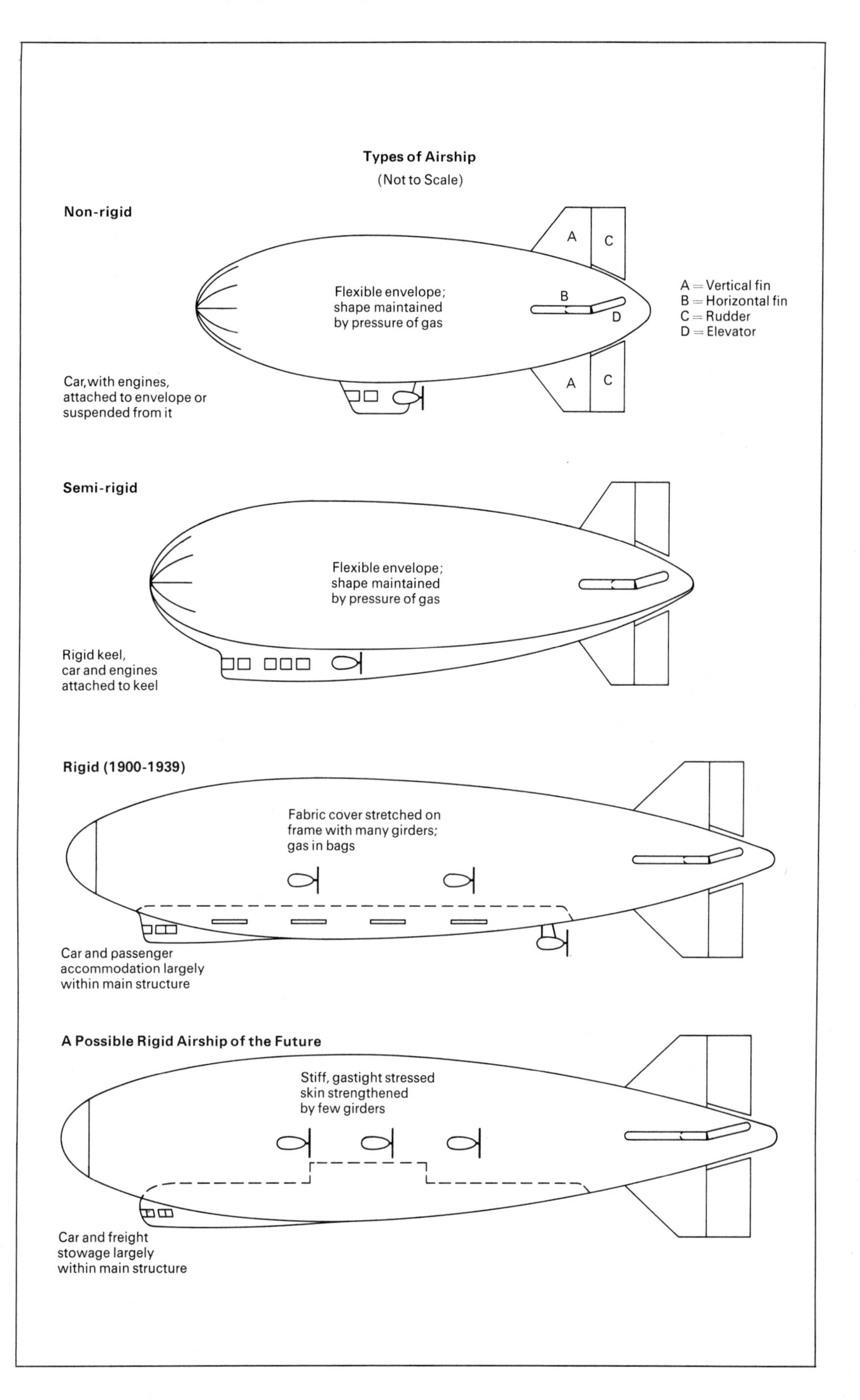

Types of Airship
(Not to Scale)
Non-rigid
A
C
Flexible envelope;
shape maintained
by pressure of gas
B
D
A = Vertical fin
B = Horizontal fin
C = Rudder
D = Elevator
Car, with engines,
attached to envelope or
suspended from it
A
C
Semi-rigid
Flexible envelope;
shape maintained
by pressure of gas
Rigid keel,
car and engines
attached to keel
Rigid (1900-1939)
Fabric cover stretched on
frame with many girders;
gas in bags
Car and passenger
accommodation largely
within main structure
A Possible Rigid Airship of the Future
Stiff, gastight stressed
skin strengthened
by few girders
Car and freight
stowage largely
within main structure

had the necessary financial support been forthcoming, but such airships could have been used on intercontinental routes only if supplies of helium for topping-up had been made available at foreign terminals or staging-posts.

In the outcome, intercontinental flights by passenger-carrying airships ceased when the *Hindenburg* caught fire in 1937 and the veteran *Graf Zeppelin* was withdrawn from service. A new *Graf Zeppelin* was completed in 1938 but was not used commercially. Since the summer of 1939, when the *Graf Zeppelin* made a few flights across the North Sea for the purpose of investigating the British radar chain, the only lighter-than-air machines used either commercially or for naval or military purposes have been relatively small non-rigid or semi-rigid airships. These have been made with gas capacities up to about 1,500,000 cubic feet, as compared with the 5,000,000 cubic feet of the R.100, the 7,000,000 cubic feet of the *Hindenburg*, and the 30,000,000 to 40,000,000 cubic feet envisaged for the large rigid airships of tomorrow.

In the account that follows, the term 'pressure airship' is applied to both non-rigid and semi-rigid airships. The distinction between these two types is sometimes hard to draw, but 'semi-rigid' implies, as a rule, that the airship in question has a rigid keel. The essential characteristic of both types is that the shape of the envelope is maintained by the pressure of the gas inside it. A rigid airship carries her gas in bags inside her hull, and her shape remains the same when the bags are deflated as when they are full.

The term 'lighter-than-air machine' is time-honoured and logical, but open to misconstruction. An airship is truly a lighter-than-air machine inasmuch as her structure weighs less than the air it displaces. When she is flying in perfect aerostatic equilibrium with fuel, crew, ballast and payload aboard her weight is, however, exactly the same as that of the air displaced. She can then rise either by shedding ballast or by putting up her elevators and using the power of her engines to raise her aerodynamically. Aerodynamic lift can also be used to hold up an airship which is overladen or has lost aerostatic lift as the result of an accident to her gas-bags, but a commander who relies on this expedient risks disaster unless he retains a reserve of ballast which can be jettisoned in an emergency.

It must also be borne in mind that the density of the air varies at different heights and is affected by changes in temperature. The term 'pressure height' is used to denote the height at which the valves of an airship are set to open so that gas is vented in order to prevent the envelope of a pressure airship, or the gas-bags of a rigid airship, from bursting as a result of expansion caused by the reduction of atmospheric pressure. As a rule the temperature of the air falls off with increasing altitude, but temperature inversions are not uncommon in mountainous areas, especially near the sea. Thus it can happen that an airship which has valved off gas in order to clear a mountain range has to valve off still more gas in order to descend into a layer of cold air on the far side of it. Since the gas lost cannot be replaced until the ship reaches her destination and is able to top up, commanders of airships do not fly over mountain ranges unless they are compelled to do so.

Such terms as 'gross lift' and 'payload' are likely to be familiar to most readers, but in case they are not the following figures for an imaginary airship with a gas capacity of some 20,000,000 to 25,000,000 cubic feet should help to make their meaning clear:

	Tons
Gross lift, say	600
Less weight of structure	250
Disposable lift	350
Less weight of crew, fuel, provisions, drinking water, spares and ballast, say	100
Payload	250

In practice, the figures would not be so neatly rounded, and the gross lift would be affected by such factors as the degree of inflation and the purity of the gas employed. The weight of the fuel, provisions and drinking water carried would, of course, depend on the length of the voyage in prospect.

In gathering material for this book I have drawn on a wide range of published and unpublished sources. In order to make the bibliography and notes as little baffling as possible to the general reader for whom the book is intended, I have excluded references to unpublished sources and published material not easily accessible, except in a few cases where no other source was available. Readers who need more bibliographic material will find valuable lists of sources, including references to material in public archives and professional libraries, in some of the books listed in my bibliography, and especially in works on particular aspects of the subject by C. F. Snowden Gamble, Robin Higham, Douglas H. Robinson and Richard K. Smith.

I owe much not only to these and other authorities cited in the notes but also to friends and correspondents who have helped me in various ways. For valuable information about current airship projects and transportation problems I am indebted to Mr B. R. V. Hughes of Airfloat

Transport Limited; Mr D. B. Jenkin of Shell International Gas Limited; Mr Arnold Nayler of the Royal Aeronautical Society and the Airship Association; Mr M. J. Rynish of Cargo Airships Limited; Mr John Wood of Aerospace Developments; and Major Malcolm Wren, Royal Engineers. The late Air Chief Marshal Dowding discussed with me on many occasions during the last twelve years of his life, the loss of the R.101 and the circumstances in which the much-canvassed Certificate of Airworthiness was issued. General Umberto Nobile has been kind enough to read the passages dealing with his polar flights, put me right on a number of points, and clear up some obscurities which have puzzled many writers on the subject. My opinion that General Nobile did not deserve the reproaches levelled at him by some critics after the loss of the *Italia* was, however, formed in the light of independent evidence long before I corresponded with him.

The sources of the illustrations are given elsewhere. I wish to acknowledge here my particular indebtedness to the Aeron Corporation, Aerospace Developments, Airfloat Transport Limited and Cargo Airships Limited for providing material not obtainable elsewhere; to the Goodyear Tire and Rubber Company for generously placing photographs from their collection at the disposal of author and publisher; and to Shell International Gas Limited for allowing a photograph of the model prepared by Aerospace Developments to be used.

B.C.

1 Beginnings

In the thirteenth century the Englishman Roger Bacon, Franciscan monk and pioneer in scientific speculation, considered the possibility of human flight with the aid of a thin-walled metal sphere filled with rarefied air or 'liquid fire'. Four hundred years later Francesco Lana di Terzi, an Italian Jesuit priest, imagined an 'aerial ship' upheld by four thin-walled copper spheres devoid of air.

This was not a practical design. The copper spheres would have collapsed under atmospheric pressure when the air was withdrawn from them, and no valid means of propulsion was suggested. Father Francesco seems not to have understood that an airship, because it floats not on but in the air, cannot be effectively propelled by oars or sails.

No real progress towards flight in lighter-than-air craft was made before the second half of the eighteenth century, when experiments with gases by Henry Cavendish, Joseph Priestley and Antoine Lavoisier led to numerous attempts at making balloons with the aid of 'inflammable air', or hydrogen. Contemporary chemists and physicists had a good understanding of the principles involved; the difficulty was to find a material for the envelope which was light enough to serve its purpose and dense enough to prevent the hydrogen from escaping through it.

A translation of a book by Priestley, *Experiments and Observations on Different Kinds of Air*, was published in France in 1776. It came to the attention of Joseph Montgolfier, a partner in a family paper-making business at Annonay, in the valley of the Rhône.[1] Montgolfier succeeded in producing hydrogen, but his attempts to imprison it in an envelope of paper or silk were fruitless. He then turned to hot-air balloons. While staying at Avignon in 1782 he made a small silken hot-air balloon which rose quickly to the ceiling of a room when burning paper was held beneath it. Not knowing that air expands and becomes lighter when heated, he supposed that combustion produced a buoyant gas akin to hydrogen.

Helped by his younger brother Etienne, Joseph Montgolfier went on to carry out experiments in the open air at Annonay with much larger balloons.[2] After trying a weird variety of combustible materials, he settled on a mixture of old rags and straw. This was moistened to make it burn slowly, and probably also in the belief that the emission of copious quantities of evil-smelling smoke was a sign that gas was being produced in abundance.

Like many an inventor before and after him, Joseph Montgolfier sought to justify the time and money spent on his experiments by pointing to a practical application in the field of military strategy. Man-carrying hot-air balloons might, he suggested, be used to mount an airborne invasion os such a place as Gibraltar, besieged at the time by French and Spanish troops who were trying to drive the British out.

Between the early winter of 1782 and the spring of 1783 the Montgolfier brothers made at least four balloons whose capacity was measured in hundreds or thousands of cubic feet. One of these flew nearly a mile at an average height of 800 feet when tested on 25 April 1783.

On 5 June the Montgolfiers demonstrated their latest balloon before a large crowd in the market square at Annonay. Almost a perfect sphere, it measured more than thirty feet across and was made of cloth lined with paper. More than 20,000 cubic feet of hot air made it so buoyant that eight men were needed to hold it down. When released it rose with what seemed majestic slowness to a height estimated at 6,000 feet before a light breeze carried it away. Ten minutes later it came to rest in a field about a mile and a half from its starting point.

The news that two provincial industrialists with no known scientific background had put a large balloon into the air came as a great shock to members of the French Academy who had been grappling with the problem of making a hydrogen balloon. The result was that they accepted an offer from a young engineer named Jacques Charles who said he would find the answer if funds were provided. The money was raised by promising ringside seats at a demonstration to subscribers willing to defray the cost of the experiment.

Charles commissioned two craftsmen, brothers named Robert, to make a suitable envelope at their workshop off the Place des Victoires in Paris. They used what is said to have been a solution of rubber, invented by themselves, to coat a silken envelope about twelve feet across and capable of holding about 900 cubic feet of hydrogen. When ready for inflation, the envelope was suspended from a rope slung between two masts in a neighbouring yard.

Charles and his helpers produced the necessary hydrogen by pouring sulphuric acid into a barrel of iron filings. The process generated so much heat that the envelope had to be drenched with water repeatedly to prevent the hydrogen inside it from catching fire. Moreover, after inflation the envelope was found not to be completely gas-tight.

The demonstration was fixed for 27 August. By 26 August a large crowd had gathered in the Place des Victoires. That night the balloon was placed on a cart and trundled under armed escort to the ampler spaces of the Champ de Mars.

Topping up with hydrogen, and other final preparations, occupied most of the following day. Spectators who had waited since dawn were showing unmistakable signs of impatience when at last, in the late afternoon, Charles was able to give the order to let go. To his inexpressible relief, the balloon rose without a hitch to a height of nearly 3,000 feet and made off to the north-east, drifting in and out of cloud. Forty-five minutes later it descended in a field near Gonesse, about fifteen miles away.

History has censured the inhabitants of Gonesse and its neighbourhood for setting about the balloon with pitchforks and other agricultural implements. But their conduct is understandable. To unlettered rustics the half-deflated balloon, writhing on the ground after descending without warning from the heavens, must have seemed like some monstrous visitor from outer space. Not surprisingly, the envelope was in shreds by the time Charles and the Robert brothers reached the spot.

Just over three weeks later, on 19 September, the Montgolfier brothers demonstrated their invention at Versailles before Louis XVI, various members of his family, and a large gathering of courtiers. A balloon intended for the purpose was

Francesco Lana di Terzi's impractical design of 1670 for an airship supported by empty metal spheres.

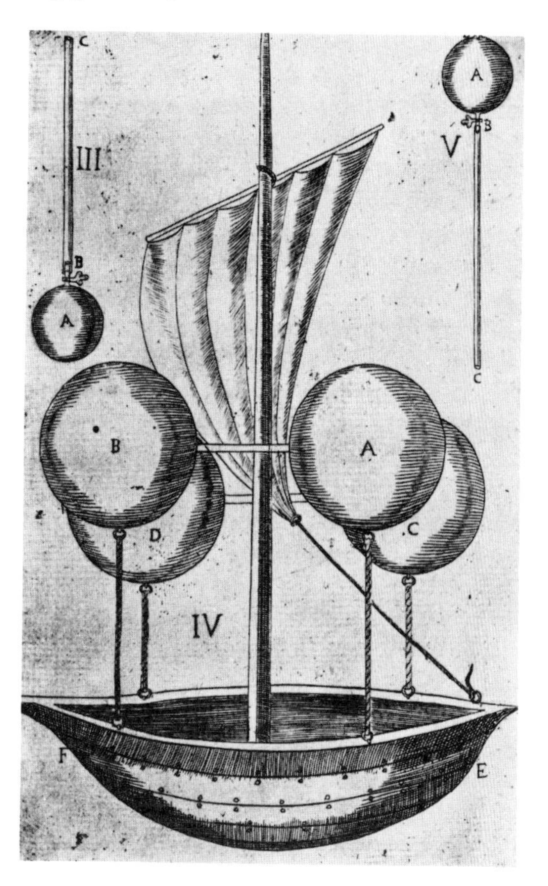

wrecked by a sudden storm on 14 September, but a new one was completed in four days, even to the painting of the royal arms on its envelope. Shaped like a fat pear, it measured fifty-seven feet from top to bottom by forty-one feet across, and carried a wicker cage containing a cock, a sheep and a duck. The Montgolfiers expected it to reach 12,000 feet and remain airborne for at least twenty minutes. Possibly because there were small holes in the fabric, it rose to no more than 1,700 feet and touched down only two miles from its point of departure after an eight-minute flight. A young enthusiast named Jean Pilâtre de Rozier, arriving first on the scene, found that the descent had broken the cage and released the passengers. The sheep and the duck were unharmed. Slight damage to one of the wings of the cock was later found to be due not to the hazards of aerial travel but to a kick from the sheep.

In the light of this experience the King was persuaded, though not without difficulty, to sanction an attempt at a manned flight. At first he insisted that the balloon should be manned by condemned prisoners, who were to be pardoned should they survive the experience. But the Montgolfiers and their friends and admirers had other ideas. Pilâtre asked a fellow-enthusiast, the Marquis d'Arlandes, to use his influence at court. Arlandes spoke to the Duchesse de Polignac, governess to the royal family. The Duchesse de Polignac spoke to the Queen, the ill-fated Marie-Antoinette. Pilâtre and Arlandes became the first men to fly in a free balloon.

The flight was made on 21 November. Pilâtre prepared for it by making a number of ascents with the balloon tethered by a rope. He found that he could control its rise and fall to some extent by feeding the brazier slung below it, or allowing the fire to die down. On the actual flight he and Arlandes carried a reserve of fuel. They also carried damp sponges with which to extinguish any sparks that might settle on parts of the envelope within their reach. Almost at the last moment an unexpected gust of wind toppled the balloon from its launching platform beside the Château de la Muette, in the Bois de Boulogne, but seamstresses among the spectators volunteered to repair the damage. By six minutes to two, when they had finished and the flight began, the wind had dropped and the sun was shining. A gentle breeze carried the balloon across the Seine at a height of less than 1,000 feet and dumped it twenty-five minutes later on the Butte aux Cailles, an eminence commemorated in the Paris of today in the name of a street near the Place d'Italie.

Ten days later, Charles and the elder of

Ascent of a hot-air balloon at Versailles, 19 September 1783.

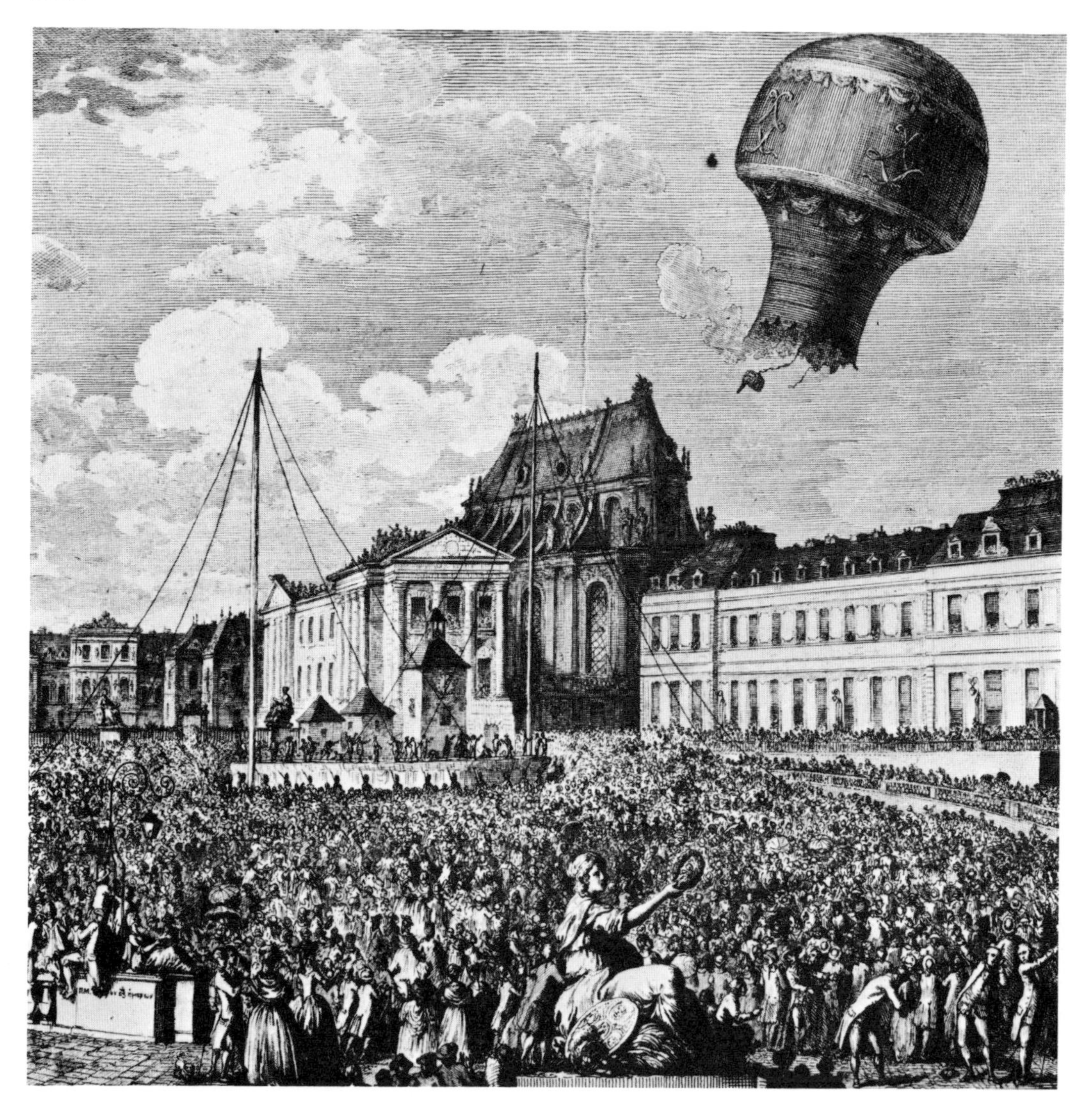

the Robert brothers made the first manned flight in a hydrogen balloon. They used a spherical balloon about twenty-seven feet in diameter, made of pieces of treated silk tapering to a point at each end. Precautions against bursting as a result of expansion of the hydrogen when the balloon rose included an open neck at the bottom of the envelope and a remotely-controlled spring-loaded valve at the top. A boat-shaped car was slung from a wooden hoop suspended by a network of cords from the upper half of the envelope. Charles and his companion made a two-hour flight in perfect weather over Paris and its northern outskirts. At sunset, after they had descended near Nesle, Charles decided on impulse to make a further flight, this time alone. He signalled to the volunteers who were holding the balloon to let go. Lightened by the reduction of its load, it shot up to a height estimated at 10,000 feet. Charles had the satisfaction of being, as far as is known, the first man ever to see the sun set twice in one day. He was also the first man to experience the discomfort which can result from too rapid an ascent to an altitude at which the reduction of atmospheric pressure becomes clearly apparent. Warned by an excruciating pain in one ear that all was not well with him, he pulled the cord which opened the valve at the top of the envelope. Half an hour after taking off on its second flight, the balloon brought its somewhat chastened pilot safely to earth in a ploughed field.

Ballooning soon became not only a fashionable pastime but also a profession. Jean-Pierre Blanchard, a native of Normandy, was among the first aeronauts to offer their services to patrons willing to pay for the privilege of accompanying them on flights which promised to go down in history. Accompanied as far as Sunbury by the celebrated anatomist John Sheldon, Blanchard flew on 16 October 1784 from Chelsea to Romsey, a distance of more than seventy miles. On 7 January 1785 he made the first aerial crossing of the English Channel, flying from Dover to Guisnes in two hours. His passenger was the American Dr John Jeffries, a generous and self-effacing patron who went out of his way to ensure that all the credit for the enterprise went to Blanchard.

Arrested in Austria during the French Revolution on a charge of spreading anti-monarchist propaganda, Blanchard escaped to the United States but afterwards returned to France, where he continued until his death in 1809 to draw a pension granted to him by Louis XVI as a reward for his cross-Channel flight. Altogether he made about sixty ascents, using mostly hydrogen balloons but sometimes hot-air

Jean-Baptiste-Marie Meusnier's classic design of 1784 for a dirigible balloon propelled by airscrews. The flexible pipes through which bellows were to pump air into internal reservoirs, or ballonnets, *are clearly shown.*

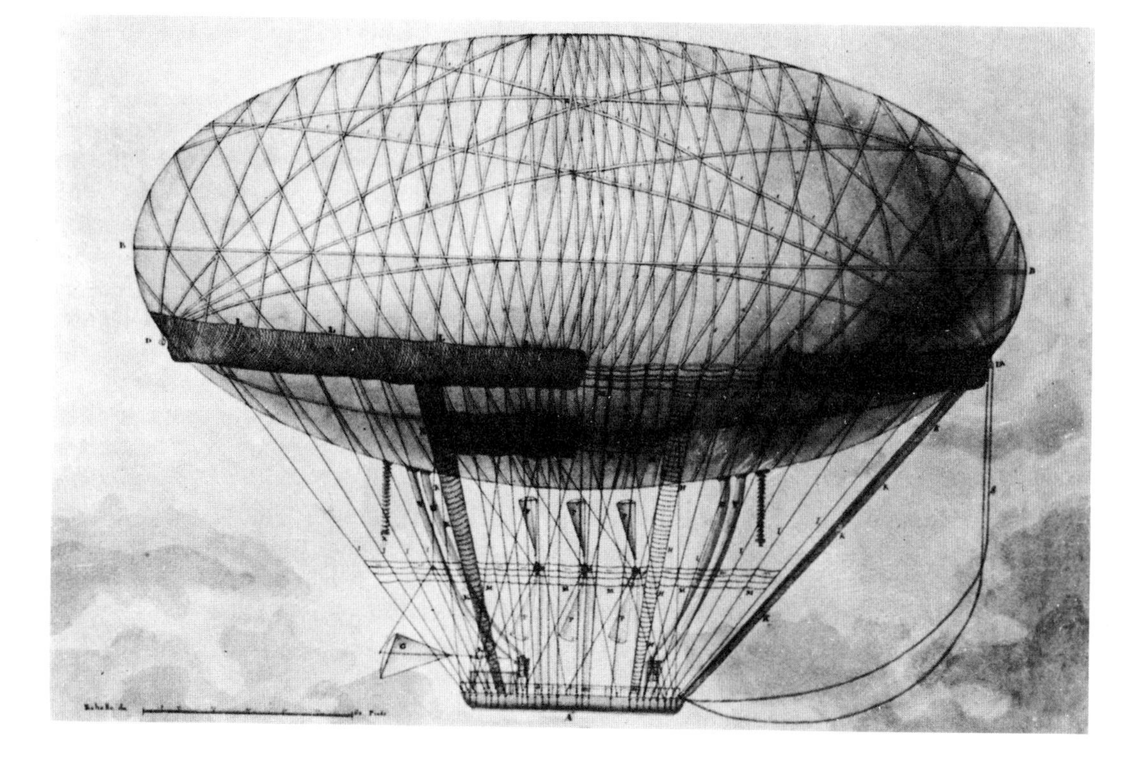

ones. The use of coal-gas as a convenient substitute for hydrogen was introduced by the English balloonist Charles Green about twelve years after Blanchard's death.

Attempts were made by some of the early aeronauts to direct balloons by means of oars or other primitive mechanical devices, but these were foredoomed to failure. In any case the spherical or spheroid form introduced by the Montgolfiers and Charles and adopted by their successors, although very suitable for a free balloon, was by no means the best for a dirigible one.

Credit for giving the airship its familiar shape belongs to Jean-Baptiste Meusnier, a young officer of the engineer corps of the

French Army. Towards the end of 1783 Meusnier submitted to the French Academy a paper on aerostatics.[3] In it he proposed that the envelope of a balloon should contain a kind of reservoir, or inner balloon, into which the balloonist could pump air for the purpose of keeping the pressure inside the envelope constant. This he called a *ballonnet.*

Meusnier first conceived of the *ballonnet* as a means of conserving gas and ballast in a free balloon. He soon saw that it could also play a part in maintaining the elongated shape appropriate to a dirigible balloon. In 1784 he designed a 260-foot-long dirigible balloon of ellipsoid form with such advanced features as a rudder, a rudimentary elevator and three large airscrews. Drawings still extant show that the design was worked out in considerable detail.[4]

When Meusnier worked out his design, the use of an airscrew to propel a boat had already been suggested. Whether he borrowed the idea of the airscrew or arrived at it independently is not known.

Meusnier charted a path followed by most of his successors to the present day, but a serious weakness of his design was the lack of an engine. His airscrews would have had to be rotated manually by members of the crew, and provision was made for this to be done by means of a rope-and-pulley mechanism. Experience with manually propelled airships in the nineteenth century suggests that this arrangement might have worked after a fashion, although probably not very well. But the speed attainable by such means would scarcely have sufficed to make the airship dirigible in anything like a wind, and the weight and bulk of the large crew needed to work the mechanism in relays would have made serious inroads on its disposable lift and the space available for passengers or freight. Moreover, while the forty men postulated by Meusnier could doubtless have been found from the ranks of the army had the military authorities adopted the design, it seems unlikely that any commercial firm could have afforded to pay so many civilian galley slaves.

Perhaps partly for that reason, some of Meusnier's immediate successors turned their backs on the airscrew and reverted to methods of propulsion which could not conceivably have been effective.

A fifty-foot-long balloon of ellipsoid form with a *ballonnet*, based on a design by Meusnier, was built in 1784 by Charles and the Robert brothers. The only means of propulsion provided was a self-defeating umbrella-like device intended to give impetus to the balloon when it was opened and shut. In the same year another elongated balloon with a *ballonnet*, also built by the brothers Robert, flew as a free balloon from Paris to Béthune in less than seven hours. The distance is about 115 miles, but the balloon is said to have covered 150 miles.

Meusnier afterwards returned to his military duties. He became a general but was killed at the Battle of Mainz in 1793.

In 1789 an Englishman named Scott put forward a design for a large dirigible balloon on the lines of Meusnier's proposals. Fore-and-aft trim was to be controlled by two *ballonnets* which would be inflated or deflated to raise or lower nose or tail. But no effective means of propulsion was proposed, and the airship was never built.

In 1816 Durs Egg, a London-domiciled Swiss who was gunsmith to George III, began work in partnership with a compatriot, John Pauly, on a large airship with an envelope made of goldbeater's skin, a material made from the intestines of oxen.

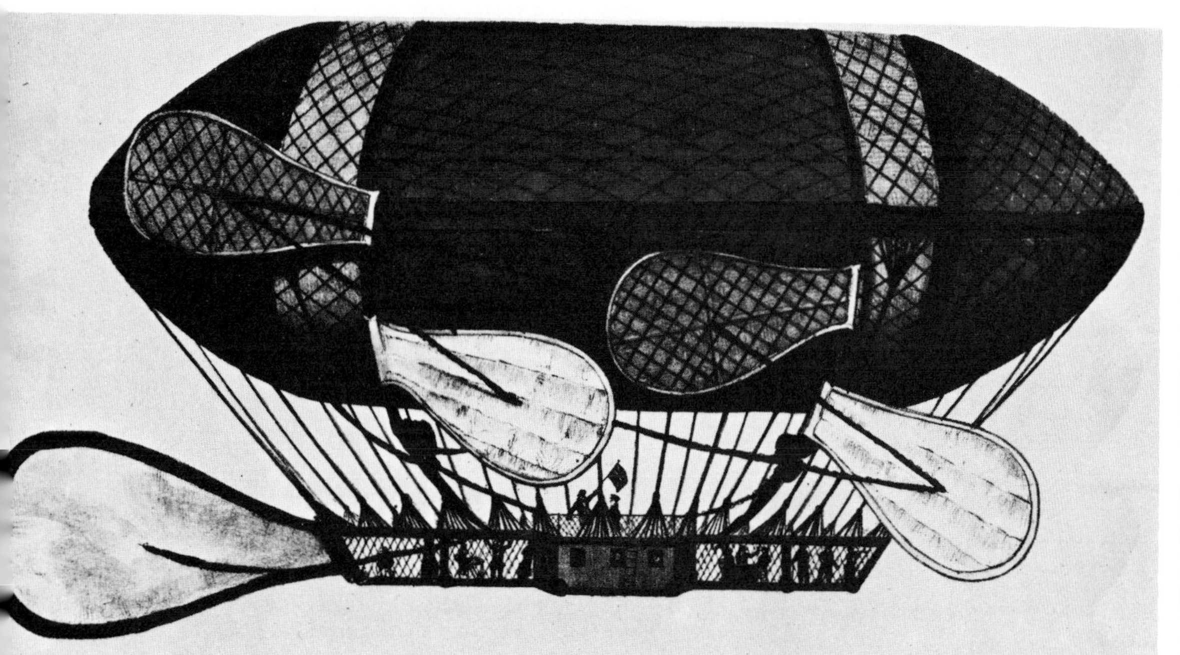

The short-lived Eagle *of 1834. Four of the eight oars, or 'wings', which were to propel the ship between Paris and London are visible, as also is a ninth oar intended to act as a rudder.*

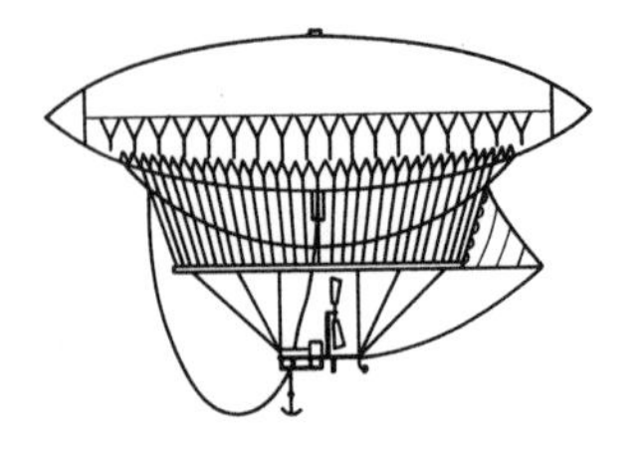

Henri Giffard's Aerial Steamer of 1852
Length 144 feet, diameter amidships 40 feet

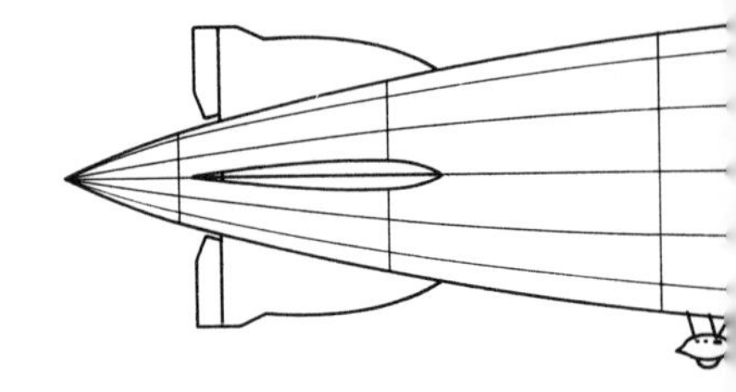

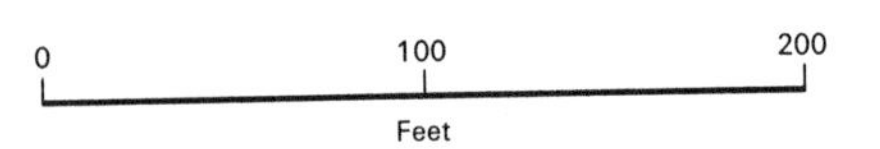

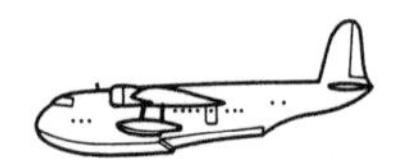

The Short S.23 Empire flying boat of 1936
Length 88 feet, height 32 feet

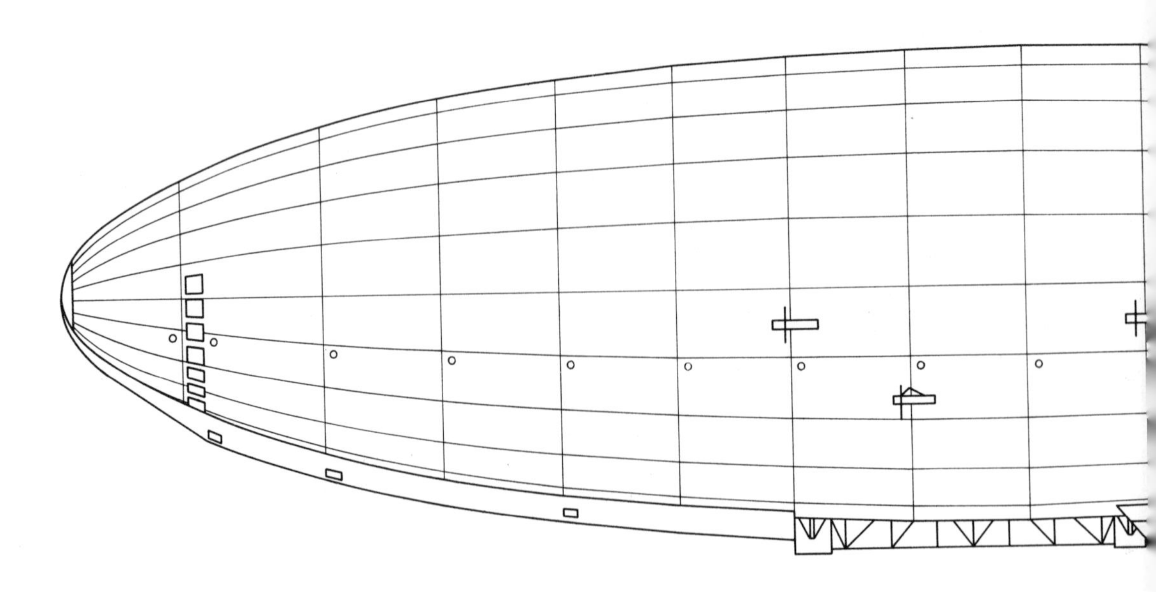

The LZ.127 (Graf Zeppelin) of 1928
Length 776 feet, maximum diameter 100 feet

The Boeing 747 (Jumbo Jet) of 1969
Length 231 feet, height 63 feet

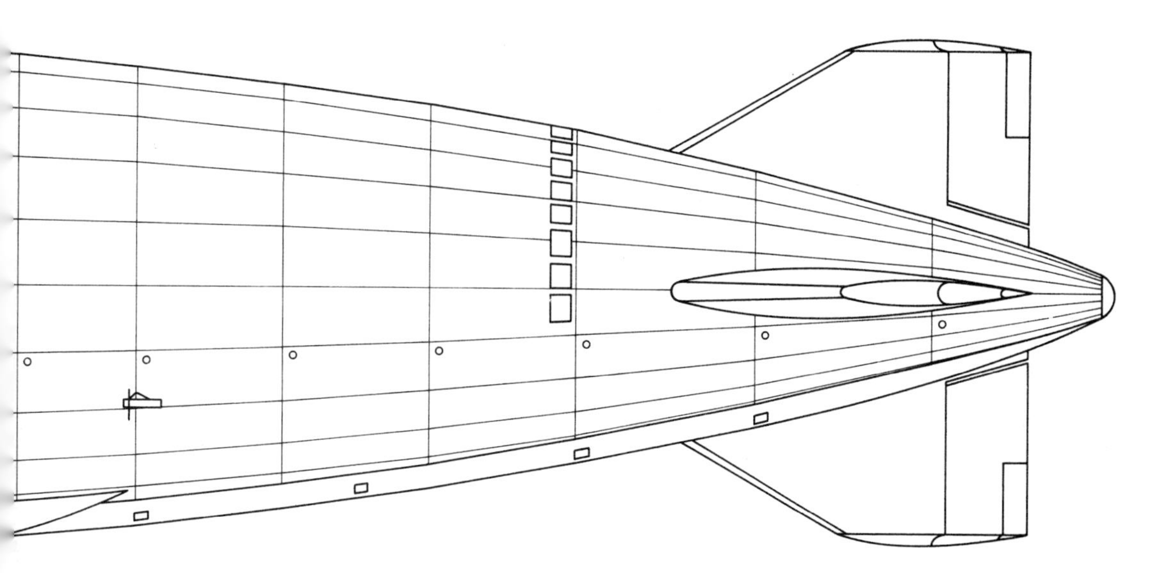

A possible airship of tomorrow
Length 1,200 feet

Hugh Bell's unsuccessful dirigible balloon of 1848, with rudder but no elevator.

The ship was known to its sponsors as the *Dolphin*, to others as 'Egg's Folly'. Propulsion was to be by rowing; fore-and-aft trim was to be controlled by a box of sand sliding on a cable. The project was eventually abandoned after a great deal of money had been spent on it.

One of the few craft of this kind actually completed during the half-century or so after Meusnier's death was the *Eagle*, designed by an adventurer named the Comte de Lennox. Lennox was a French nobleman of Scottish descent who either believed, like Egg, that an airship could be propelled by oars, or professed to do so. He invited public support for an airship service between London and Paris and opened offices in both cities where patrons would be able to book passages when scheduled flights began.

The *Eagle* was due to make her maiden flight from the Champ de Mars in Paris on 17 August 1834. Just as she was about to cast off, she broke from her moorings and rose so rapidly that she burst her envelope and was wrecked. Her destruction was completed by angry spectators, some of whom had invested money in the project.

Lennox then transferred his activities to London. He found quarters in Kensington and built a second airship, but ran out of money. The ship was seized by the Sheriff of Middlesex on behalf of his creditors, and its ultimate fate is unknown. Probably it was sold for scrap.

In 1848 a Dr Hugh Bell built a fifty-foot-long airship with a manually rotated airscrew, but it was not successful.

As long as the means of propulsion was the stumbling block, it was only to be expected that more would be achieved with models – which could be driven by clockwork or other simple mechanisms – than with airships designed to carry men.

In 1840 Charles Green, already well known as a balloonist, exhibited at the Polytechnic Institution in London a model airship with two airscrews rotated by the unwinding of a spring. After the envelope had been filled with coal-gas, the model was ballasted so that it hung motionless in the air until its airscrews began to turn. It then rose to the ceiling and stayed there until the spring ran down.

Three years later another English balloonist, Monck Mason, showed a model airship with a single clockwork-driven airscrew. It is said to have been an uncertain flier but to have attained a speed of five miles an hour.

In the following year a steam-driven model airship built by a certain Dr Le Berrier with the help of an engineer named Henri Giffard was tested in Paris. Giffard specialized in steam engines, but he had a long-standing interest in airships and had

worked with Lennox on the ill-fated *Eagle*. After witnessing trials of Le Berrier's model he ceased for a time to concern himself with flying machines, doubtless because his time was fully occupied by his professional work. But in 1850 a French clockmaker named Pierre Jullien, of Villejuif, built a clockwork-powered model airship which aroused enormous interest in Paris. A visit to the Hippodrome to see Jullien's model demonstrated set Giffard on a course which led to the construction of the first successful man-carrying aircraft ever made.

2 The airship flies

he sight of Jullien's model re-awakened Henri Giffard's dormant enthusiasm for powered lighter-than-air craft. After seeing it fly he decided to design and build an 'aerial steamer' large enough to carry a man.[1] He succeeded in completing by 1852 a pressure airship with an envelope 144 feet long, tapering from a diameter of forty feet amidships to a sharp point at each end. The engine delivered about three horsepower and weighed, with its boiler, about as much as two fair-sized men. This was a poor power-to-weight ratio by present standards, but to make such an engine well over a century ago was a considerable achievement.

Unlike some of his successors, Giffard took great pains to minimize the risk of setting the envelope on fire. The gondola which housed engine, boiler, pilot and controls was slung from a long pole suspended from the upper part of the envelope by a net, and was separated from the nearest part of it by more than forty feet. The fire-door of the boiler was screened, like a miner's safety-lamp, with wire gauze except when stoking was in progress, and the chimney pointed downwards and rearwards so that sparks from it were unlikely to reach the envelope.

Ceremonially attired in top hat and frock coat, Giffard climbered into the gondola at the Paris Hippodrome on 24 September 1852 and gave the order to let go. To the astonishment of all beholders, the ship gained height and made off at a dignified pace to the south-west, hissing gently and leaving a trail of steam in her wake. After covering about seventeen miles Giffard brought man's first flight in a powered machine to a close by landing safely at Trappes.

Giffard afterwards subjected his first aerial steamer to further trials, including a circular flight over Paris to test the efficacy of her canvas rudder. She acquitted herself well, but Giffard was not blind to her shortcomings. He knew that, with a maximum speed of five or six miles an hour in still air, she was truly dirigible only in a calm. Had even a light breeze been blowing when he attempted his circular flight, no manipulation of her rudder, would have enabled him to bring her back to her starting point.

The obvious remedy was to build a larger airship capable of carrying a heavier and more powerful engine and still providing a useful lift. As a first step, Giffard installed his existing engine in a ship with a longer and more streamlined envelope. Just as the new ship was about to make her maiden flight, she was wrecked as the result of an escape of gas which distorted the envelope and culminated in its breaking away from the gondola and bursting.

Giffard then designed an enormous

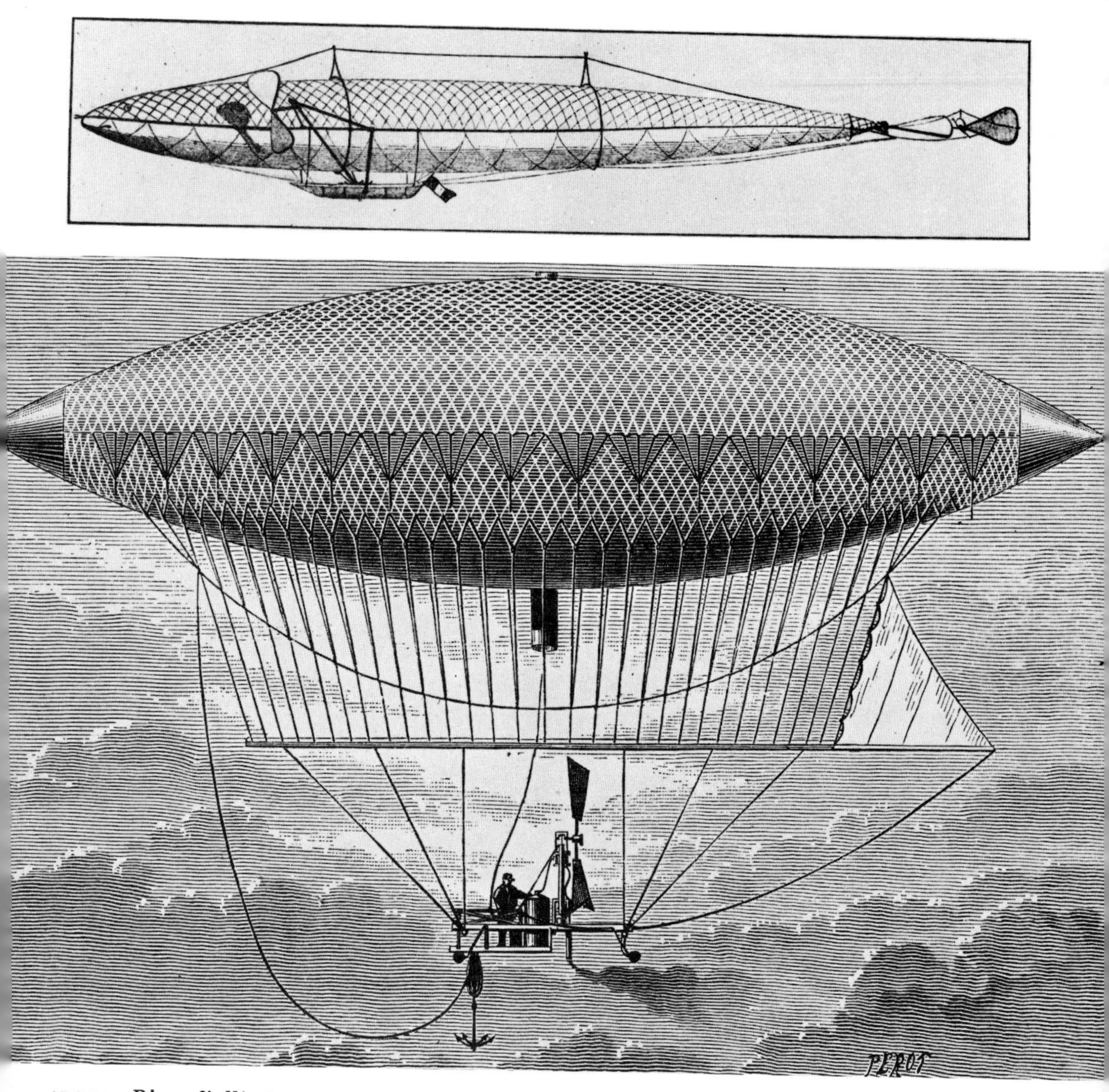

ABOVE: *Pierre Jullien's clockwork-driven model of 1850.*
BELOW: *The first successful man-carrying powered aircraft: Henri Giffard's Aerial Steamer of 1852. The single airscrew was driven by a three-hp steam engine designed by the inventor.*

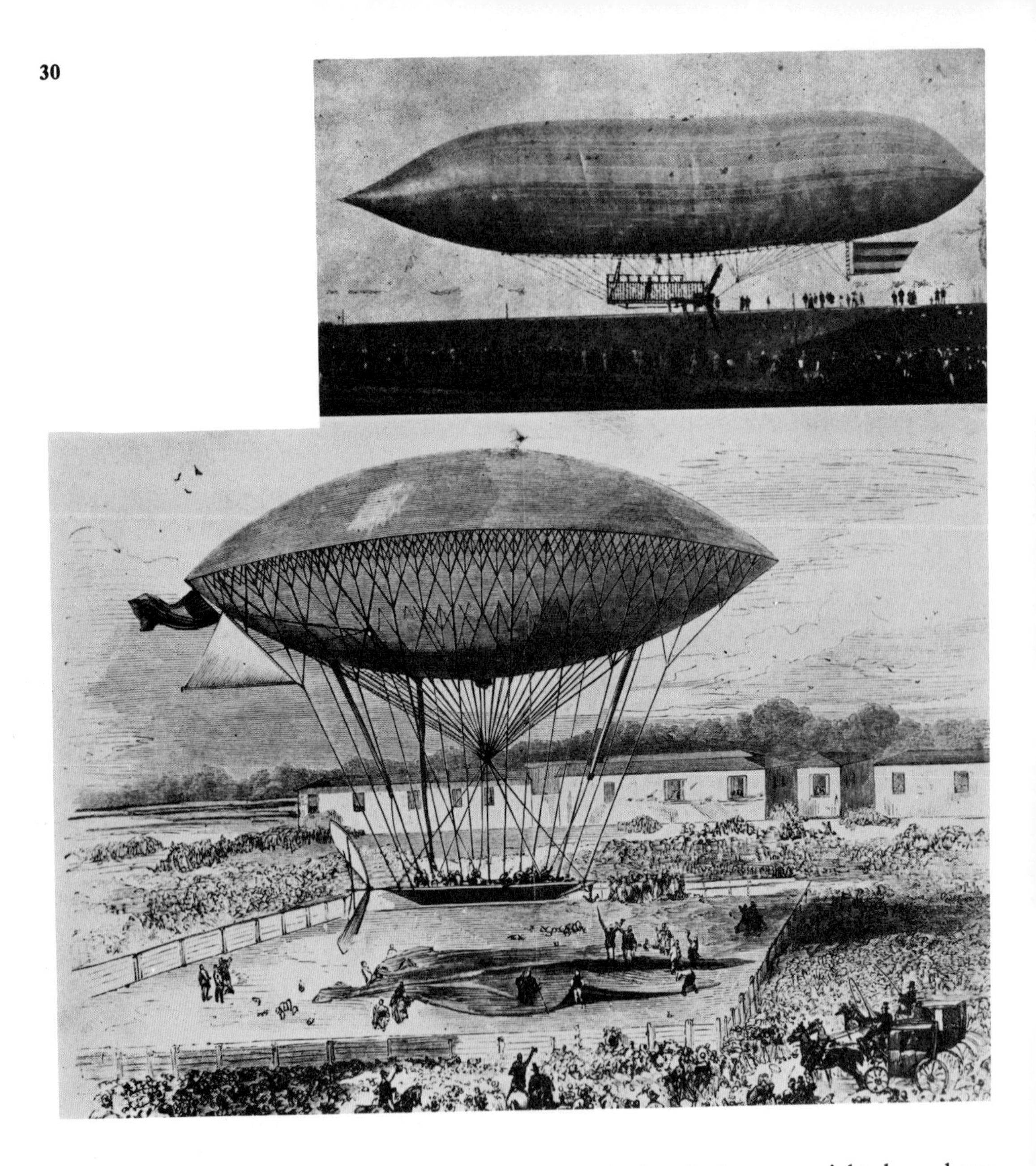

pressure airship with an envelope nearly 2,000 feet long. He aimed at installing a massive engine which would give the ship a maximum speed of forty-five miles an hour in still air, but was unable to complete the project for lack of funds.

The success of Giffard's first airship, limited though it was, might have been expected to convince designers that the steam-driven airship had a future. As things turned out, little attempt was made to follow up Giffard's experiments. Perhaps because they felt that the weight of the steam engine, with its heavy boiler,

ABOVE LEFT: *The first airship with an internal combustion engine: Paul Haenlein's dirigible balloon, with gas engine, on test at Brno, December 1872.*
BELOW LEFT: *The first government-sponsored airship: Stanislas Dupuy de Lôme's man-powered dirigible balloon of 1872.*
BELOW: *Car of Dupuy de Lôme's airship.*

would always be against it, designers preferred to go on casting about for some other means of propulsion.

The gas engine, invented by Étienne Lenoir in 1860, seemed for a time to promise a solution. It was not particularly efficient, but at least it was boilerless. Paul Haenlein, an Austrian, took out a patent in 1865 for a pressure airship driven by a gas engine, but the project hung fire. When Haenlein's airship was at last tested at Brno in Moravia in 1872, the results were disappointing. The ship, which drew the fuel for its engine from its own envelope, made two flights while still fastened to ropes held by soldiers. A speed of nine miles an hour in still air was claimed, but the ship was noticeably deficient in lift. Had the inventor been in a position to spend money on further experiments this weakness might perhaps have been overcome, but he was not.

In the same year the French naval authorities tested an airship ordered during the Franco-Prussian War and designed by Stanislas Dupuy de Lôme, a marine engineer and naval architect. No engine was installed, but eight sailors liberally

Car of Albert and Gaston Tissandier's man-carrying electrically-propelled dirigible balloon of 1883–4.

The Aerial Bicycle: a man-powered dirigible balloon designed by Charles F. Ritchel, of Corry, Pennsylvania, and tested at Hartford, Connecticut, in 1878.

supplied with rum rotated a large four-bladed airscrew by means of cranks and gears. A speed of approximately five miles an hour with a total of fifteen men aboard was attained, but the authorities were not favourably impressed and no further tests were made.

Another airship which depended on manpower for its propulsion was tested at Hartford, Connecticut, in 1878. This was a one-man aerial bicycle designed by Charles F. Ritchel, of Corry, Pennsylvania. With a vigorous youth at the pedals, the machine made a circular flight in a complete calm at a speed of three and a half miles an hour.

Other designers turned to electricity for an answer to their problems. At an exhibition in Paris in 1881, two brothers named Albert and Gaston Tissandier showed an electrically-propelled model airship which seemed so promising that influential backers offered to meet the cost of a man-carrying version. The ship was completed in 1883 and tested in October and November of that year, when two flights were made. Since the brothers relied on batteries which weighed considerably more than Giffard's engine and boiler, it is not surprising that their airship was a good deal slower than his.

Electrical propulsion was used much more successfully by Charles Renard and Arthur Krebs, two officers of the engineer corps of the French Army who were backed by the redoubtable Léon Gambetta. Their airship, just under 170 feet along and named *La France*, was of advanced design, although her appearance was not very

pleasing. When tested in 1884 *La France* made three circular flights in two days and proved fast enough to be truly dirigible in winds up to Force 3 on the Beaufort Scale. She made four more flights in the early part of 1885, but on two occasions was prevented by unfavourable winds from returning to her starting point.

About the same time, attempts by H. A. Otto and others to improve upon

TOP: *Renard and Knebs' airship* La France *returning to Chalais-Meudon.*
BELOW: La France.

Lenoir's gas engine culminated in the development by Gottlieb Daimler of an internal combustion engine which used as fuel the volatile liquid known as petrol or gasoline. In 1887 Daimler read in a newspaper that trials of an airship designed by a man named Wölfert had been disappointing because no means of propulsion better than manual rotation of her airscrews was available. Feeling that his boilerless engine might be suitable, he wrote to Wölfert offering his collaboration.

Karl Wölfert was a former Protestant pastor who had quitted the pulpit to become first a bookseller and afterwards an inventor. He had received some help from the Berlin Aeronautical Society, but by 1887 a series of setbacks had almost exhausted his resources. Gladly accepting Daimler's offer, he sent his latest product to the Daimler factory at Seelberg to be fitted with a single-cylinder two-horsepower engine. This was installed in a car immediately below the hydrogen-filled envelope. Like all Daimler's early engines, it relied for ignition of the explosive mixture fed to it on a tube which projected through the wall of the cylinder and was kept hot by a naked flame.

After a series of tests on the ground, a trial flight was made on Sunday, 12 August 1888. The weather was calm. The pilot, who was also sole occupant of the car, was a young man named Michael, chosen for his light weight. The airship made a successful flight of nearly three miles. Nothing untoward occurred, except that the flame of the burner which heated the ignition tube blew out and had to be rekindled from a candle which Michael shielded with his hand.

Two more flights were made in November. They were successful, but only because there was no wind. Even a light breeze would have made them hazardous.

The next few years brought growing demands for internal combustion engines for horseless carriages. Daimler did not withdraw his support from Wölfert, but measured in financial terms it fell short of expectations. Wölfert managed none the

Gondola of Wölfert airship tested in 1888.

less to build an improved version of his airship, powered by a six-horsepower twin-cylinder Daimler engine, again with hot-tube ignition. When exhibited at the Berlin Trade Fair in the late summer of 1896 it attracted so much attention that Kaiser Wilhelm II – the 'Little Willy' of the First World War – was moved to inspect it in person. He arranged for Wölfert to be given facilities for its further development at the headquarters of the Prussian Balloon Corps at Tempelhof.

A demonstration flight was scheduled for 12 June 1897. Representatives of the armed forces and members of the diplomatic corps were invited to attend. An officer of the Balloon Corps was to have accompanied Wölfert and his mechanic, but he stood down in order to improve the distribution of weight when the net connecting the car with the envelope was found to have broken in two places. Perhaps Wölfert forgot, in the excitement of the moment, to take on additional ballast after the officer left the car. However that may be, when released the airship climbed so rapidly to 3,000 feet that spectators doubted whether she was under control. Some said afterwards that they saw fabric trailing from her rudder. A few seconds later, flames shot from the engine and licked the envelope. The fuel tank exploded. The whole airship became a mass of fire. One terrible scream was heard, and then no more. What was left of the ship came down in a timber yard beside Tempelhof Station. The charred bodies of Wölfert and his mechanic were found amidst the wreckage.

Wölfert cannot be dismissed as a mere foolhardy adventurer. The scant regard he paid to his own safety was characteristic of a man inclined to be heedless for the future. Pioneers are not to be judged by the standards applied to other men. Even so, it seems fair to suggest that a little more regard for the safety of his unfortunate mechanic might have been desirable. Wölfert was surely remiss in taking none of the precautions against fire which Giffard had thought necessary nearly half a century earlier. The car of his airship was not slung well below the envelope, and the envelope contained no *ballonnet.* Critics had pointed out that any deformation due to loss of gas by valving might cause it to sag towards the heads of the occupants and the naked flame they tended. Wölfert's disregard of this warning is hard to understand unless he counted on always flying so low that no gas would be vented.

Wölfert has also been censured for not insisting on a safer means of ignition than that provided. This criticism seems harder to justify. Daimler, not Wölfert, was responsible for the design of the engine.

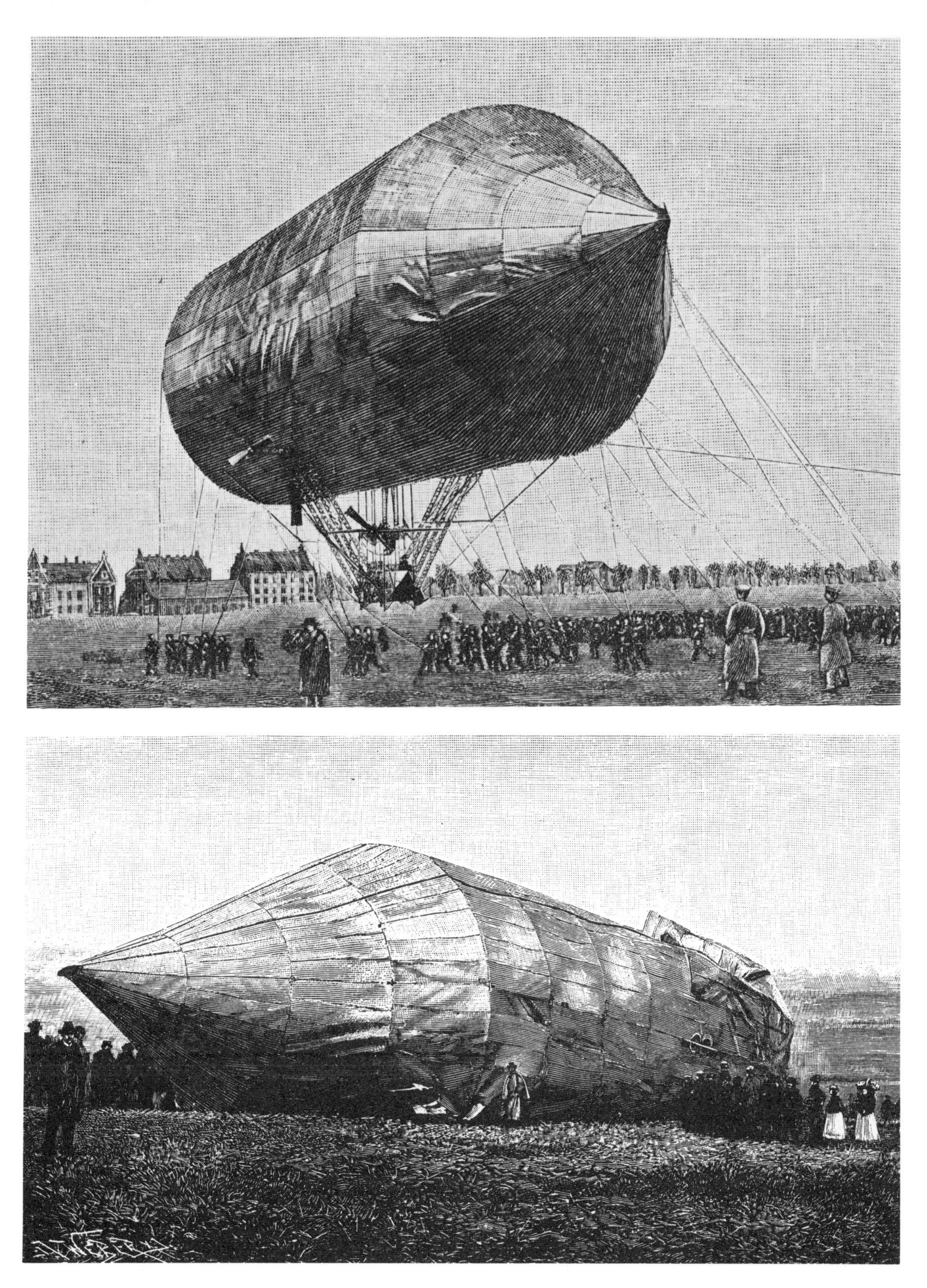

Disaster at Tempelhof: Karl Wölfert's Daimler-powered dirigible balloon of 1897 before and after its fatal flight.

All engines offered to the public by Daimler before 1900 had hot-tube ignition. After accepting Daimler's help in 1887 and using his engines from the summer of 1888, Wölfert was scarcely in a position in 1897 to insist that an engine with hot-tube ignition should not be used.

The Tempelhof disaster put airships out of favour with many people for some years. It did not lead, as might have been expected, to strenuous attempts to make steam engines and electric motors more suitable for use in the air. The petrol engine soon became the standard means of propulsion for airships. It continued to be used by practically all designers until, much later, its supremacy was challenged by the diesel engine.

The closing years of the nineteenth century and the first decade of the twentieth saw the introduction of airships with envelopes which did not rely on internal pressure to maintain their shape. But the story of the origin and early development of the rigid airship belongs to another chapter.

In the year of the Tempelhof disaster, there arrived in Paris a small, dapper Brazilian named Alberto Santos-Dumont. The son of a rich coffee-planter, he came to taste the pleasures of fashionable life in Europe. These included ballooning and also motoring, then in its infancy. Santos-Dumont was taken up in a balloon and became an enthusiastic aeronaut. He bought a De Dion tricycle driven by a petrol engine with an electrical ignition system. An intelligent man with a mechanical bent, he soon saw that such an engine might be used to propel an airship.

As a designer of airships, Santos-Dumont was not among the great innovators like Meusnier and Zeppelin.[2] But he had the advantage over most of his rivals of possessing both ample private means and an almost instinctive understanding of what an airship could be made to do. When his first airship was taken to the Paris Zoo to be tested on 18 September 1898, he proposed to take off upwind and under power in order to derive as much lift as possible from 'the fulcrum of the air'. Veteran aeronauts persuaded him to start by allowing the ship to drift downwind, with the result that it became entangled in the branches of a tree before it could be brought under control. At his next attempt a couple of days later, Santos-Dumont took off into the wind with his engine running, gained steerage way almost from the outset and cleared the tree-tops without difficulty. When loss of gas by valving caused the ship to begin jack-knifing as it was landing, he again summoned the 'fulcrum of the air' to his aid by shouting to boys playing in a field to seize ropes

Santos-Dumont rounding the Eiffel Tower.

Triumph at Saint Cloud: Alberto Santos-Dumont begins his prize-winning flight to the Eiffel Tower and back in 1901.

thrown to them and bring the ship's nose into the wind by running as hard as they could in that direction.

For a novice in any field to believe that he knows better than the experts is not unusual. The difference between Santos-Dumont and most novices was that he *did* know better than the experts.

He went on to build a whole series of small petrol-driven airships which he used for pleasure flights: to call on friends, to visit a favourite café. While drinking his *porto* or eating his ice, he left the airship tethered to a lamp-post or a railing. He became famous by winning in 1901 a large prize offered by Henri Deutsch de la Meurthe for the first flight from the premises of the Aéro Club de France at Saint Cloud to the Eiffel Tower and back in half an hour or less. Two years later he gave military strategists food for thought by flying immediately above the heads of troops parading at Longchamp on Bastille Day.

Santos-Dumont's feats led to a revival of interest in pressure airships after some years of neglect. The results were not always happy. In 1902 a French-domiciled Brazilian balloonist named Augusto Severo completed an airship which he called *Pax*. Accompanied by his mechanic, he took her for her maiden flight on 12 May. The ship climbed so fast that Severo and his companion lost their heads and threw out ballast instead of venting gas. The result was that the ship climbed still faster, the envelope burst, and both men were killed. A subsequent investigation showed that Severo had put one of the ship's two safety valves out of action by stuffing it with wax.[3]

In the same year an airship with a horizontal rotor underneath its car was built to the design of Ottokar de Bradsky, Secretary to the German Embassy in Paris. Bradsky and his engineer, a man named Morin, took the ship into the air on 13 October. At a height of some hundreds of feet, the car began to rotate. The steel cables by which it was slung from the envelope became twisted and eventually gave way. The car fell to the ground and both occupants were killed.[4]

About a fortnight later Henri Julliot, chief engineer to a firm of sugar refiners, completed for its principals, Paul and Pierre Lebaudy, a large airship which became known as the *Lebaudy I*. The 187-foot-long envelope was attached to a rigid keel from which the car or gondola was hung. A triple *ballonnet* was provided, and a Daimler engine capable of developing about forty horsepower gave the ship a maximum speed of approximately twenty-five miles an hour in still air.

Julliot's was the first airship truly dirig-

The first truly dirigible airship: a version acquired by Britain of Henri Julliot's Lebaudy *of 1902.*

ible in a fresh breeze. Between the early winter of 1902 and the summer of 1903 she made twenty-nine flights, including one of sixty-one miles.[5] Running before the wind in the following November, she covered thirty-nine miles in forty-one minutes before landing close to the spot from which Charles had released his first hydrogen balloon in 1783.

A week later she was damaged by a forced landing and had to be dismantled. Rebuilt under contract by a firm of balloon manufacturers, the Société Astra des Constructions Aéronautiques, she was named *Lebaudy II* and went on to make a large number of successful flights. In the summer of 1905 she completed a two-stage flight of 126 miles in six hours thirty-eight minutes. The Astra company built more than a dozen airships based more or less on the Lebaudy airship before switching to a method of construction introduced by a Spaniard, Torres Quevedo, who gave his name to the Astra-Torres airships used in the First World War.

Other manufacturers who produced airships in France during the first decade of the twentieth century included the firm of Clément-Bayard and the Société Zodiac. The second of these firms specialized in the manufacture of balloons, but also built small airships which found some favour with sportsmen and industrialists at home and abroad.

In Britain, the well-known balloonist Stanley Spencer built in 1902 a one-man airship with an envelope seventy-five feet long and a three and a half horsepower water-cooled Simms engine. Carrying only enough fuel for two hours' flying, Spencer flew on 22 September 1902 by a roundabout route from the Crystal Palace, in south-east London, to Eastcote in Middlesex. The ship passed over East Dulwich, Battersea, Earls Court and Acton, among other places. Spencer claimed that this was the route he meant to follow, but spectators had the impression that the ship was more or less at the mercy of the wind. A large airship built later by Spencer was less successful. The envelope jack-knifed during a demonstration flight at Ranelagh, and the ship was afterwards flown without its engine as a free balloon.

In 1903 a medical practitioner and amateur balloonist, Dr F. A. Barton, took out a patent in London for a pressure airship and demonstrated a clockwork model to the military authorities.[6] The War Office made a tentative offer of £4,000 for an airship capable of remaining airborne for three days with a crew of three and attaining the moderate speed of sixteen miles an hour. In a shed at Alexandra Palace in north London, Barton built a ship 180 feet long with a capacity of nearly a quarter of a million cubic feet. Each of its two engines

was said to develop fifty horsepower, but nothing like that output seems in fact to have been attained. With Barton and four other men aboard, the ship took off safely for her maiden flight on 22 July 1905, but she proved so seriously underpowered as to be unable to do more than run before the wind. Barton was about to make an emergency landing when the envelope folded up and the ship was wrecked. The car was so near the ground at the time that none of the five men was hurt.

The same year saw the maiden flight of a much smaller but far sounder airship designed and built by the firm of E. T. Willows, manufacturers of envelopes for balloons. No longer than Green's first airship and powered by a Peugeot engine rated at only seven horsepower, the first Willows airship provided experimental data which enabled the firm to tackle with confidence the design of bigger craft. On 8 August 1910 their second airship flew from Cardiff to London in nine hours at an average speed of approximately fifteen miles an hour. The same ship, now named

LEFT: *Before and after: Dr F. A. Barton's unsuccessful airship of 1905.*

BELOW: *One of the first successful British airships: the* Willows II (*City of Cardiff*) *of 1910.*

the *City of Cardiff*, left London at 3.30 p.m. on 4 November of that year and landed at Douai ten and a half hours later after crossing the Channel in darkness and fog.[7] Two more Willows airships were completed in 1912.

In the early part of the twentieth century the British military authorities made somewhat halting attempts to provide themselves with a pressure airship of their own. Two envelopes were designed by Colonel J. L. B. Templer, Commandant of the British Army's Balloon Factory at Farnborough, and were made to specifications which called for the use of goldbeater's skin, supplied by a family in which the craft of handling this expensive and durable material was hereditary. The first, with five layers of goldbeater's skin, was so heavy that it failed to rise from the ground when inflated. The second, with three layers, was much more satisfactory, but the project came to a halt for lack of funds before it could be used.

In 1907 the authorities agreed to spend £2,000 on a fresh attempt. A quarter of

British military airship pre-1914: Beta, *an enlarged version of* Baby *with a gas capacity of 35,000 cubic feet.*

The Farnborough-built British Army Dirigible No 1, *or Nulli Secundus, of 1907.*

the money was devoted to the purchase of a fifty-horsepower Antoinette engine of French design and manufacture. This was fitted to the second of the envelopes designed by Colonel Templer. Samuel F. Cody, a Texan who could neither read nor write but had done some work for the British Army on man-lifting kites and other projects, was employed to marry engine to hull and design a gondola and steering gear.

The result was British Army Dirigible No. 1, or *Nulli Secundus.* Her capacity was 56,000 cubic feet, she was 111 feet long, and her maximum speed in still air was about sixteen miles an hour. She made a brief, disappointing first flight of merely 1,000 yards on 10 September 1907, but flew much more satisfactorily on 30 September and 3 October.

On Saturday, 5 October, Cody and Colonel Templer's successor, Colonel John Capper, left Farnborough in the *Nulli Secundus* with the intention of taking her to London and back. They hoped to show her not only to the British public but also to the Kaiser, who was staying in London at the time. Flying at heights between 800 and 1,400 feet, they reached Westminster soon after midday. King Edward VII and his imperial guest failed to appear on the balcony of Buckingham Palace, but civil servants and serving officers waved enthusiastically from the roof of the War

Office. The delighted aeronauts continued eastwards and rounded the dome of St Paul's Cathedral before heading back for Farnborough. They soon found that they could make little progress against a freshening wind. They decided, therefore, not to attempt the return flight that afternoon, but to make for Clapham Common. Unable to land there because the motor car carrying their ground crew was held up by the crowds that thronged the streets, they went on to the Crystal Palace, where they made a successful landing in the area enclosed by the track used for bicycle races. They still hoped to resume their flight to Farnborough in the near future, but the weather remained unfavourable and the envelope was damaged by heavy rain. After five days of frustration the ship had to be deflated and taken to Farnborough by road.[8]

She was afterwards rebuilt as *Nulli Secundus II*, with a capacity of 85,000 cubic feet. She made two or three short flights in her new form in the summer of 1908, and was then dismantled.[9]

In the same year the military authorities began work on a ship with a capacity of only 21,000 cubic feet, called *Baby*. Enlarged to 35,000 cubic feet in the winter of 1909–10, she was given a thirty-five-horsepower British-made engine and flew from Farnborough to London and back in 244 minutes. *Gamma* (75,000 cubic feet) and

Another pre-1914 British military airship: Delta, *with a gas capacity of 175,000 cubic feet.*

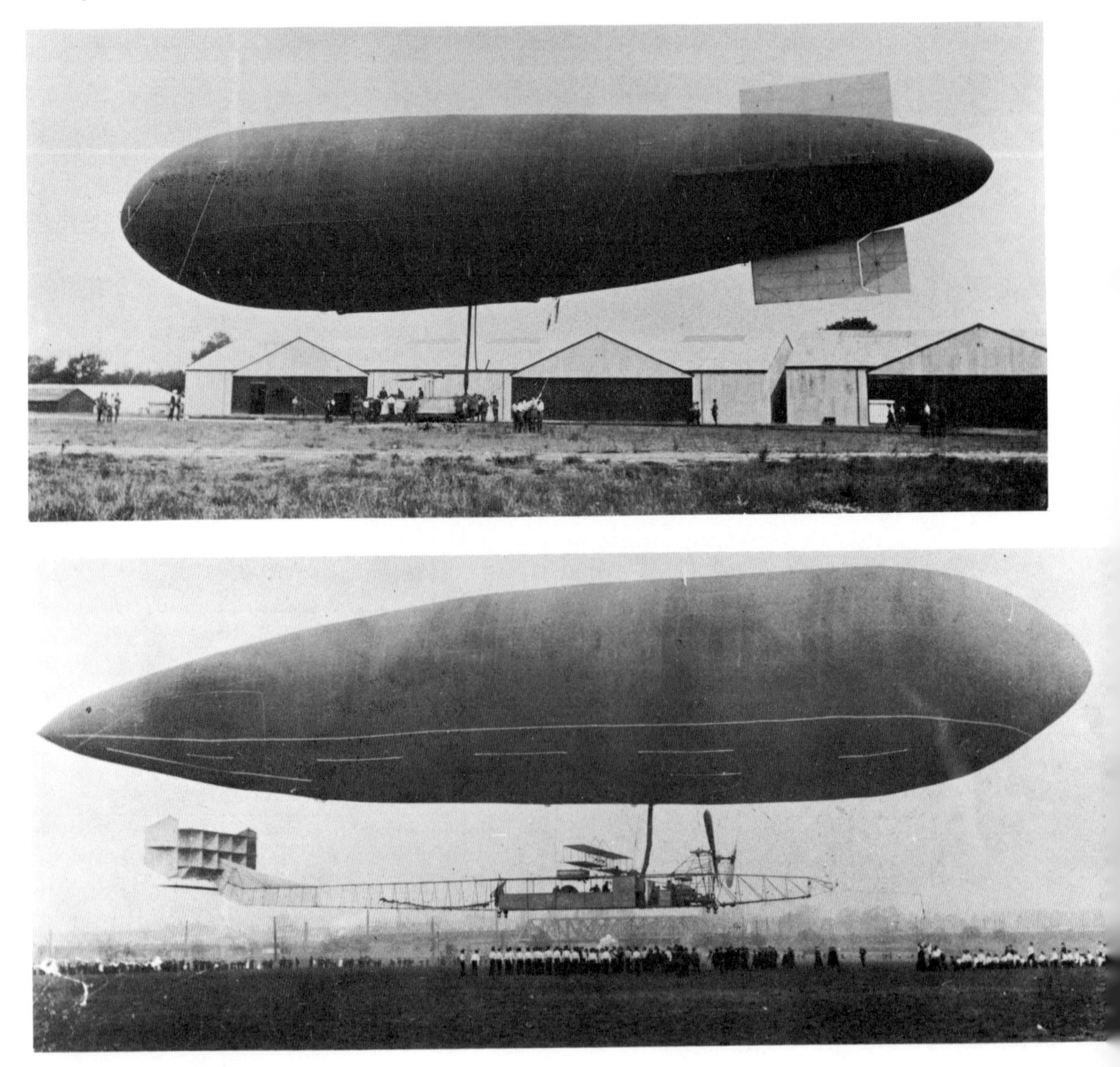

The first airship to cross the English Channel: the Clément-Bayard acquired by the British government in 1910.

Delta (175,000 cubic feet) followed in 1910 and 1912 respectively. In addition the War Office acquired two French pressure airships, one a Clément-Bayard whose cost was partly defrayed by a public-spirited Member of Parliament, Arthur du Cros, the other a Lebaudy paid for by the *Morning Post*. The Clément-Bayard made her delivery flight from Compiègne to Wormwood Scrubs, in north London, about a fortnight before the *City of Cardiff* crossed the Channel in the opposite direction. She was found when closely examined after her arrival to have suffered so much wear and tear at the hands of the French, who had used her on military manoeuvres, that the War Office declined to put her into service.[10]

The Parseval airship delivered to the British government in 1913.

The Lebaudy presented to the nation by the *Morning Post* also failed to give satisfaction. She was built at Soissons to a War Office specification, tested in France, and flown on 26 October 1910 to Farnborough. While she was being taken into a shed there the officer in charge of the handling party noticed that she looked too big to go through the entrance. He told his men to wait while he made a closer examination, but a staff officer who was not abreast of the situation shouted to them to carry on. The result was that she struck the roof of the shed and was badly damaged. A subsequent investigation showed that her diameter exceeded the specified figure by ten feet.[11] She was afterwards rebuilt with modifications which made her so hard to control that she became unmanageable during a trial flight and suffered irreparable damage.[12]

In 1912 the Admiralty placed an order through the firm of Vickers for an airship of the type made by a German company to a design by Major August von Parseval. The ship was delivered in June 1913.[13] In the following month the Admiralty decided to buy three more Parsevals. One of these was to be built in Germany; the others were to be built by Vickers with

An Italian semi-rigid airship, c. 1911, designed by Enrico Forlanini.

An early Gross-Basenach airship, c. 1910. Her resemblance to the Lebaudy 1 *is unmistakable.*

envelopes made in Germany. In the event, the German-built ship was requisitioned by the German Army and three Parsevals were completed by Vickers after the outbreak of war.[14]

In Italy, two small pressure airships designed by an engineer named Forlanini were completed by 1912 and used in Tripolitania during the Italo-Turkish War. Their tasks included artillery reconnaissance, tactical reconnaissance and some rudimentary bombing.

In Germany, more than twenty Parseval airships were built between 1906 and 1914 by the firm which held the manufacturing rights in Major von Parseval's designs. The Parseval delivered to the British in 1913 was one of a number sold to foreign governments. Those completed during the last two years of peace, although not comparable in endurance with the large rigid airships described in the next chapter, were substantial craft which could make some forty knots in still air. In addition, a government balloon factory managed by a Captain von Gross produced four pressure airships designed by Nikolas Basenach. These were designed with the army's needs in mind, but one of them was used by the airship division of the German Navy from November 1914 to November 1915.

A Gross-Basenach built for the German Navy.

Airships were not manufactured commercially in the United States before 1911, but in 1906 an American named Walter Wellman placed an order in France for a pressure airship which was completed to his specification in the summer of that year. Called by Wellman the *America*, she was 228 feet long and driven by two engines rated at ninety horsepower each. Wellman at first intended to use her for polar exploration, but his attempt to reach the North Pole from Spitzbergen in the late summer of 1907 was defeated by strong headwinds which forced him to return to base after only three hours' flying.

Wellman then planned a transatlantic flight from west to east. Accompanied by his engineer, Melvin Vaniman, and four other men, he set out from Atlantic City on 10 October 1910, but soon ran into atrocious weather. Eventually he was obliged to ditch the ship off the coast of New England. He and his companions took to a small lifeboat and were picked up by a British ship.[15]

Wellman's interest in long-range airships did not survive this experience, but Vaniman was not discouraged. He persuaded the Goodyear Tire and Rubber Company, of Akron, Ohio, to finance the building of a semi-rigid airship with an envelope 285 feet long, made of fabric

The first America*:*
Walter Wellman's
French-built airship
shown at Olympia,
1909.

The American-built
Akron *of 1911–12.*

coated by a process invented by the North British Rubber Company. This was a Scottish firm which granted Goodyear American rights in the process in return for reciprocal benefits.[16] Two modified motor-car engines, supplemented by an engine made in France, drove three pairs of airscrews.

The ship, named the *Akron*, was completed in the autumn of 1911 and laid up for the winter after making a short trial flight in the first week of November. The opportunity was taken to make a number of modifications to her ancillary equipment.

In the following summer Vaniman yielded to demands for a demonstration flight, although some of the equipment adopted during the winter had not yet undergone all the pre-flight tests he would have liked to make. With Vaniman and three other men aboard, the ship left Atlantic City on 2 July and headed out to sea. After only fifteen minutes' flying, the envelope exploded and the blazing hulk of the airship plunged into the sea. The bodies of the four men were seen to fall from the gondola and strike the water. The cause of the accident was never established beyond question, but the most probable explanation is that valves of a kind not previously used were too tight to allow gas to escape as the airship rose.[17]

This experience did not destroy the faith in airships which Vaniman's enthusiasm had engendered in the breasts of Goodyear's directors. When the opportunity came their way, they succeeded in making their company the leading manufacturer of airships in the United States.

3 The rigid airship: 1895-1914

In 1886 an electrolytic process by which aluminium could be produced in commercial quantities was invented almost simultaneously by Paul Héroult in France and C. M. Hall in the United States.

The introduction to industry of this light, strong metal during the next few years opened up new possibilities for designers of lighter-than-air craft. One of the first to explore them was an Austrian engineer named David Schwartz.

In 1895 Schwartz began work on an airship made almost entirely of aluminium. He built a tubular aluminium framework shaped like the fully inflated envelope of a pressure airship and covered it with thin sheets of aluminium to form a gas-tight seal. To this envelope, or hull, were added the usual controls and a twelve-horse-power Daimler engine driving three tractor airscrews by means of a belt-and-pulley mechanism. Elliptical in cross-section, the hull was 156 feet along and held 130,000 cubic feet of hydrogen.

Schwartz died early in 1897, but the airship was completed later in the year under the supervision of his widow. About five months after the loss of Wölfert's airship she was taken to Tempelhof, where the specified quantity of hydrogen was pumped into her hull. To the astonishment of critics who had declared that a metal airship would never fly, the ship proved buoyant.

Some doubt exists as to the identity of the pilot chosen to take the ship on her maiden flight on 3 November. He may have been an officer of the Prussian Balloon Corps, but is perhaps more likely to have been Schwartz's engineer or mechanic.[1] Whoever he was, it seems fairly certain that he had never handled an airship before.

When the flight was due to begin, a fifteen-mile-an-hour wind was blowing. Since the fastest airships hitherto tested were incapable of making headway against winds of much more than twelve miles an hour, conditions for the test could scarcely be called promising. Nevertheless the ship was released, rose quickly to a height of eighty feet or so, and began to drift downwind at what must have seemed to the pilot an alarming speed. While he was struggling to gain control, the driving belt came off its pulley. Losing his head, he opened the release valve so smartly that the ship dropped like a stone. The pilot managed to jump clear at the last moment, but the ship was damaged beyond repair. The designer's unfortunate widow had nothing to show for the large sums expended on her husband's brain-child but a mass of twisted metal.

The much more successful rigid airships designed by Count Ferdinand von Zeppelin

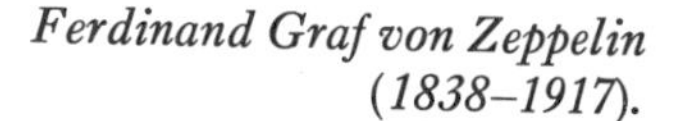

Ferdinand Graf von Zeppelin (1838–1917).

were constructed on a different principle. Like Schwartz, Zeppelin used a tubular aluminium frame, but instead of covering it with sheets of metal he made a fabric cover not intended to be gas-tight. The gas was enclosed in bags in compartments of the hull separated by transverse aluminium girders.

A soldier by profession, Zeppelin was commissioned in a cavalry regiment in 1857, when he was nineteen. Most of his service career was spent with the engineer corps. His interest in airships dated from 1874 or earlier, but it was not until after 1890, when he was prematurely retired after making some indiscreet comments on the Prussianization of the army, that he became seriously concerned with problems of construction and design. In 1893 he submitted to the military authorities a design prepared in collaboration with an engineer named Theodore Kober for a 384-foot-long rigid airship propelled by two eleven-horsepower Daimler engines. The project was considered by a scientific commission specially appointed for the purpose, but was turned down on the ground that too many problems were left unsolved and that Zeppelin's estimates of performance were too optimistic.

Five years later Zeppelin formed a joint stock company for the promotion of flight in lighter-than-air machines. An association of German engineers provided some capital, but more than half the total of £40,000 came from Zeppelin's personal fortune. Construction of an airship designated LZ.1 began in 1899, in a shed on the surface of Lake Constance near Friedrichschafen. The hull was 420 feet long and about thirty-eight feet in diameter amidships. It was divided into seventeen compartments, all but two of which held gas-bags containing between them 400,000 cubic feet of hydrogen. Weak features of the design were the two Daimler marine engines which had a combined output of only thirty horsepower or less, rudders too small to give much directional control, and an unsatisfactory method of controlling fore-and-aft trim by means of a sliding weight – a method similar to that proposed by John Pauly and Durs Egg in 1816.

On 2 July 1900 a steam-launch hauled the LZ.1 from her floating hangar for her maiden flight. Zeppelin was one of five men aboard her. When released she rose under power to a height of approximately 1,000 feet, but then she proved difficult to control both directionally and in elevation, and the sliding weight caused her frame to buckle slightly. Nevertheless she landed safely on the surface of the lake after remaining airborne for some eighteen minutes.[2]

With her frame strengthened, the LZ.1 made a second flight of some eighty minutes on 17 October, and a third of twenty-three minutes four days later. Her second flight was witnessed by Hugo Eckener, a young economist who had been commissioned by the *Frankfurter Zeitung* to write a report on the flight and assess the airship's qualities. Eckener had been brought up at Flensburg on the Baltic, was descended on his mother's side from a Danish seafaring family, and had done a fair amount of sailing. He wrote in his article that the LZ.1, with her maximum speed of sixteen miles an hour in still air, was too slow to make much progress against even a moderate wind.

Zeppelin was reluctant to admit that the ship was underpowered, but had to agree after the third flight that her performance fell short of expectations. Soon afterwards the company folded up for lack of funds. The LZ.1 was dismantled after logging only just over two hours' flying. Hangars, workshops, stocks of aluminium and the LZ.1's engines were sold. What little money remained after creditors had been paid was distributed to stockholders. Sole rights in Zeppelin's designs reverted to Zeppelin himself, but most of his capital was lost.

His next airship was built in 1905 with funds provided by a state lottery and a contribution from a manufacturer of aluminium. Designated LZ.2, she was similar in size and appearance to her predecessor, but her engines were five times as powerful. Orthodox elevators replaced the clumsy sliding weight.

Unfortunately the engines which ought to have given the new ship an outstanding performance proved a source of weakness. At the very beginning of her first flight, on 30 November 1905, her forward engine cut out. Her stern struck the surface of the lake and rebounded into the air. Making off with a damaged rudder which put her out of control, she was rescued by the crew of her attendant launch, who managed to overtake her, seize her trail rope, and haul her to safety.

At the next attempt, on 17 January 1906, her engines at first refused to start. By the time they were running smoothly, a fresh breeze was blowing and an hour of daylight had been lost. Nevertheless the flight went well until the forward engine again cut out. Zeppelin and his crew succeeded in making an emergency landing about twenty miles from their point of departure, but the ship was slightly damaged by contact with a tree. They decided to leave her where she was for the night and make repairs in daylight on the following day. Through inexperience they moored her in such a way that she was not free to turn her nose into the wind. The result was that she was irremediably damaged during the night and the early hours of the morning by a violent storm.

Appalling though this disaster seemed at the time, it turned out not to be an unmixed evil. Touched by a sympathetic article in the *Frankfurter Zeitung*, Zeppelin paid Eckener a formal visit for the purpose of introducing himself, thanking him for his courtesy, and congratulating him on writing seriously and objectively about a subject which other journalists saw only as a matter for ridicule. The visit laid the foundations of an association which not only changed the course of Eckener's life but proved of great benefit to Zeppelin and his successors.

The first British rigid airship: the Mayfly *immediately after emerging from her shed on 22 May 1911.*

By scraping up the remnants of his fortune and borrowing from friends, Zeppelin succeeded in completing by the following autumn a new ship, the LZ.3. She was very similar to the LZ.2, but proved far more successful. When tested on 9 October 1906, she made a circular flight of sixty miles in two hours. In September 1907 she set a new standard of achievement for airships by remaining airborne for eight hours. Zeppelin received a grant of half a million marks from public funds to enable him to continue his experiments, and the German military authorities placed a tentative order for an airship capable of making a twenty-four-hour non-stop flight.

To meet this requirement, Zeppelin designed and built a rigid airship 450 feet long, with a capacity of more than 500,000 cubic feet and two 105-horsepower Daimler engines. Completed by the summer of 1908 and designated LZ.4, she was instantly successful. After undergoing trials on 20 and 23 June, she made a flight of nearly 200 miles in twelve hours on 1 July.

At 7 a.m. on 4 August, with twelve people aboard, the LZ.4 left Friedrichshafen to attempt the twenty-four-hour flight of 450 miles or so which would qualify her for acceptance by the military authorities. Zeppelin decided to fly first to Basle, thence down the Rhine to Mainz

and back to Friedrichshafen by a cross-country route.

For the first eleven hours all went well, except that the heat of the sun caused the ship to lose a good deal of gas by valving. Then, as she was approaching Oppenheim, about ten miles short of Mainz, the forward engine spluttered and stopped. Zeppelin was obliged to make an emergency landing in a field in order to give his mechanics a fair chance of putting matters right. After an hour or two he was able to resume the flight, but he took the precaution of disembarking some of his passengers to compensate for the gas lost during the heat of the day. Again all seemed to be going well when the trouble recurred. Although the ship was only about ninety miles from home, Zeppelin decided to make for the Daimler factory at Stuttgart on one engine rather than risk another emergency landing in open country. He managed, with some difficulty, to reach the outskirts of Stuttgart and land at Echterdingen. Soldiers from a neighbouring barracks volunteered to hold the ship down while mechanics from the factory took the recalcitrant engine apart. They had not yet reassembled it when a thunderstorm, followed by torrential rain, compelled them to stop work. Before running for shelter, they and the soldiers fastened the ship to a makeshift mooring. When she was seen to be insecure, the volunteers returned to their posts and hung on grimly, but the wind became so strong that the ropes were wrenched from their grasp. The ship lurched into the air, caught fire and was reduced in a few minutes to a burnt-out wreck.

This calamity proved a blessing in disguise. The sight of the great airship flying overhead in the August sunshine had stirred the hearts of patriotic Rhinelanders. Newspaper editors throughout Germany followed Eckener's lead in representing the loss of the ship as a setback not merely for her designer but for Germany. Appeals for funds to enable Zeppelin to carry on his work attracted enormous support. Subscribers vied with each other in pressing their contributions on an elderly retired officer who cared little about money but was determined to miss no opportunity of enhancing the might and splendour of the Fatherland.

Finding himself with 6,000,000 marks at his disposal, Zeppelin began by establishing a trust called the Zeppelin Foundation. Its purpose, he told his intimates, was to safeguard his organization against governmental interference. He then set up a company to manufacture airships, another to manufacture engines specially designed by Carl Maybach for lighter-than-air machines, and another to

Two approaches to the rigid airship: Ironclad airship proposed by Prosper Mellow in 1851, and the successful LZ.3, completed in 1906 and modified in 1909.

manufacture ancillary equipment.[3] In 1909 he was prevailed upon to form yet another company, Deutsche Luftschiffahrts-Aktien-Gesellschaft, or DELAG, to organize commercial flights. The role of DELAG, however, was not merely, nor perhaps even mainly, to bring in revenue. Besides making the airship manufacturing company to some extent independent of the army by providing an alternative outlet for its products, DELAG gave Zeppelin a means of instilling air-mindedness into members of the public and especially of the armed forces. Even as early as 1909 he may have foreseen a time when officers and other ranks of the army and the navy would be sent to DELAG to learn how an airship should be handled.

Eckener had left Friedrichshafen in 1907 to return to his native Flensburg and become editor of a newspaper owned by a member of his wife's family. Finding that some of the staff regarded him as an interloper, he was not altogether happy there. After the Echterdingen disaster, Zeppelin invited him to come back to Friedrichshafen and join the new organization. At first he declined. Later he accepted an arrangement which would, in theory, enable him to combine part-time employment as a kind of public relations officer to the Zeppelin organization with long hours of work on a book on economics and social problems, which he had been intermittently engaged upon since his student days. Still regarding himself as an economist and sociologist by vocation and a journalist from necessity, he soon found that being Zeppelin's right-hand man was a full-time job. His book was destined never to be completed.

In the meantime Zeppelin made substantial modifications to the well-tried LZ.3 and completed a new ship, the LZ.5. After a series of trials in the early summer of 1909, the German military authorities took delivery of the rebuilt LZ.3 in July and called her the Z.1. Thereafter she was used mainly as a training ship. The LZ.5 made her maiden flight on 26 May. A few days later she completed a record-breaking flight of more than 600 miles in just under thirty-eight hours. She, too, was acquired by the army, and was called the Z.2.

In the same year Zeppelin completed the LZ.6. On 27 August, only two days after making her maiden flight, she set off on a demonstration flight to Berlin. Delayed by technical troubles, she did not reach her destination until 29 August. Further hitches occurred during the return flight in September. The army's refusal to buy her was partly responsible for Zeppelin's decision to form DELAG in the following November. The lack of interest taken by the military authorities in Zeppelin's latest product was due, however, not so much to any technical shortcomings she might be supposed to possess as to their temporary preoccupation with the smaller and cheaper pressure airships which Major von Gross was building on government account to Basenach's designs.

In May 1910 Zeppelin completed the LZ.7. The first airship built for DELAG, she was named the *Deutschland*. Her maiden flight on 22 June was made with thirty-two people aboard and lasted two and a half hours. She completed a number of other successful flights during the next few days, but was wrecked on 28 June, when the failure of one of her engines at a moment when she was beating against a strong westerly wind led her commander to attempt an emergency landing in the Teutoberg Forest. No one was hurt, but the commander was held to have made the wrong decision.

As a result of this incident, Eckener found himself not only holding a full-time administrative post but called upon to take command of the *Deutschland*'s successor. He received his pilot's licence on 6 February 1911, only a few weeks before the new ship was completed.[4] Her official designation was LZ.8, *Deutschland II*, or *Ersatz Deutschland*, but the name painted on her hull was simply *Deutschland*.[5] She made a number of successful flights in the spring of 1911, but on 16 May Eckener ordered her ground-crew to walk her out of her shed in a strong cross-wind rather than disappoint the passengers who were to have travelled in her. She was blown against the side of the shed and seriously damaged.

This experience convinced Eckener that commanders or flight directors must never hesitate to cancel flights if conditions were unfavourable. A weather-forecasting service was set up so that decisions could be made in advance and intending passengers be warned of cancellations.

Between the summer of 1911 and the outbreak of the First World War the Zeppelin factories completed another seventeen airships, including four built for DELAG. These were the *Schwaben* (1911), the *Viktoria-Luise* (1912), the *Hansa* (1912) and the *Sachsen* (1913). Zeppelin also had the satisfaction of adding the German Navy to his customers. His first naval airship, designated LZ.14 by the factory but known to the navy as L.1, made her maiden flight on 7 October 1912. After completing a thirty-hour flight on 13 and 14 October, she moved to a training establishment near Berlin, where she remained until the following summer. In August and September 1913, she took part in naval manoeuvres off the German North Sea coast. While reconnoitring the Heligoland

Bight on 9 September, her commander was warned by wireless that bad weather was approaching. He turned for home, but was overtaken by the storm. Battered by turbulent winds, the ship plunged into the sea and broke in two. Of the twenty men aboard her, six were rescued and fourteen drowned. Little more than a month later the LZ.18, specially built for the navy and given the service designation L.2, exploded while undergoing an altitude test and crashed in flames.[6] An investigation showed that gas vented from valves on the underside of her hull had been sucked into the gondola carrying her forward engine. There were no survivors.

Mishaps to DELAG's airships included the loss of the *Schwaben* on 28 June 1912, when she broke up in a gale and caught fire shortly after completing a flight to Düsseldorf; but she had already disembarked her passengers and crew, and no one was hurt. Indeed, not one of the 10,000 passengers carried by DELAG's fleet suffered any injury during nearly sixteen hundred flights completed between 1910 and 1914. Pleasure flights were made throughout the spring and summer months from stations at or near large towns and holiday resorts by airships equipped to carry twenty or more passengers in considerable comfort. On most flights a meal was served in the air. The outbreak of war prevented DELAG from introducing regular return flights between places inside and outside Germany, but an experimental flight to Vienna and back was made in the summer of 1913. Besides attracting fare-paying passengers, these flights gave DELAG opportunities of training service crews by arrangement with the naval and military authorities.

The German Army was not content to rely solely on the Zeppelin organization for its rigid airships. In 1909 the firm of Schütte-Lanz was founded with the backing of the German War Office for the purpose of producing airships in competition with Zeppelin. The firm took its name from Dr Johann Schütte, Professor of Naval Architecture at the University of Danzig, and Heinrich Lanz, who represented a group of industrialists financially interested in the venture. The distinctive feature of Schütte's designs was the use of plywood instead of aluminium for the framework of the envelope. His first ship, the SL.1, made her maiden flight in 1911, three days before Zeppelin's ninth. Her hull, 420 feet long and fifty-nine feet in diameter at its widest, contained gas-bags holding between them three-quarters of a million cubic feet of hydrogen. His second, the SL.2, was completed in 1914. Beautifully streamlined, she was notable for her freedom from needless excrescences and

An early passenger airship: the LZ.13 (Hansa) *of 1912.*

also for the relatively comfortable quarters provided for her commander and crew. Many of the good features of the SL.2 and her successors were reflected in ships built by the Zeppelin organization after the outbreak of war, when Schütte's patents were taken over by the government. The Schütte-Lanz organization, with factories at Mannheim, Leipzig and Zeesen, succeeded in retaining its separate identity until 1917, and the last Schütte-Lanz airship was commissioned as late as the summer of 1918.

Outside Germany, Zeppelin had scarcely any rivals worthy of the name. Some rather half-hearted experiments with rigid airships were made in France, but they led nowhere.

In Britain, the interest taken by the German government in large rigid airships from 1907 caused a good deal of concern. Such craft as the LZ.3 and the LZ.4 could fly not only higher but also much further than contemporary heavier-than-air machines. At a time when Anglo-German naval rivalry was at its height, British strategists feared that their use for maritime reconnaissance might turn the scale in Germany's favour. They might also be used to attack shipping and perhaps dockyards and other installations ashore. The Royal Navy, it was argued, ought to possess at least one airship of comparable performance, if only for the purpose of testing the practical utility of such monsters.

On the initiative of Captain R. H. S. Bacon, Director of Naval Ordnance, the Admiralty therefore proposed in the summer of 1908 that a large rigid airship should be built in Britain. The Committee of Imperial Defence accepted the proposal in the following February. Tenders were invited, and eventually a contract was placed with Vickers Sons and Maxim Limited (afterwards Vickers Limited).

By the time the contract was signed, a team of naval officers was working with engineers employed by Vickers on problems of design and construction. Specifications were drawn up by the Director of Naval Construction, but it was chiefly to Captain Bacon that the Vickers engineers looked for help and guidance in translating them into a practical design.

As things turned out, Bacon was soon compelled to relinquish his appointment because of a dispute between senior officers about strategy. Captain Murray Sueter then assumed the post of Inspecting Captain of Aircraft, which Bacon had been expected to hold until the ship was ready. Sueter was convinced that air power had a part to play in naval warfare, but he did not claim to understand airships, and he accepted the post on the express understanding that he was to be absolved of responsibility for the design of the Vickers airship.

The result was that an unexpected burden was thrown on the shoulders of the manager of the marine division of Vickers, who had no knowledge of aeronautics. His task was not made easier by the choice of duralumin, an alloy developed in Germany and not previously used for airships, as the material of which the framework of the hull was to be made.

Construction of the 512-foot-long airship began in 1909 in a floating shed built specially for the purpose at Barrow-in-Furness. Specially treated silk was used for the outer cover of the hull, and the gasbags were made of layers of cotton and rubber. Gondolas designed to float were built of copper-sewn mahogany planking. Two 160-horsepower Wolseley engines were to drive three airscrews.[7]

In the course of the work a number of departures were made from the original design to meet problems of construction. When the ship – officially designated His Majesty's Airship No. 1 but widely known as the *Mayfly* – was approaching completion, a member of the design staff, H. B. Pratt, investigated the cumulative effect of these changes. His calculations led him to predict that her main structure would col-

Pioneers of British naval aviation: Captain R. H. S. Bacon (drawn after his promotion to flag rank).

lapse under stress unless still further and more radical modifications were introduced.[8]

However, the decision was made to carry out mooring trials which would entail no loss of life even if this prediction were fulfilled. The ship was duly hauled from her shed on 22 May 1911. She was brought without mishap to a thirty-eight-foot mast, spent two nights in the open, and withstood winds rising in gusts to Force 9 on the Beaufort Scale. All that seemed to be wrong with her was that she was too heavy by three tons. Accordingly, she was returned to her shed so that structural alterations could be made and superfluous equipment be removed. A proposal to insert an additional bay in order to increase her lift was turned down, partly on the ground that the shed was not long enough.

Arrangements were then made to begin a further series of trials on 24 September. While she was being walked from the shed on that day, she was struck by a sudden squall and broke her back. She is said to have been 'almost out of the shed' when the accident occurred, but a photograph taken just as she began to break up shows her apparently well clear of it.[9] Precisely what happened may never be known, for evidence that might settle the point is not available. Winston Churchill, First Lord of the Admiralty when the causes of the ac-

Captain Murray Sueter.

cident were investigated, refused to allow the minutes and proceedings of the Court of Inquiry to be published, and the report was afterwards described as 'lost'.[10]

No further attempt to build a rigid airship in Britain was made before 1913, when the Admiralty asked Vickers to undertake the design and construction of a ship to be known as His Majesty's Airship No. 9. H. B. Pratt, who had left Vickers after the *Mayfly* disaster, returned to take charge of the design staff. He brought with him a young apprentice named B. N. Wallis, afterwards better known as Dr Barnes Wallis. Good progress was made until the outbreak of war, but thereafter the work went on spasmodically.[11] The result was that in the early stages of the war Germany alone possessed the large rigid airships which were then the only aircraft capable of reconnoitring or attacking distant objectives.

The Mayfly *being hauled from her shed on 24 September, 1911.*

The LZ.10 (Schwaben) *passenger airship of 1911, with box-like elevator-and-rudder assembly characteristic of early Zeppelins.*

4 Airships in World War 1: 1914-15

When the murder of an Austrian archduke at Sarajevo in the summer of 1914 precipitated a European war, the Germans had been preparing for many years for a two-front war against France and Russia. Even so, their preparations were in some respects still far from complete. The German General Staff had drawn up an elaborate plan to invade France through Belgium and Luxembourg while the Austrians held the Russians at bay on the Eastern Front. German naval strategists, aware that such a move was likely to bring Britain into the war on the side of France, hoped that the navy's possession of large airships capable of reconnoitring the Heligoland Bight and its approaches might do something to offset the numerical inferiority of the German High Seas Fleet to the British Grand Fleet. Yet in August 1914 the Naval Airship Division had only about seven-eighths of its authorized establishment of 414 officers and other ranks, and only one naval airship was in service.[1] This was the L.3, completed in the previous May to replace the ill-fated L.1 and L.2. One Parseval and one Gross-Basenach, the latter handed over by the army, were acquired soon after the outbreak of war, and later two more Parsevals were commissioned; but these non-rigid airships were seldom used outside the Baltic, except for training. Pending the completion of a new airship base at Nordholz, near Cuxhaven, the Heligoland Bight and its approaches could, in any case, by reconnoitred only from a station at Fuhlsbüttel, owned by a subsidiary of DELAG but rented by the navy since 1913.

The German Army, on the other hand, possessed at the outbreak of war no less than seven large rigid airships, not counting ships requisitioned from DELAG and later either retained or transferred to the navy as training ships. The Z.4, Z.5 and SL.2 were stationed on the Eastern Front; the Z.6, Z.7, Z.8 and Z.9 were in west Germany. Especially on the Western Front, these large ships proved extremely vulnerable to fire from the ground when used in daylight at heights suitable for tactical reconnaissance or the bombing of tactical targets. On 6 August, when the Germans were trying to capture the Belgian forts commanding the crossings of the Meuse at Liège without undertaking a regular siege, the Z.6 was sent to attack one of them. She was hit by artillery fire and crashed on her return to Germany. Just over a fortnight later the Z.7 and Z.8 were destroyed by the same means within the space of a single day. On the Eastern Front the SL.2 made some useful sorties for the benefit of Austrian troops, but the Z.5 was hit by artillery fire on 28 August and landed behind the Russian lines. Her

commander was killed and the rest of her crew surrendered. Finally, on 8 October the Z.9 was destroyed by bombs dropped on her shed at Düsseldorf from a British naval aircraft. This was particularly pleasing to the Belgians, who could not forget that in August bombs dropped on Antwerp from the Z.9 had killed or injured twenty-six people and damaged a building in which the Belgian royal family was staying.

The French began the war with one small pressure airship built in a government factory at Chalais-Meudon, two bought from Zodiac, and about a dozen bought from Astra-Torres or Clément-Bayard.[2] Their attempts to use these ships for direct or indirect support of troops were not very successful. Besides proving vulnerable to attacks by German gunners and airmen, the ships were repeatedly hit by fire from French troops. New ships, defensively armed with machine-guns mounted on platforms above their envelopes, were introduced in 1915, but the great disadvantage of the airship as a low-flying army support weapon continued to be the ease with which it could be brought down by fire from guns and even small arms.

The Italians, as signatories to a thirty-year-old pact which pledged them to support Germany and Austro-Hungary should either be attacked by Russia, had been expected before the outbreak of war to take up arms against the Entente powers in the event of a clash between Britain, France and Russia on the one hand and Germany and Austro-Hungary on the other. In the event they refused to do so, pointing out that nothing in the pact obliged them to join an offensive war which their allies had launched without consulting them. When they decided in 1915 to throw in their lot with France and Britain, they had about a dozen pressure airships broadly similar to those possessed by the French.[3] Some were used to hunt for submarines in the Mediterranean, but most were devoted to reconnaissance of positions held by Austrian troops. Again, this proved an expensive method of providing air support for land forces. Several Italian airships were shot down by Austrian airmen, and others by fire from the ground. The Austrians themselves made little or no use of airships, but derived some benefit from information about Russian dispositions provided by German airships on the Eastern Front. At least two airships bought in France were at the disposal of the Russian Army on the outbreak of war, but the use made of them remains obscure.

The British differed from the Germans, the French and the Italians in making no use of airships to support their armies in the field. About seven months before the

ABOVE: *Astra-Torres airship, c. 1914.*

outbreak of war the British government, observing that lighter-than-air machines seemed likely to be more useful for maritime reconnaissance than for any other warlike purpose, directed the War Office to part with its airships for the benefit of the navy.[4] As a result of this decision and of orders placed by the Admiralty, the newly formed Royal Naval Air Service began the war with seven airships.[5] The smallest was a Willows with an envelope holding only 20,000 cubic feet of hydrogen. At the other end of the scale were the Parseval delivered in 1913 and an Astra-Torres bought in the same year. Farnborough-built airships taken over by the navy included the somewhat antiquated *Beta*, *Gamma* and *Delta* and the more modern *Eta*, completed about twelve months before the outbreak of war.

From the Willows the British developed in 1915 a fleet of small, low-powered airships which they used to hunt for submarines in and near the English Channel and the Irish Sea. These diminutive craft, called Sea Scouts or Blimps, were driven by a variety of engines. With a seventy-horsepower Renault engine, a Sea Scout was capable of speeds up to about forty-five miles an hour in still air and could remain on patrol for at least eight hours.[6] The Coastal, a larger and more powerful ship designed to withstand such weather as crews could expect to meet off the East Coast and based substantially on the Astra-Torres, was introduced towards the end of the year. Two powerful Sunbeam engines and a big reserve of fuel gave the Coastal a top speed of more than fifty miles an hour and an endurance of twenty-four hours or more with four or five men aboard.[7] Standard versions of the Sea Scout carried two or sometimes three men in a car made from the fuselage of a Farnborough-designed aeroplane; the Sea Scout Zero had a specially designed car which could be used in an emergency as a boat. Airships developed from the Sea Scout and the Coastal included the Sea Scout Twin, with two engines and a crew of five, and the C-Star, an improved version of the Coastal with a larger envelope and a maximum speed of just under sixty miles an hour.

By the autumn of 1915 Sea Scouts were making daily patrols whenever the weather was suitable from stations in Kent, Sussex, the Pas de Calais and Anglesey. These were not very successful so far as the destruction of submarines was concerned, but they made the work of submarine commanders more difficult and had a considerable moral effect on crews of British and Allied merchant vessels and on passengers in troopships. More than one member of the British Expeditionary Force confessed after the war that he had never felt happy

A more sophisticated version of the Sea Scout, the Sea Scout Zero. The surface vessel is a minelaying sloop.

British Sea Scout airship, c. 1916. The envelope was based on the Willows; the car was the fuselage of a B.E.2c aeroplane, without wings but with tractor airscrew and aero engine. The first airship designed expressly as a submarine spotter and the ancestor of all blimps.

when crossing the English Channel unless there was a Blimp about.

Meanwhile the Germans wrestled with the problem of turning the large rigid airship into the decisive weapon that Ferdinand von Zeppelin had always hoped to make it.

Within a few days of the outbreak of war, the naval authorities took advantage of a partial relaxation of financial controls to place a large order with the Zeppelin organization before its entire output was bespoken by the War Office. The experts wanted ships at least twenty-five per cent larger than any yet produced. The manufacturers could not undertake to build such ships until they were able to use new sheds whose construction the naval authorities were willing to finance. In the meantime they could offer only ships similar to the L.3.[8]

The outcome was that between 1 September 1914 and the end of 1915 the navy commissioned six ships of the L.3 class, numbered from L.4 to L.9, and ten larger ships numbered from L.10 to L.19.* During the same period seven ships were written off as lost on active service, accidentally destroyed, or damaged beyond repair. In the same period the army commissioned nineteen new ships and wrote off nine of these for one reason or another.[9]

The result was that before long both the army and the navy either had, or expected to have in the foreseeable future, more airships than they could usefully employ unless new tasks were found for them. Once the troops in France and Flanders settled down to trench warfare, the army's airships were not needed for tactical reconnaissance on the Western Front. In any case, experience had shown that they were not very suitable for such work. As for the navy's airships, they were intended primarily to help the High Seas Fleet by scouting ahead of it and establishing the whereabouts of the enemy's naval forces. But the navy's policy after the outbreak of war was to keep the High Seas Fleet away from waters where it might meet the British battlefleet. Thus there was a risk that naval airships might be relegated largely to defensive patrols, which would tend to stifle the initiative of commanders and crews unless they were sometimes given more interesting work to do.

In these circumstances both the naval and the military authorities were attracted by the idea of using some of their airships to attack objectives in England. For

* The L.20, commissioned in December 1915 and first ship of a new class, has been excluded from this reckoning.

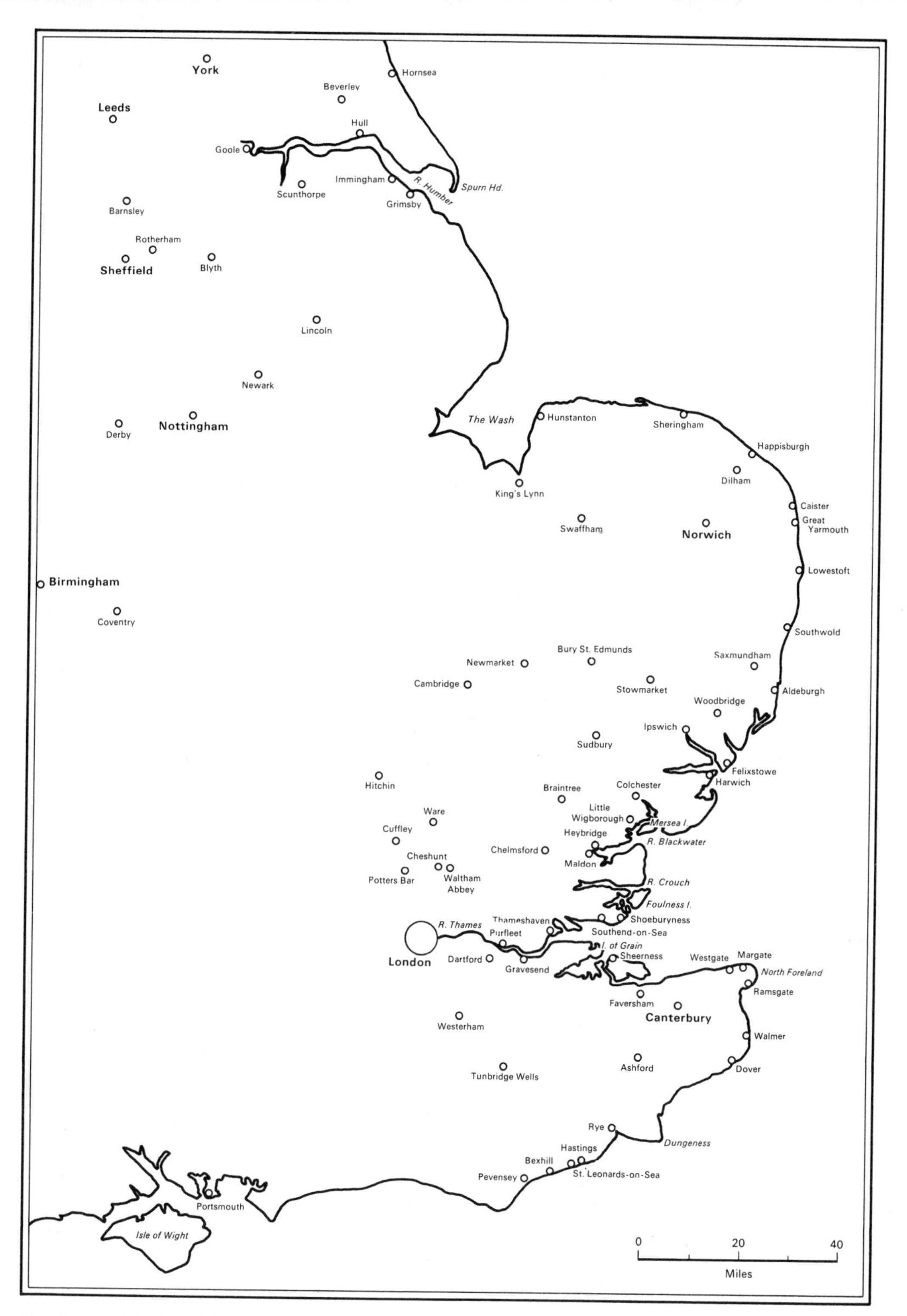

South-east England showing some airship bases in use during World War I.

The German naval airships L.11 (foreground) and L.6.

various reasons they were unable at first to agree on a common policy, and in any case it was not until some six months after the outbreak of war that the Kaiser could be persuaded to sanction an offensive against the British homeland. He then did so, with the proviso that crews were to take special care not to damage historic buildings or private property. He stipulated that London should not be attacked.[10]

The plan proposed by the Chief of Naval Aviation and approved by the Chief of Naval Staff envisaged attacks on dockyards and military installations in areas which included Tyneside, the Humber and the Thames Estuary. Great Yarmouth, Lowestoft and Harwich was also mentioned, although there were no dockyards or military installations of major importance at either of the first two of these places. The attackers were to cross the North Sea in daylight, drop their bombs at or after dusk, and return under cover of darkness.

Britain's air defences in 1915 were rudimentary in the extreme. A month after the outbreak of war the Admiralty had, at the request of the War Office, assumed responsibility for the air defence of the United Kingdom.[11] About thirty quick-firing guns and pom-poms, manned by naval reservists, were available for the defence of government offices, Woolwich arsenal, naval dockyards and other objectives of interest to the navy. The Admiralty undertook to provide, with such help as the Royal Flying Corps might be able to furnish, aircraft for the purpose of defending London and the chief ports and of intercepting hostile aircraft which reached the coast; but nothing like the number of aircraft needed to give continuous cover was available. Moreover, even if hostile aeroplanes or airships were intercepted, the chances of destroying them with the weapons carried in the aircraft of the day would be slender.

The first attempt by naval airships to attack objectives in Britain proved abortive. The L.3, L.4, L.5 and L.6 set out from Fuhlsbüttel and Nordholz on 13 January, but turned back on running into unfavourable weather over the North Sea.

Six days later the L.3 (Kapitänleutnant Hans Fritz) and L.4 (Kapitänleutnant Magnus Graf von Platen-Hallermund) left Fuhlsbüttel with the Humber as their objective. On the same day the L.6 (Oberleutnant Horst Freiherr Teusch von Buttlar-Brandenfels) started from Nordholz for the Thames Estuary, carrying Korvettenkapitän Peter Strasser, commander of the Naval Airship Division and organizer of the venture, in addition to her crew, fuel and bomb-load.

After five hours, engine trouble forced Buttlar to turn for home. Fritz and Platen-Hallermund continued to the English coast, but reached it many miles further south than they intended. Fritz dropped bombs at Great Yarmouth from 5,000 feet, wrecking some cottages and killing two elderly people. Platen-Hallermund dropped some of his load in the neighbourhood of Sheringham and Hunstanton and the rest at King's Lynn, where a woman and a boy were killed and thirteen people injured.

Platen-Hallermund reported on his return that he had been attacked near King's Lynn by anti-aircraft guns and followed by a searchlight. There were in fact no anti-aircraft guns in that neighbourhood, and according to British accounts not a shot was fired at either airship.[12] Three aircraft were ready for action at the Royal Naval Air Station at Great Yarmouth, but none of them was capable of reaching the heights at which airships could fly, or carried any armament apart from the small arms which pilots often took into the air. As a result of the raid the authorities did, however, add some mobile anti-aircraft machine-guns and searchlights to the air defences of East Anglia.

In the following month the Kaiser authorized attacks on the London docks and on oil installations, military establishments and naval and military stores, adding that objectives in London west of the Tower were not to be attacked.[13] Strasser, determined not to be forestalled, promptly sent the L.8 to the army's airship base at Düsseldorf. Her commander, Kapitänleutnant Helmut Beelitz, set out for London on 26 February, but was forced by contrary winds to land near Ghent. When ordered a few days later to return to Düsseldorf, Beelitz decided without consulting Strasser to fly first to England and drop bombs there. On reaching the Belgian coast and losing height to get his bearings, he was met by small-arms fire from Belgian troops. He jettisoned his bomb-load and made for Germany, but the ship crashed near Tirlemont and was completely wrecked.[14]

In the course of the next few days four of the army's airships moved to forward bases in Brabant and Flanders. They set out for England on 17 March, but turned back on running into dense fog. On the following day the Kaiser once again forbade attacks on London. The ban was afterwards lifted, but meanwhile one of the airships in the forward area was shot down while returning from a raid on Paris, a second was wrecked by a forced landing, and a third – the SL.2 – was withdrawn for overhaul and reconstruction. For the moment, therefore, the army was not in a position to do much.

As for the navy, Strasser's faith in the ability of his crews to carry out the Kaiser's instructions had been somewhat shaken by the poor results of the raid on 13 January and the loss of the L.8. It was revived by a curious episode on 14 April. On that day the L.9, commanded by Kapitänleutnant Heinrich Mathy, made a long and uneventful reconnaissance of the southern part of the North Sea. The ship carried ten bombs, each weighing about a hundredweight, in addition to forty small incendiaries. Mathy asked to be allowed to drop his bombs on an objective in England before coming home. Permission was granted. The ship crossed the Northumbrian coast at Blyth, which Mathy mistook for Tynemouth. Mathy then dropped his bombs, which fell mostly in open country. On his return to base he reported, erroneously but in good faith, that he had made a successful attack on shipyards near the mouth of the Tyne.[15]

Thus encouraged, Strasser sent three ships to England on the following day. These were the L.5 (Kapitänleutnant Alois Böcker), the L.6 (Buttlar) and the L.7 (Oberleutnant Werner Peterson). Böcker flew over the neighbourhood of Lowestoft and Southwold during the night and dropped bombs there, apparently in the belief that he had reached the Humber. Buttlar, going even further astray, dropped bombs in the neighbourhood of Maldon and Heybridge, in Essex. Peterson, with

Gondola of L.6.

Strasser aboard his ship, confessed that he was unable to find his objective and carried his bomb-load back to Germany. An aircraft was sent from the Royal Naval Air Station at Great Yarmouth during the night to search for the airships, but they were not intercepted. The L.6 was, however, hit by rifle and machine-gun fire. Bombs damaged a number of buildings and a woman was injured, but no one was killed.

When making a further attempt to reach the Humber on 12 May, the L.5 suffered from severe icing and narrowly escaped disaster. In the light of this experience Strasser ruled that no more raids on Britain should be undertaken until the new, large airships ordered just after the outbreak of war were ready. The first of these, the L.10, was commissioned on 13 May.

During the night of 29–30 April four aircraft were despatched from the Royal Naval Air Station at Great Yarmouth to search for an airship which had dropped bombs at Ipswich and Bury St Edmunds. The ship, afterwards identified as the LZ.38, was not intercepted. The conclusion drawn by the British was that in future they must try to intercept airships before nightfall and before they reached the coast. A trawler equipped to carry a seaplane was stationed between fifty and sixty miles off the Norfolk coast, but frequent patrols during the rest of the year proved completely ineffective.[16]*

The LZ.38, commanded by Hauptmann Erich Linnarz, returned on 10 May to drop bombs at Southend. Some buildings of no military value were damaged or destroyed, a woman was killed and two men were injured. Linnarz also attacked Ramsgate, where he dropped bombs on and near a public house in the early hours of 17 May, and on 26 May he made a second visit to Southend, dropping a large number of bombs which did little damage. Finally, on the night of the 31st he flew to London by way of Kent and Essex. Passing over Stoke Newington, Hoxton, Shoreditch, Whitechapel, Stepney, West Ham and Leytonstone, he dropped about a ton of bombs which killed seven people and injured thirty-five.

* The army began by giving airships bought from the Zeppelin organization numbers prefixed by the letter Z, and allotting to ships bought as replacements the designations of the ships they replaced. After reaching Z.12 they switched to factory designations, beginning with the LZ.33 and omitting ships assigned to the navy. On taking delivery of the LZ.42 they decided to call her the LZ.72. Thereafter they added thirty to the factory number of each ship bought from Zeppelin.

The navy's first attempt at a raid on London followed on 4 June. The newly commissioned L.10, commanded by Kapitänleutnant Klaus Hirsch, came within sight of the target area, but Hirsch mistook the lights ahead of him for those of Ipswich. Troubled by a strong head-wind, he decided to turn to port, drop his bombs on a place which he thought was Harwich, and then make for home. In fact, his bombs fell on Gravesend. On the same night Kapitänleutnant Fritz Boemack took the SL.3 to the neighbourhood of the Humber, Flamborough Head and Hull, but dropped only three bombs which did no damage.

Two nights later, both naval and army airships raided Britain. The L.9, still commanded by Heinrich Mathy, made the navy's contribution. Mathy's primary target was London, but on finding when he reached the English coast that a strong wind was blowing from the south-west, he set course for the Humber. After going as far north as Bridlington he returned to aim bombs at the docks at Kingston-upon-Hull, using flares to illuminate the target area. About forty houses and shops were destroyed and sixty-four people were killed or injured. This raid was by far the most destructive suffered up to that time by any English town.

No such success attended the army's efforts. The ships used were the LZ.37, 38 and 39, and their target was London. The LZ.38 flew only a short distance before engine trouble forced her to return to her base at Evère, near Brussels. The other ships continued towards the target area, but they too turned back before reaching the English coast. During the homeward flight the LZ.37 was seen by Flight Sub-Lieutenant R. A. J. Warneford, whose Morane monoplane was laden with bombs which he had intended to drop on airship sheds in Belgium. He followed the LZ.37, climbed above her, and released his bombs. She burst into flames and crashed near Ghent. On the same day the LZ.38 was destroyed by bombs dropped on her shed by two other pilots of the Royal Naval Air Service, Flight lieutenant J. P. Wilson and Flight Sub-Lieutenant J. S. Mills.

Immediately after destroying the LZ.37, Warneford was compelled by a broken petrol pipe and other mishaps to land behind the enemy's lines. He managed to elude capture, repair the pipe and return to his base at Dunkirk, after landing at Cap Gris Nez to find out where he was. Ten days later he was killed when his aircraft crashed near Paris.

Mathy's attack on Kingston-upon-Hull caused intense excitement and indignation in the town and indeed throughout the country. Troops had to be called in to quell rioters who sacked shops owned or thought to be owned by Germans.[17] For some time after the raid thousands of inhabitants of Hull left the town every evening and slept in fields, woods or barns. A great many innocent people were accused by their neighbours of signalling to or otherwise aiding the enemy. The authorities were deluged with complaints and suggestions, some of them far-fetched to the verge of lunacy.

The raid might have been expected to lead to much stricter control of lighting in British towns and cities. Mathy and his crew reported that Hull and Grimsby were 'a blaze of lights' on the night of 31 May, and their success was attributed by their superiors partly to the failure of local authorities to impose an effective blackout. In fact, this responsibility had been transferred more than six weeks before the raid from local authorities to the Home Office.[18] A good many months were to elapse, however, before drastic restrictions on lighting were applied to the whole of England except six western counties which seemed unlikely to be attacked.

In Germany, Mathy's success brought demands from the Naval Staff for more and bigger raids on Britain, and especially on London. The General Staff agreed that a vigorous offensive was desirable, but drew attention to the difficulty of mounting attacks on short summer nights. They proposed that in favourable conditions raids should be made by airships of both services under the army's control. The Naval Staff did not take kindly to this proposal. They pointed out that attempts to co-ordinate attacks by naval and army airships from bases far apart had not been successful in the past and seemed unlikely to prove so in the future. Adding that the army did not possess enough airships to make a valuable contribution, they concluded that in all probability the navy would do better on its own.[19] Some point was given to their argument by a successful raid on Tyneside by the L.10 during the night of 15–16 June.

After a good deal of argument the Kaiser and the Imperial Chancellor, Theobald von Bethmann-Hollweg, sanctioned vigorous attacks on London by naval airships, stipulating on humanitarian grounds that, in principle, they should be made on Saturdays or Sundays, when the City of London would be almost deserted.[20]

The new phase began on 9 August. Strasser's intention was that the L.10, L.11, L.12, L.13 and L.14 should bomb London; the L.9, the SL.3 and the SL.4 were to attack objectives on the Humber and the Tyne. As things turned out, not one ship reached London. The L.13 turned back with engine trouble and the L.10, L.11, L.12 and L.14 dropped their bombs more or less at random on places far outside the target area. About forty people were killed or injured, most of them by bombs dropped by the L.9 at Goole. The L.12 was hit by gunfire over Dover and came down on the sea off the Belgian coast. She was towed to Ostend by a patrol boat and withstood attacks by three aircraft of the Royal Naval Air Service, but caught fire while she was being dismantled. Commanders and crews attributed their troubles to heavy rain which robbed their ships of buoyancy and made it even more difficult than usual to find their targets.

A further attempt to bomb London a few nights later was equally unsuccessful, but on the night of 17–18 August one of four ships despatched succeeded in reaching the target area. This was the L.10, commanded on this occasion by Oberleutnant Freidrich Wenke. Wenke dropped some bombs at and near Leyton, Leytonstone and Wanstead, all in the Greater London area, and also some at Chelmsford. In addition bombs were dropped on various places in Kent by the L.11, but with little effect, and in the sea off the Norfolk coast by the L.14. The commander of the L.14 reported on his return to base that he had attacked blast furnaces and factories at or near Ipswich and Woodbirdge, in Suffolk. Fifty-eight people were killed or injured, all in London.

The next month began badly for Strasser. On 3 September the L.10 blew up and was lost with all her crew only a few miles from the German coast, when she ran into a thunderstorm while returning from a routine flight over the Heligoland Bight.

A moderately successful raid on London followed on the night of 7 September, when two army airships, the LZ.74 and the rebuilt SL.2, reached the target area. The commander of the LZ.74 dropped most of his load prematurely in Hertfordshire and had only small incendiary left when he arrived over his intended target. But Hauptmann von Wobeser, commanding the SL.2, carried his to the dockland area round Millwall, Deptford, Greenwich and Woolwich. Fifty-six people were killed or injured, but no objective of military importance was seriously damaged. A pilot from the Royal Naval Air Station at Great Yarmouth, Flight Sub-Lieutenant C. E. Wood, patrolled for two hours in search of a third airship, afterwards identified as the LZ.77, but saw nothing of her.

A few hours later it was the navy's turn. Three ships, the L.11, L.13 and L.14, set out for London on 8 September. The L.11 soon turned back with engine trouble and

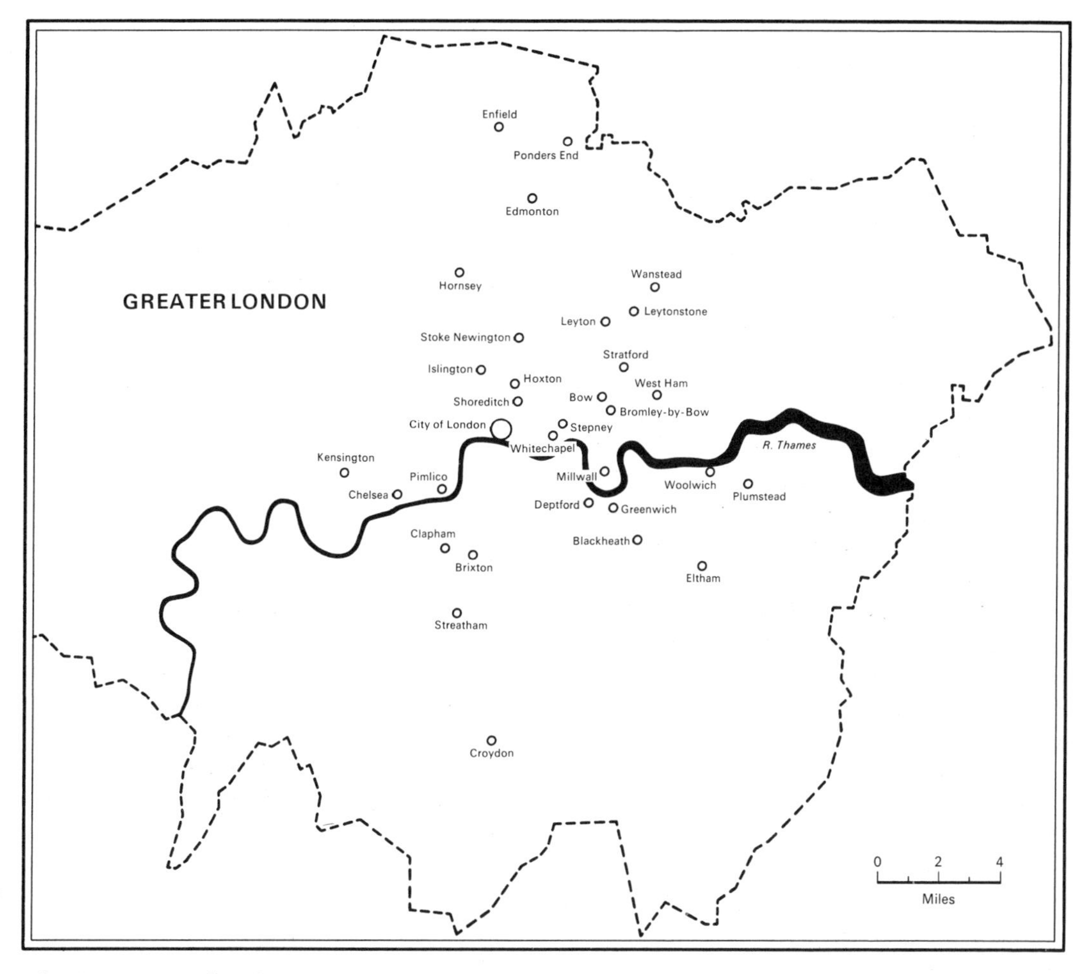

The Greater London Area.

the L.14 went no further than the neighbourhood of Norwich, where her commander shed his bomb-load before setting course for home. But the L.13, commanded by the redoubtable Mathy, continued to the target area and dropped bombs which started an immensely destructive fire amidst textile warehouses near St Paul's Cathedral. Every high-angle gun within miles opened fire on Mathy's ship, but he returned safely to his base and was able to assure the imperial court a few days later that no harm had come to Buckingham Palace and that none of his bombs had hit churches or historic buildings.[21] He could not conscientiously have added that only military objectives had been damaged.

On the same night Mathy's old ship, the L.9, crossed the Yorkshire coast near Whitby. Her commander, Kapitänleutnant Odo Loewe, had orders to bomb a factory at Skinningrove, where large quantities of highly inflammable benzol were stored. He complained afterwards that he could not find the factory and had to drop his bombs more or less where he guessed it was. In fact, he attacked it with uncanny precision, but luck was against him. A high-explosive bomb fell ten feet away from a building containing benzol, but neither damaged it not set fire to another 45,000 gallons of benzol in adjacent tanks. The same building was struck by an incendiary bomb which also did no harm. Another bomb scored a direct hit on a store containing TNT, but failed to explode. Minor damage done to the factory included the fracture of a water-main.

For his last raid of the year, on the night of 13 October, Strasser used five ships. Again, London was the target area. Two ships failed to reach it, and two of those that did dropped bombs at places remote from the objectives their commanders thought they were attacking. Kapitänleutnant Joachim Breithaupt, commanding the L.15, made no such mistake, although he was flying over England for the first time. He carried most of his load to central London and dropped it with devastating effect north of the Strand and near the Law Courts. Altogether 149 people were killed or injured in London and fifty elsewhere. Although hotly engaged by anti-aircraft guns and chased by airmen who hoped to get above the ship and drop small bombs on her, the L.15 escaped unscathed.

In an age when acts of terrorism and the slaughter of civilians by bombing are almost daily occurrences which occasion no more than a passing regret, it is difficult to form an adequate conception of the horror and indignation aroused in Britain by these events. The Kaiser had stipulated when he first authorized attacks on Britain that only 'military shipyards', arsenals, docks and military establishments in general should be bombed. Later, he had added oil installations to the list. But he must have known by the time he sanctioned raids on London that no airship commander could aim bombs at such an objective as the Millwall docks or Woolwich arsenal without endangering civilian lives and property. Long after experience had shown that selective bombing of precisely defined objectives in built-up areas at night was beyond the skill of even the most painstaking crews, the raids were continued because the German authorities saw in them a means of keeping up the spirits of their aeronauts, disrupting Britain's war economy, and weakening the will of the British people to carry on the war.

Notwithstanding the importance attached to the raids by students of air power, they constituted only a very small proportion of Germany's air effort in 1915. As compared with some forty to fifty sorties devoted in that year to raids on Britain, the naval airship division devoted some 300 to reconnaissance of the Heligoland Bight and its approaches, and some fifty or sixty to reconnaissance of the Baltic and raids on objectives in the vicinity of the Gulf of Finland.[22] Sorties against Britain by the army's airships were still more heavily outnumbered by those expended on such tasks as reconnaissance of the Eastern Front and the bombing of objectives behind the Russian lines and in France. Moreover, the entire effort against Britain resulted in only twenty-seven flights over British soil by the navy's airships and ten by the army's.

Most patrols over the Heligoland Bight and its approaches were uneventful, but there were exceptions. Klaus Hirsch was making a routine flight in the L.5 on 24 January when he learned that Rear-Admiral Franz Hipper, who had put to sea on the previous evening with four battlecruisers, four light cruisers and nineteen destroyers, was in action with a force of British battlecruisers near the Dogger Bank. He flew to the spot, was fired upon by British cruisers, and saw the German cruiser *Blücher* sink, but was not aware that the British battlecruiser *Lion* had been damaged. Conceiving it to be his duty to cover Hipper's retreat, he placed himself in a position which did not enable him to give his superiors any useful information about the enemy's strength or movements.[23] Indeed, such information as he did provide was misleading. Nevertheless, the experience was enough to suggest that he might conceivably have made a worthwhile contribution had he been fully briefed before his flight began.

As things turned out, the Battle of the

Dogger Bank was the only major naval action of the entire war at which a German naval airship was present and its commander given an opportunity of making such a contribution. The L.6, the L.7 and the L.9 covered a sortie towards Terschelling by part of the High Seas Fleet at the end of March, but they were not sent far enough for their commanders to stand any real chance of finding out what the enemy was doing. Patrols later in the year brought occasional contacts with British submarines or surface craft, but all such encounters were inconclusive. Airships were also used to warn German minesweeping forces of the approach of hostile warships, and in this role the L.5 scored a notable success on 2 June, when a signal from her commander enabled minesweepers and their escort of destroyers to escape interception by British cruisers.

On the debit side of the account, Strasser suffered a serious loss on 17 February. Arrangements had been made for a merchant vessel carrying supplies consigned to German East Africa to run the gauntlet of the British blockade by passing along the Norwegian coast. Strasser was ordered by the Naval Staff to send two airships to keep watch for British warships. He sent Fritz in the L.3 and Magnus von Platen-Hallermund in the L.4. Neither saw anything of the enemy, but both ran into trouble. Turning back with one engine out of order, Fritz faced a strong headwind. When a second engine failed, he made an emergency landing on the Danish island of Fanö, destroyed his confidential papers and set fire to his ship. No one was hurt, but he and his entire crew were interned. The L.4, also with two engines out of order, fared still worse. As dusk was falling she crashed in shallow water off the Danish coast and four members of the crew were lost. Eleven survivors, including her commander, struggled to the shore to face internment.

On balance, the Germans concluded from their varied experience in 1915 that the large rigid airship had an important part to play in the war against Britain. Britain was the enemy whose intervention in 1914 had disrupted the plans of the German General Staff and whose economic blockade threatened to deprive Germany of imports essential to her war effort and the welfare of her people. To bring her to her knees, the Germans relied largely on attacks by their submarines on shipping bound for the British Isles. In the light of events in August, September and October, it seemed to them that attacks by their airships on British cities might also make a valuable contribution.

5 Airships in World War I: 1916

On 1 January 1916 seven German naval airships of the L.10 class and one airship of a new class, the L.20, were in service.* A second airship of the L.20 class, the L.21, was commissioned on 19 January. In addition three ships of the L.3 class – the L.6, L.7 and L.9 – were still in use, but these old ships were more suitable for defensive than offensive purposes. Of the three Schütte-Lanz airships delivered to the navy in 1915, two had come to grief before the end of the year, so that only the SL.3 remained. The Naval Airship Division also had one Parseval in commission and one in reserve, but had lost its other Parseval on the Eastern Front and had taken its only Gross-Basenach out of service.[1]

On 18 January Strasser discussed the future of the Naval Airship Division with Vice-Admiral Reinhard Scheer, who was about to succeed Admiral Hugo von Pohl in command of the High Seas Fleet. In general, Scheer favoured a more aggressive strategy than his predecessor. He and Strasser agreed that widespread raids on Britain should be made by as many naval airships as possible and as many army airships as the military authorities might think fit to provide. For the purpose of giving broad instructions to commanders, Britain was to be divided into a northern, a midland and a southern target area. Commanders ordered to the northern area were to give preference to objectives near the Forth and Tyne, those ordered to the southern area to objectives in London and East Anglia. In the midland area Liverpool was to be the primary and the Humber the secondary objective, but commanders on their way to Liverpool would be free to attack suitable objectives in undefended built-up areas in the industrial Midlands.[2]

On 31 January Strasser sent all nine available airships of the L.10 and L.20 classes to Britain, himself embarking in the L.11. He told his commanders to attack objectives in either the midland or the southern area, adding that, 'if at all possible', Liverpool was to be attacked.

Their attempts to carry out these orders were not very successful. Fog and mist over the North Sea and parts of Britain forced them to rely on direction-finding stations at Nordholz and Bruges to fix their positions before, and in some cases after, they reached the English coast. Many of them crossed the coast at points far from the places where they thought they were.

* The surviving airships of the L.10 class were the L.11, L.13, L.14, L.15, L.16, L.17 and L.19. The L.10 had blown up (p. 80), the L.12 had caught fire while being dismantled at Ostend (p. 80) and the L.18 had been accidentally destroyed only eleven days after she was commissioned.

Objectives which, on their return to Germany, commanders claimed to have attacked included docks, factories and other installations at Liverpool, Manchester, Goole, Immingham, Nottingham and Great Yarmouth. In fact, no bombs fell at any of those places. The bombs which Kapitänleutnant Max Dietrich, commanding the L.21, believed he had dropped at Liverpool and Birkenhead fell seventy-five miles away at Birmingham. Windows were broken at Stoke-on-Trent, and ten people were killed or injured at Scunthorpe, by bombs which Mathy, in the L.13, thought he was aiming at Manchester and Goole. The experienced Peterson, now commanding the L.16, claimed to have dropped two tons of bombs on 'such factories as could be made out at Great Yarmouth'. So far as is known, the only bombs from the L.16 which fell on land came down at Swaffham, a good forty miles from Yarmouth.[3]

As if difficulties of navigation and target-finding were not enough, at least four of the ships sent to Britain on 31 January had engine trouble.[4] The L.15 and later ships of the L.10 class, as well as all ships of the L.20 class, were fitted with 240-horsepower Maybach HSLu engines instead of the 210-horsepower Maybach C-X engines previously used. Early engines of this series were notoriously unreliable, and some of them broke down for long or short periods during the January raid. Nevertheless all but one of the ships despatched on 31 January returned safely to their bases in Germany on the following day, completing flights whose duration ranged from just under twenty to well over twenty-four hours.

The exception was the L.19. Her commander was the Kapitänleutnant Odo Loewe who had taken the L.9 to Skinningrove the previous September. Between nightfall on 31 January and daybreak on 1 February Loewe made an inordinately long and curiously roundabout flight over East Anglia and the Midlands. His course, as tracked by observers on the ground from the sound of the ship's engines, was like that of a man groping his way blindfold through a maze. In the early hours of the morning he reported by wireless that he had flown as far as the west coast but, finding Liverpool shrouded in fog, had returned to drop his bombs on factories at Sheffield. In fact, he seems never to have gone further west than Bewdley, in Worcestershire, and most of his bombs fell in the suburbs of Birmingham.[5]

At 6.41 a.m. by Central European time on 1 February, when Loewe was bound for home, he asked for his position. He was then about ten miles off the Norfolk coast. More than eighteen hours had elapsed since he set out from Germany; but he was only about 300 miles from his base at Tondern, in Schleswig-Holstein, and his ship was capable of a speed of more than sixty miles an hour in still air. During her acceptance trials she had logged the highest speed attained in test conditions by any airship delivered to the navy up to that time.[6]

The next nine hours brought no further message from Loewe. Destroyers were leaving port to search for him when, a few minutes after 4 p.m. by Central European time, he at last broke silence. He reported that three of his four engines were out of order and that his wireless equipment had been working only intermittently. He gave his approximate position as Borkum, the most westerly of the East Frisian Islands and just inside German territory. But bearings from the direction-finding stations indicated a position about twenty miles north of Ameland, in the West Frisians. The inference was that, while Loewe believed himself to be already over Germany or German territorial waters, he was in fact uncomfortably close to neutral Holland.

About an hour later, Dutch troops saw an airship flying low over Ameland. Although they sensed that she was in difficulties and had lost her way they opened fire on her, presumably because they had been told to resist any infringement of their country's neutrality. They continued to fire at her until she disappeared in gathering mist and darkness over the North Sea.

From that moment Loewe must have known that he had only a remote chance of getting his ship back to Tondern. With only one engine working, and presumably with her gas-bags riddled with holes made by Dutch rifle bullets, she had become too heavy and sluggish to gain height.[7] But Loewe could still hope that he and his crew of fifteen would not be left to drown in the cold waters of the North Sea.

At midnight the German naval authorities ordered a search by destroyers and all available airships. But the airships were prevented by an unfavourable wind from leaving their sheds, and the destroyers found only one of the L.19's fuel tanks, floating in the sea about twelve miles north of Borkum and not quite empty. Aeroplanes were sent out from Borkum, but their pilots saw nothing and two of them failed to return.[8]

In Britain, a report that a German airship in difficulties had been seen off the Norfolk coast was received at dusk on 1 February. Destroyers and light cruisers from Harwich searched the southern part of the North Sea from daybreak on 2 February until the late afternoon, but without success.[9]

Nevertheless the missing airship *was* seen on that day. At 7 a.m. the master and crew of the British trawler *King Stephen*, fishing in a prohibited area more than a hundred miles east of Spurn Head, caught sight of a 'white object' on the surface of the water. On coming close they found it was the hulk of the L.19. Some men were in a rough shelter on top of the envelope, and the sound of hammering came from below. Loewe hailed the skipper of the *King Stephen* and asked him to take his crew aboard. The skipper refused to do so, fearing that Loewe and his fifteen officers and men would overpower his crew of nine and sail his ship to Germany. According to his subsequent account of the matter, he then set off in search of a patrol vessel whose commander would know what to do in such circumstances, but failed to find one. Hence it was not until he returned to the Humber on the following day that he was able to report the incident to the naval authorities.[10]

How much longer the wreck of the L.19 remained afloat is not known. Some months later a bottle containing a 'last report' from Loewe was washed up on the Norwegian coast and found its way to the headquarters of the naval airship division at Nordholz.[11] Loewe wrote that he and his crew were awaiting the end 'about one o'clock in the afternoon'.[12] He attributed the loss of his ship to engine failure and an adverse wind which not only delayed his homeward flight but was also responsible for carrying him over Dutch territory, 'where I was received with heavy rifle fire'.[13]

As a result of the loss of the L.19, Scheer ruled in February that future raids on Britain by naval airships should be made in conjunction with sweeps by destroyers. Airship commanders were to report movements of British warships for the benefit of the destroyers, which in turn would help any airships that might be crippled.[14]

The January raid left the British with the impression that the Germans had wasted a good deal of their effort on targets of no strategic value. At the same time, it convinced them that Britain's air defence needed to be substantially improved if the enemy's airships were not to be free to wander over the country, dropping bombs on any building or open space which their commanders might mistake for a factory or dockyard. In the past thirteen months bombs dropped from airships had killed or injured 922 people, and not one airship had been brought down on British soil.

The arrangement by which the navy was responsible for air defence and the army gave what help it could had never been regarded by the military authorities as one which ought to be perpetuated. From the outset they had intended to end it as soon as the Royal Flying Corps and the Royal Artillery had enough weapons to stand on their own feet, but they were understandably reluctant to shoulder the burden in the meantime. Early in 1916, after a good deal of argument and counter-argument, the change was made. Field-Marshal Lord French, Commander-in-Chief, of the Home Forces, assumed responsibility on 16 February for the air defence of the London area, and a few days later for that of the country as a whole.[15]

At that time 295 guns were available for the air defence of all parts of the United Kingdom. Only eighty of these were true anti-aircraft guns, but orders had been placed for 326 three-inch and sixty-two thirteen-pounder guns of recent design. The War Office had already drawn up a scheme for the local defence of factories, magazines and arsenals in eight areas between the Firth of Forth and Portsmouth and of specially important or vulnerable objectives outside those areas. For this 475 guns and five hundred searchlights would be needed, including sixty searchlights to be deployed for the benefit of pilots of aeroplanes sent to intercept airships before they reached the gun-defended areas. Twelve squadrons of such aeroplanes, nominally with eighteen or twenty-four aircraft apiece, though in practice few had more than half that number, were formed between November 1915 and November 1916. They were equipped with Farnborough-designed aircraft, nearly all manufactured under contract by commercial firms. At first pilots carried small incendiary bombs or explosive darts, but these were gradually replaced by machine-guns, and in the summer of 1916 incendiary and explosive bullets were introduced. Thirty-three home defence airfields equipped with rudimentary flare-paths for night flying were in service by the end of 1916.[16] Among those whose names became familiar to a later generation of airmen because they were used as fighter bases in the Second World War were Turnhouse, Catterick, Kirton-in-Lindsey and North Weald (then called North Weald Bassett), Rochford and Hornchurch (then called Sutton's Farm).

As a direct result of the January raid, the authorities used the powers conferred on the Home Office in the previous year to extend restrictions on lighting to the whole of England except Cumberland, Westmorland, Hereford, Monmouth, Somerset and Cornwall. Some local authorities in these areas asked that the restrictions should be applied to districts for which they were responsible, and eventually this was done.[17]

A further consequence of the January raid was that some local authorities, especially in the Midlands, pressed the central government to set up a reliable early-warning system which would enable them to take prompt action when hostile airships or aeroplanes were known to be approaching their areas, and at the same time would obviate the wasted efforts sometimes caused by false alarms. Their arguments received powerful reinforcement when, on 10 February, a false report that a Zeppelin had been seen during the afternoon off Scarborough led to the extinction of railway lights during the night at places as far apart as Nottingham and Bath and brought work to a standstill at two government factories at Gloucester.[18]

As a result of this incident Field-Marshal French was summoned to a meeting of the Cabinet and asked to prepare a scheme which would 'stop the spreading of rumour and of false reports'.[19] Knowing that members of his staff were already at work on the problem, French was able to promise an answer within three days. The outcome was an early-warning system based on the national telephone network and devised by Lieutenant-Colonel Philip Maud of GHQ, Home Forces. Warnings from observer posts and supplementary reports from police forces, railway officials, troops and naval stations were passed by telephone to Warning Controllers. Those parts of England, Wales and Scotland deemed liable to attack were divided into eight areas, and each Warning Controller was responsible for one of these. In the light of the information he received, the Warning Controller instructed the telephone exchange manager in the town where he had his headquarters to pass warnings to authorized persons, firms and authorities in one or more of a number of specified districts within his area. Telephone lines were kept open at appropriate times for the passing of warnings, and authorized recipients were required by regulations which had the force of law to answer a call within fifteen seconds. Coloured lights displayed behind a transparent map in a central control room at the Horse Guards in London told watch-keeping officers of Home Forces which parts of the country were under warning at a given moment, and whether a particular area had received only a preliminary warning or an order to take full precautions.

Whether warnings should be extended to the general public was a controversial question. Responsible men who had studied the behaviour of civilians during the early airship raids called attention to the danger that public warnings might prompt the uninitiated to venture into the streets to see what was going on, or to crowd together in places where they would be more vulnerable than if they stayed at home. There was also a risk that, until the system was perfected, a high proportion of false alarms might destroy the credibility of the warnings, so that by the time they became trustworthy the public would have acquired the habit of disregarding them. Still worse, the system might be utterly discredited if a town were bombed without warning and its inhabitants were aware that a public warning system was in operation.

However, by the spring of 1916 these arguments had lost much of their force. Doubtless some members of the public would always be inclined to act heedlessly in an emergency; but the vast majority, it was thought, could be trusted to take cover when hostile aircraft were approaching if they were told that that was the right thing to do. Above all, the adoption of a unified early-warning system under the direction of a responsible commander meant that, although in future there might still be warnings not followed by raids, raids not preceded by warnings were very unlikely to occur. The government was not yet prepared to sanction the issue of warnings in all areas, but ruled that they should be issued in areas where there was a manifest demand for them.[20] Warning Controllers were then authorized to order the sounding of hooters, as a signal to the general public to take cover. At the same time the sounding of hooters without the authority of a Warning Controller was forbidden. The issue of public warnings in the London area was not sanctioned until the late summer of 1917.[21]

Strasser's first raid with destroyer support was scheduled for early March. The plan was that submarines should lay mines off Dover and Harwich and in the Thames Estuary and that destroyers should sweep not only in the path of the returning airships but also further south for the purpose of engaging any light naval forces which the British might send out as they had done when the L.19 was in difficulties on 2 February. Cover was to be provided by the High Seas Fleet, and additional submarines were to lie in wait for the British in the southern part of the North Sea and the approaches to the Dover Strait.

In the outcome the submarines duly laid their mines and the German surface ships carried out their allotted tasks. But no British warships were seen, although plenty were at sea, and a brief sortie by the High Seas Fleet was completely ineffective. Two fishing smacks, however, were sunk by submarines off Lowestoft.

The start of the operation, originally fixed for 3 March, was postponed until 5 March.[22] On the intervening day Strasser took the L.15, L.16, L.17, L.20 and L.21 temporarily out of service and sent their engines to the Maybach factory at Friedrichshafen for inspection.[23] The SL.3 having moved at the end of January to Seddin, on the Baltic, only the L.11, L.13 and L.14 were available for raids on Britain.

About noon on 5 March all three of these ships left their bases at Nordholz and Hage with orders to fly to the northern target area, report the composition, positions and headings of any British naval forces seen in the North Sea or Scottish waters, and attack either the British naval base at Rosyth or other suitable objectives in the neighbourhood of the Forth, Tyne or Tees. Over the North Sea they met an unpredicted north-westerly wind of gale force. All three commanders then gave up the idea of going to Rosyth. Korvettenkapitän Viktor Schütze, who had succeeded Buttlar in command of the L.11, decided to make for Middlesbrough, and Mathy and Böcker in the L.13 and L.14 for the Tyne.[24]

Both Schütze and Böcker seriously underestimated the strength of the wind. Böcker crossed the English coast near Flamborough Head, recognized that he was far south of the Tyne, and after trying in vain to make good a northerly course, turned towards the Humber. He dropped six bombs in open country near Beverley and went on to drop at least twenty more on Hull. Schütze, after crossing the coast near Tunstall in Lincolnshire, flew southwestwards to Lincoln, but then turned back and made his way to the Humber by a zig-zag course. He reached the neighbourhood of Hull to find Böcker already there, stood off for a while, and eventually added his bombs to Böcker's. Guns had been assigned to the local defence of Hull in the scheme prepared by the War Office, but none had arrived and the place was completely undefended.[25] The bombs dropped from the two airships wrecked houses near the docks, damaged a ship under construction, set fire to an almshouse, broke the windows of a church and killed or injured sixty-nine people. The L.14 received one hit, probably when she passed over the Humber defences on her way out.

Mathy went even further astray. He crossed the Lincolnshire coast near Spurn Head, heading almost due west, but was carried by the wind in a south-westerly direction. Having mistaken the Humber for the Tees, he believed when he caught sight of the ground about an hour later that he was near Carlisle. In fact, he was near Newark, about 150 miles from

Carlisle.[26] He then turned to the southeast. After running before the wind for more than two hours, he estimated that he was near the Humber, but found when the clouds parted that he was over the Thames Estuary, where he was engaged by guns at Shoeburyness and Sheerness, but received no hits. He tried to double back, but could make no progress against the wind and was held in the glare of searchlights for five minutes while he hung almost motionless over the Isle of Grain. Finally he flew over Faversham and Canterbury, crossed the coast at Walmer, and took refuge at one of the army's airship stations in Belgium.[27]

Besides having to battle with gales which brought flurries of snow and hail, Mathy was dogged by trouble with his engines. While he was over England with one engine useless, another temporarily out of order and his ship weighed down with snow, he was forced to jettison fuel and bombs in order to gain height. He reached Belgium with only two engines running, and was unable to return to his base at Hage until 10 March.

Encouraged by exaggerated reports of the damage done at Hull, Strasser went ahead with an elaborate plan for a series of raids on Britain during the moonless period at the beginning of April. Seven naval airships, including three with HSLu engines, left Germany about noon on 31 March with orders to make London their main target. With tardy caution, Strasser told his commanders not to transmit stereotyped messages which on previous occasions had made it clear to anyone who intercepted them that a raid on Britain was impending. Nevertheless the British became aware, from other indications, not only that naval airships were on their way to the south of England but that there were seven of them. At 8 p.m., after two of the ships had been sighted from a minesweeper, the Admiralty ordered destroyers from Harwich to be ready on the following day to deal with any airships that might be brought down.[28]

As things turned out, only five arrived. The L.9, making what was then for her a rare sortie outside the Heligoland Bight, had to return to base when a bracing wire fouled one of her airscrews and nearly caused her to crash, and the L.11 also turned back after only a few hours' flying.

Mathy, still commanding the L.13, decided after crossing the coast near Aldeburgh to lighten his load by bombing a munitions factory at Stowmarket before continuing his flight to London. He was unable to find the factory, and while searching for it was picked up by a searchlight and engaged by anti-aircraft guns. Twelve bombs which he hoped would silence the guns fell near the factory, but did no damage apart from breaking windows. With two of his gas-bags holed, he then made for home. Just before crossing the coast he dropped six more bombs, which also did no damage. Next morning the British picked up near Stowmarket a signal form on which Mathy or one of his subordinates had written a message intended for transmission to the Chief of Staff of the High Seas Fleet and conveying the information that the L.13 had been hit and was returning to base.[29]

The L.14, with Böcker in command and Strasser as a passenger, dropped bombs at Sudbury in Suffolk (which Böcker mistook for Cambridge) and at various places in Essex. Seventeen people were killed or injured at Sudbury and Braintree. Böcker scored hits with incendiary bombs on two oil tanks at Thameshaven, but both were empty. Claiming on his return to have attacked London, he was credited with causing buildings to collapse and fires to break out 'in the vicinity of Tower Bridge and the docks'.[30]

Breithaupt, in the L.15, was in trouble almost from the start. Even after throwing all his ballast overboard, he was unable to gain what he considered a safe height. Approaching London from the east after flying over Suffolk and Essex, he was picked up by searchlights and engaged by guns of the London and Thames defences.

Kapitänleutnant Martin Dietrich, commander of the German naval airships L.22 and (later) L.42.

Turning to starboard in a vain attempt to escape from the guns, he dropped bombs on what he thought was north-east London, but succeeded only in cratering fields in Essex. A few minutes later, his ship was hit by a shell from a gun at Purfleet. He was also intercepted by two aircraft from neighbouring airfields, but it was damage done by the shell that brought the L.15 down in the sea off the mouth of the Thames. An armed trawler guarding a flotilla of netdrifters fired a few rounds at her, but ceased on finding that there was no return fire.[31] Breithaupt and his crew, less one man drowned, were taken as prisoners of war to Chatham. Destroyers of the Nore command took the airship in tow, but she broke up and sank off Westgate.

Peterson, commanding the L.16, also claimed to have bombed London, but the bombs he believed he was aiming at the suburb of Hornsey fell sixty miles away at Bury St Edmunds, where thirty-seven houses were wrecked and twelve people killed or injured. On his way out Peterson dropped one bomb at Lowestoft, damaging a shed but harming no one.

There remained the L.22. Commissioned only three weeks before the raid, she gave so much trouble that her commander, Kapitänleutnant Martin Dietrich, did not try to reach London but made for Grimsby. His bombs landed well short of the target, but one of them killed or injured eighty-two soldiers quartered in a Baptist chapel at Cleethorpes.

Three of the army's airships were detailed to take part in the raid, but their contribution was negligible. One, the LZ.90, flew as far as Ipswich but dropped no bombs on land, although her commander claimed on his return to have attacked Norwich. A second approached the Suffolk coast but did not cross it. The third turned back so soon that the British did not realize at the time that she had left her base.

When the raid was over the British, observing that no bombs had fallen on London and that one airship had been destroyed and a second damaged, regarded it as a setback for the enemy. The Germans took a different view. Misled by inaccurate claims and supplied by their agents with false reports of damage done to the West India Docks, the Surrey Commercial Docks and Tilbury Docks, they believed that the raid was by far the most successful they had yet made. At the same time, they acknowledged that London's defences had been much improved and that future raids would have to be carried out at greater heights.[32]

Only a few hours after the raid the L.11 and the L.17 set out for London. When the wind was found to be blowing from the wrong quarter, they were ordered by wireless to switch their attacks to the north or Midlands. The L.17, after reaching the neighbourhood of Flamborough Head without difficulty, was forced by engine trouble to jettison her bombs in the sea and return to base. Viktor Schütze took the L.11 across the coast at Seaham Harbour and dropped bombs on villages north-east of Durham and at Sunderland and Middlesbrough. Damage and casualties were light except at Sunderland, where houses and shops were wrecked and forty-seven people killed or seriously injured. Another hundred or so suffered minor injuries. Trawlers patrolling near the Dogger Bank fired at the L.11 on her way in, but only one gun engaged her in the target area.

Schütze returned to base at 9 a.m. on 2 April. Three hours later the L.13, L.14, L.16 and L.22 left Nordholz and Hage with orders to attack Rosyth, the Forth Bridge or other objectives in the neighbourhood of the Firth of Forth. During their outward flight they transmitted signals which enabled the British to give appropriate warnings to the naval authorities at Scapa Flow and Rosyth.

Engine trouble soon forced Mathy to take the L.13 back to Hage. The other ships went on, but only Böcker in the L.14 escaped being blown off course. Martin Dietrich, in the L.22, approached the English coast near the Farne Islands, dropped bombs on fields near Berwick-on-Tweed in the belief that he was attacking Newcastle, and eventually found his way to the Forth by way of St Abb's Head and the Bass Rock. Before returning to base he dropped three bombs which did no damage apart from breaking windows in the suburbs of Edinburgh. Peterson, in the L.16, dropped his load in open country north-west of Newcastle, but reported on his return that he had attacked blast furnaces south of the Tyne.[33]

Böcker, a naval reservist employed in peacetime as an officer of the mercantile marine, had the advantage of having sailed up the Forth before the war in a ship of the Hamburg-Amerika Line. He made an accurate landfall at St Abb's Head, was chased and fired upon by destroyers but eventually outdistanced them. Approaching Leith and Edinburgh from the north-east after turning to starboard off Dunbar and then wheeling westwards, he saw some lights ahead of him which were turned off before he reached them.

At that moment the L.14 was picked up by a searchlight. Unable to see anything of Rosyth or the Forth Bridge, Böcker dropped about twenty bombs on Leith in the hope of damaging docks and harbour works. These killed a man and a child, wrecked or set fire to three houses, damaged a grain-store and a tannery, and destroyed a bonded warehouse containing some thousands of gallons of whisky whose owners took the risk of attack so lightly that neither warehouse nor whisky was insured against war damage. One small bomb went through the floor of a room in which an old lady was in bed, and started a fire in the room below. She got out of bed and poured water through the hole until the fire went out.[34]

Böcker then passed over Edinburgh, where he dropped about twenty-four bombs before recrossing the coast south-east of Dunbar. Eight buildings, including three hotels, were seriously damaged, Princes Street Station was hit and thirty-five people were killed or injured. The only rounds fired at the L.14 while she was over Leith or Edinburgh came from two machine-guns.[35]

An attempt by the LZ.88 and the LZ.90 to bomb London on the same night was unsuccessful. The LZ.88 crossed the coast near Orfordness, flew briefly over Ipswich, and dropped about seventy bombs in open country on her way back. The LZ.90 came in by way of Mersea Island and headed towards London, but dropped her entire load of ninety bombs when guns at Waltham Abbey opened fire on her. Four houses were damaged, but no one was hurt and no bombs fell on the magazine which the guns were defending. The commander of the airship, believing himself to be over London, was unaware that an objective of major importance lay beneath him.

On 3 April the L.11 and the L.17 left Nordholz in the early afternoon with orders to attack London, but were met by strong winds over the North Sea. The L.17 turned back, but the L.11 crossed the coast near Sheringham in the early hours of 4 April. Observing that visibility was poor and that much time had been lost, Viktor Schütze decided to attack Norwich, Great Yarmouth and Lowestoft instead of going on to London. But he was unable to find any of those places and dropped most of his bombs in the sea off Caister. The few that fell on land did no damage.

A raid on the Midlands was ordered for the night of 4 April, but the five airships despatched were recalled soon after their departure because of unfavourable weather. Fog over Nordholz compelled the authorities to divert two of them to landing-places far from the coast.

Finally, on 5 April the L.11, L.13 and L.16 left Nordholz and Hage for the last raid of the series. The L.13 turned back with engine trouble and the L.11, bound for the Firth of Forth, was driven so far off her course that she came under fire from anti-aircraft guns newly installed at Hull.

A typical wartime Zeppelin, the L.30. Commissioned in 1916, she survived the war but was dismantled and surrendered to the Belgian government in 1920.

Schütze, disconcerted by the change that had occurred since his last visit, dropped four bombs and turned away with the intention of making a further attempt to reach the Firth of Forth when the crescent moon had set. When one of his engines failed, he decided not to go so far but to make for Hartlepool. Skirting the Yorkshire coast, he was almost abreast of Middlesbrough when another engine failed. Thereupon he made a wide turn to port in order to pick out a landmark from which to set his course for home. This manoeuvre brought him to within sight of the brightly lit smelting-furnaces of Skinningrove. He aimed nine high-explosive and twenty incendiary bombs at them, but succeeded only in wrecking a laboratory and damaging two houses and a shop. A gun had been installed at Skinningrove, but it did not open fire because the crew had not yet received their searchlight and could not see the airship. There were no casualties.

Peterson, in the L.16, crossed the Yorkshire coast, heading south-west, at a point which he thought was just north of Scarborough but which was in fact about five miles north of Hartlepool. He claimed on his return to base to have attacked Leeds and rail junctions between Leeds and York. In fact his bombs fell on mining villages and near collieries in the neighbourhood of Bishop Auckland, demolishing or damaging miners' cottages and killing or injuring six people of whom four were children.

Had accurate information about the effects of their bombing during the past week been available to the Germans, they would have been forced to recognize that their attempt to inflict damage of military importance on the enemy had failed. As things were, they relied on commanders' claims and reports from agents. Both were seriously misleading. Strasser had complete confidence in the integrity of his subordinates, and it does not seem to have struck him that they might be mistaken in claiming to have attacked objectives which airships in which he himself was a passenger had repeatedly failed to reach. Nor does it seem to have occurred to the German authorities that circumstantial reports of damage done to the London docks and other vital objectives could scarcely be genuine if British security was as good as the German agents said it was.[36]

At the same time, it had become obvious to the Germans that they could no longer afford to leave the British defences out of account when planning raids on Britain. Breithaupt admitted during his interrogation that the days when airship commanders could expect to be met by no more than a little innocuous gunfire were

over.[37] Strasser looked forward, however, to the arrival of new 'super-Zeppelins' whose performance might tip the scales in his favour.

The first of these new ships, the L.30, was commissioned at the end of May. With six HSLu engines and a capacity of nearly two million cubic feet, she was slightly faster and carried more bombs than ships of the L.20 class, but her bulk made her rather difficult to handle on the ground. Moreover, she and the other nine ships of the L.30 class commissioned before the end of 1916 were too big to use the revolving shed which had been built at Nordholz until it was lengthened early in 1917. This was a serious disadvantage at a time when, for lack of the mooring masts introduced after the war, German airships had to return at the end of each flight to sheds from which they could not emerge if a strong cross-wind was blowing.

In the meantime three airships of the L.3 class, four of the L.10 class and three of the L.20 class were detailed to take part in an operation scheduled for the latter part of April. The German General Staff had arranged to support an insurrection in Ireland, due at Easter, by sending rifles, machine-guns and ammunition to County Kerry. Sir Roger Casement, a retired British consular official associated with the Irish Republican movement, was also to be put ashore there. The naval authorities, besides providing a submarine to carry Casement from Wilhelmshaven to Tralee Bay, undertook to demonstrate their sympathy with the oppressed by despatching a battlecruiser force to bombard the fisher-folk and lodging-house keepers of Lowestoft and Great Yarmouth. Cover was to be provided by the main body of the High Seas Fleet. To help the High Seas Fleet and to cause additional trouble and injury to the British, the L.6, L.7 and L.9 were to reconnoitre towards the English coast, and the L.11, L.13, L.16, L.17, L.20, L.21 and L.23 were to stage a raid on London.

In the outcome, very little of this went according to plan. The arms ship, carrying 20,000 old rifles of Russian manufacture and more than a million rounds of ammunition but only a few machine-guns, was intercepted by the British. Casement disembarked from the submarine U.19 early on 21 April with two companions, but was arrested within a few hours of his arrival. The insurrection did not begin on 23 April, as the Germans had told Casement it would, but was postponed until 24 April, and the bombardment of Lowestoft and Great Yarmouth was not carried out even on that day. As the result of a sweep by the British Grand Fleet during the night of 22–23 April, the German battlecruisers held back until the early hours of 25 April. They then pumped enough shells into Lowestoft to wreck two hundred houses, fired a few rounds at Great Yarmouth, and made off at high speed. Neither the battlecruisers nor the main body of the German battlefleet made any serious attempt to close with the enemy, although one of the objects of the operation, according to Scheer, was to create an opportunity of engaging British warships on favourable terms. Of the three airships which were to have co-operated directly with the High Seas Fleet, the L.6 was carried off course by the wind and the L.7 turned back at an early stage to escort a battlecruiser which had struck a mine. The L.9, after warning the battlecruisers of the approach of British naval forces, was chased away by aircraft based in Norfolk and could provide no further information.

Of the ships assigned to attacks on Britain, all except the L.20 – which seems to have flown only a short distance before returning to base – crossed the English coast towards midnight on 24 April or in the small hours of 25 April. A strong wind from the south-west prevented them from reaching London, and fog, rain, banks of cloud and lighting restrictions made target-finding in East Anglia extremely difficult. Two commanders claimed on their return to Germany to have attacked Norwich and Cambridge, but no bombs fell at either of those places. Others reported that they had made no attacks, but some of these seem in fact to have dropped bombs more or less at random over Britain, perhaps in the belief that they were dumping them in the sea. The bombing did very little harm except at Newmarket, where a man was injured and houses were badly damaged, but a woman at Dilham in Norfolk died of shock when bombs fell in the neighbourhood.

The army detailed five airships to attack objectives in Britain on the night of 25–26 April. Two turned back near the English coast; two dropped bombs in open country in Kent and Essex. Erich Linnarz, commanding the LZ.97, reached the outskirts of London, but sheered away when engaged by anti-aircraft guns and approached by two of the eight aircraft which had taken off from airfields in the London area.[38]

One army airship, the LZ.93, flew over Kent on the following night. Engine trouble caused her commander, Hauptmann Wilhelm Schramm, to return to base without dropping any bombs on land.

On 2 May Strasser made a further attempt to get his airships to the Firth of Forth and back while the nights were still long enough to give them some protection. Meeting adverse winds over the North Sea, six of the eight ships despatched sought alternative objectives in the north of

England or the Midlands. Viktor Schütze, in the L.11, made a brief flight over Northumberland, but could find nothing worth attacking and carried most of his bombs home with him. The two he dropped fell harmlessly in open country. The L.23, commanded by Kapitänleutnant Otto von Schubert, dropped her first bomb on Danby High Moor in Yorkshire, starting a heath fire at which at least two other commanders aimed bombs in the belief that they were attacking blast furnaces, marshalling yards or factories. Max Dietrich, in the L.21, bombed York, but reported on his return to base that he had attacked Middlesbrough and Stockton.[39]

The two ships which went to Scotland were the L.14 (Böcker) and the L.20 (Kapitänleutnant Franz Stabbert). Böcker reached the Firth of Tay, mistook it for the Firth of Forth, and aimed some bombs without effect at what he thought were warships but were presumably fishing vessels. Stabbert crossed the coast even further north, lost his way over the Highlands and returned by way of Peterhead after dropping some of his bombs in open country and others near a remote country house. After further misadventures he found that he was too far from his base to have any hope of reaching it with the fuel left in his tanks. He managed to bring his ship down on the surface of the water in a fjord near Stavanger and did his best to destroy what was left of her. Six members of the crew were rescued by fishing vessels and repatriated as 'shipwrecked mariners'. Stabbert, with other survivors, waded ashore and was interned, but afterwards escaped and made his way to Germany.[40]

Strasser assured Scheer after the raid that, notwithstanding the loss of the L.20 and damage suffered by a number of other ships, he considered that it had been 'fully successful'.[41] This verdict was founded on his mistaken belief that factories and other objectives had been destroyed.

The raid coincided with an attempt by British seaplanes to bomb the airship sheds at Tondern under cover of a mining expedition to the Heligoland Bight and a sortie by the Grand Fleet towards the Skagerrak. No hits were scored on the sheds, but the operation led to the loss of the L.7. When British warships approached Horn Reefs early on 4 May after spending the night at sea, the L.7 (Kapitänleutnant Karl Hempel) left Tondern in haste to reconnoitre. She was engaged at long range by the light cruisers *Galatea* and *Phaeton* and forced to alight on the surface of the water. The British submarine E.31 completed her destruction and picked up seven survivors.[42]

From early May until late July the

nights were too short for raids on Britain. In the meantime Scheer planned an operation by which he hoped to destroy the British battlecruiser squadron based on Rosyth. Unrestricted submarine warfare, begun by the Germans early in 1915, had been discontinued in the autumn of that year as a result of protests from the United States government, but resumed when Scheer assumed command of the High Seas Fleet. The sinking of the cross-Channel steamer *Sussex* on 24 March brought Germany so close to a diplomatic breach with the United States that once again their submarines had to be recalled. Scheer decided to station some of them off the English coast and try to draw the British battlecruiser squadron towards them by using his own battlecruisers to bombard Sunderland. Any of the enemy's battlecruisers which survived the encounter were to be enticed towards the German battle fleet and sunk. Strasser's airships were to reconnoitre the North Sea and warn Scheer of any threat to his surface warships from the main body of the Grand Fleet.

Scheer hoped to be ready by 17 May, but unfavourable weather and damage done to the battlecruiser *Seydlitz* when she struck a mine on 24 April forced him to postpone the operation until the end of the month. On 30 May Strasser warned him that conditions unfavourable for air reconnaissance might persist for another two days. Scheer then decided to forego the bombardment of Sunderland and substitute a sortie towards the Skagerrak. Vice-Admiral Franz von Hipper, commanding the German battlecruiser force, was ordered to leave the estuary of the Jade early on 31 May and show himself before nightfall off the Norwegian coast for the purpose of luring the British battlecruiser squadron in that direction.

As it happened, knowledge gleaned by

The German naval airship L.20 after making a forced descent in Norwegian territorial waters as the sequel to an attempted raid on the Firth of Forth on the night of 2/3 May, 1916.

the British from intercepted signals made this gesture unnecessary. By 11.30 p.m. on 30 May both the battlecruiser squadron (Vice-Admiral Sir David Beatty) and the main body of the Grand Fleet (Admiral Sir John Jellicoe) were steaming towards the area in which Scheer hoped to meet the former but not the latter. Beatty had with him the small seaplane carrier *Engadine*, with three aircraft. The larger carrier *Campania*, with ten aircraft, was to have accompanied Jellicoe, but had been left behind in consequence of the failure of an order to reach its destination. She started about two hours late, and might conceivably have joined the fleet by the time she was needed had not Jellicoe ordered her to return to port. The result was that he was without the means of air reconnaissance at a time when knowledge of the enemy's whereabouts was vital to him.

The airships L.9, L.14, L.16, L.21 and L.23 managed to leave their sheds during the morning of 31 May, but they were many hours behind schedule, and visibility was so poor that they saw nothing of the enemy. All were recalled during the afternoon. Five more ships, the L.11, L.13, L.17, L.22 and L.24, were despatched late on 31 May and during the ensuing night. Early on 1 June the L.11 (Viktor Schütze) transmitted a fairly accurate account of Beatty's position, but Scheer was confused by a misleading report from the L.24 (Kapitänleutnant Robert Koch). Convinced that further attempts to engage the enemy in difficult conditions offered no prospect of success, he ordered his fleet to return to base.[43]

On the British side, an aircraft from the *Engadine* saw part of the German battlecruiser force change course just before Beatty went into action during the afternoon of 31 May. The aircraft transmitted three reports which might have proved valuable if the *Engadine* had been able to pass them on without delay. As things were, she was unable to make contact with Beatty's flagship, and Beatty received news of the enemy's change of course from one of his cruisers.[44]

Thus the Battle of Jutland was fought by both sides without the benefit of effective air reconnaissance. Nevertheless the battle demonstrated, if only in a negative way, the importance of the part that aircraft could play in naval warfare. The conclusion drawn by the British was that a fleet going into action should be accompanied by at least one carrier from which aeroplanes could take off and to which they could return. The large German airships, the British thought, would not have proved of much value even if the weather had been good. To make useful observations, they would have had to fly so low that they would

Ferdinand von Zeppelin (third from left) with Hugo Eckener (bearded) and members of the crew of the L.31. Photograph taken in 1916.

have been vulnerable to fire from ships' guns.

The Germans, on the other hand, were by no means of the opinion that their airships could make no useful contribution to a naval battle. At Jutland, Scheer had stumbled on the British battlefleet without warning. The conclusion he drew was that far-reaching air reconnaissance was an essential prerequisite of any future sortie by the High Seas Fleet, and that no sortie should be attempted unless the weather was good enough for airships to reconnoitre freely.[45]

On the British side, small single-seater aircraft could already be flown from the *Campania*. Successful experiments were made in June with aircraft large enough to carry an observer as well as the pilot, but persistent trouble with her engines prevented the *Campania* from putting to sea when she was next needed.

By the middle of August Scheer was ready for a fresh attempt to lure the British battlecruiser squadron to its doom by bombarding Sunderland. On 16 August he ordered nine submarines to take up positions off Blyth and Flamborough Head. Strasser warned him that the weather on the following day would be unfavourable for air reconnaissance, but was able to report on 17 August that the outlook was better, and on 18 August that it was good. Accordingly, Scheer left port at 9 p.m. by Central European time on 18 August with the intention of presenting himself off Sunderland at sunset on the following day.

To guard against a surprise attack by the Grand Fleet, Strasser arranged an elaborate programme of reconnaissance for 19 August. In the north, the L.22, L.24, L.30 and L.32 were to patrol a line from Peterhead to the Norwegian coast while the L.31 kept watch off the Firth of Forth for the battlecruiser squadron. At the same time, the L.11 and the L.21 were to cover the southern flank by patrolling off the Tyne and the Humber. Finally, the L.13 was to reconnoitre the southern part of the North Sea as far south as the Belgian coast so that British warships would not be able to debouch from the Thames Estuary or the English Channel without detection.

Since visibility on 19 August was generally good, this would have been an excellent plan if the British had waited until that day before putting to sea. Unfortunately for the Germans, they did not. They were able to read Scheer's signals well enough to know by the afternoon of 18 August that he was about to make a sortie, although they were not sure where he was going. The main body of the Grand Fleet left Scapa Flow some hours before Scheer was ready to start, and was well past Strasser's northern patrol line by the time

his airships reached it. Similarly, the battlecruiser squadron emerged unseen from the Firth of Forth during the hours of darkness.

Jellicoe's intention was to assemble his battlefleet 100 miles to the east of the Firth of Forth at 5 a.m. on 19 August, and to place the battlecruiser squadron about thirty miles to the south of it. He would then move with his whole force towards the southern part of the North Sea. Even without the *Campania*'s aircraft to scout for him, he would stand a good chance of catching Scheer at a disadvantage and thus gaining the decisive victory which had eluded him at Jutland.

However, Scheer was not destined to be caught and destroyed by the Grand Fleet. It happened that Commodore R. Y. Tyrwhitt, commanding the Harwich Force of light cruisers and destroyers, had put to sea at 10.30 p.m. by British time on 18 August, with the intention of patrolling a line running from north-east to south-west in the neighbourhood of the Brown Ridge, about midway between Lowestoft and the Dutch coast. Tyrwhitt reached the Brown Ridge at 3 a.m. by British time or 4 a.m. by Central European time. About three and a half hours later Kapitänleutnant Eduard Prölss, in the L.13, saw and was fired upon by Tyrwhitt's force, which was then moving towards the south-western end of its patrol line. He reported that two destroyer flotillas, followed by a cruiser squadron, were steaming at high speed in a southwesterly direction. Scheer, observing that the force reported by Prölss was moving away from him, concluded that the British did not know that he was at sea.[46]

Prölss then moved away from Tyrwhitt's guns. He saw no more of the Harwich Force until some two hours later, when he caught sight of one of its ships and reported it as a light cruiser moving east-south-east.[47] About the same time Mathy, in the L.31, saw some of the cruisers and destroyers screening Beatty's battlecruiser squadron. He reported them as two light cruisers and two destroyers moving north, adding shortly afterwards that a hostile force already reported by a

German submarine was heading in a north-easterly direction. Mathy's reports were accurate, for Jellicoe had decided to hold to the north for a while before making the southward turn by which he hoped to bring Scheer to action. But they proved misleading, inasmuch as they seemed to Scheer to confirm his belief that an enemy whose forces were moving away from him could not know that he had put to sea.

Scheer concluded that he could safely continue towards Sunderland. Unaware that Jellicoe had turned and was steaming towards him on a course which would bring the two battlefleets into contact in the early afternoon if neither turned away, he held to his intention until dramatic news from the south seemed to open up fresh possibilities.

The news came from the L.13. About midday Prölss regained contact with the Harwich Force after losing touch with it for some hours. He reported that a hostile force 'about thirty units strong' was moving towards the High Seas Fleet. Soon afterwards he added, incorrectly, that the thirty units included battlecruisers and battleships.[48] Scheer decided to seize what seemed a heaven-sent opportunity of engaging a detached squadron of the Grand Fleet on favourable terms. Abandoning his intention of bombarding Sunderland, he changed course and set off to the south-east. Since his and Jellicoe's scouting forces were only about thirty miles apart when he made this turn, he thus averted what could scarcely have failed to be the most spectacular naval battle since Trafalgar.

In due course Tyrwhitt reached the northern limit of his patrol and reversed course. Unencumbered by the heavy ships imputed to him, he was soon far out of Scheer's reach. After an hour or so Scheer gave up hope of catching him, and turned for home.

Thereafter Scheer made no serious attempt to challenge the Grand Fleet. Once again he had to rely on airship raids and attacks on merchant shipping to give him a decision.

Airship raids on Britain had in fact been resumed on 28 July, when ten ships were despatched but ran into thick fog over the North Sea. Six made brief flights over the eastern counties, but visibility was so poor that only random bombing was possible. Apart from killing or maiming cattle and breaking a few panes of glass, their bombs hurt no one and did no damage.

Similar raids on the nights of 31 July and 2 August were equally ineffective. On both nights the weather was so bad that even the experienced Mathy dropped bombs off the coast of Kent in the belief that he was attacking London. No one was killed in either raid, but on the second night some cottages were damaged and a boy was injured.

Strasser made a further attempt on 8 August, when eleven airships were despatched. Two turned back without reaching the English coast. Of those which crossed it, eight dropped bombs which did no damage apart from wrecking two buildings and injuring five people. Only Robert Koch, commanding the L.24, found his way to an objective worth attacking. The bombs he dropped at Hull did no significant military damage, but they destroyed a number of shops and houses and killed or injured twenty-one people.

Thus encouraged, Strasser assured Scheer on 10 August that airships offered 'a sure means of victoriously ending the war'.[49] He added that all he needed to deprive the British of the means of existence was a small addition to his fleet. Scheer did not promise him the four additional crews he asked for, but agreed that two ships, the SL.8 and SL.9, should move from the Baltic to the Western Front. They reached Nordholz on the eve of Scheer's second and last attempt to bring the British battlecruiser squadron to action by moving towards Sunderland.

One army airship, the LZ.97, visited England on the night of 23 August. Her bombs fell harmlessly in open country.

On the following day, the British learned from intercepted signals that a big raid was in prospect. They detected twelve airships over the North Sea, but only four crossed the coast. Of the commanders who failed to complete their missions, at least two turned back in face of gunfire from ships waiting off the coast. Others attributed their inability to reach the target area to engine failure, structural defects or strong winds. The primary target was London, but only Mathy, in the L.31, succeeded in getting so far. He dropped bombs north and south of the Thames at Millwall, Deptford, Greenwich, Plumstead, Blackheath and Eltham. Forty-nine people in the London area were killed or injured, but bombs dropped from the L.16, L.21 and L.32 in Essex and Suffolk and off the coast of Kent harmed no one and did little damage. The L.21 and the L.23 were damaged by rough landings, and the L.13 narrowly escaped destruction when a shell from a three-inch gun went clean through her hull and burst above her.

Not even the ever-hopeful Strasser can have regarded this raid as an unqualified success, though the fact remained that an airship had bombed London for the first time since the previous October. Undeterred by an abortive raid on 29 August, when eight airships were despatched but had to be recalled because the weather was unsuitable, the Germans planned for the night of 2 September the most ambitious raid on London yet attempted. Twelve naval and four army airships were despatched with orders to make the City of London their primary objective.

The outcome was a setback which shook the army's airship service to its foundations and led ultimately to its disbandment. One of the first ships to cross the English coast was the SL.11, commissioned barely a month earlier and commanded by Hauptmann Wilhelm Schramm. A Londoner by birth, Schramm must have viewed the prospect of bombing his native city with mixed feelings. After crossing the coast almost due east of London, he made a wide sweep over Essex and Hertfordshire in order to avoid the Thames and Medway defences by approaching the target area from the northwest. Perhaps mistaking the outskirts of London for the city itself, he began to drop his bombs so soon that he had shed more than half his load by the time he reached the northern suburbs. He was then heavily engaged by gunfire and picked up by searchlights. Pursued by Lieutenant W. Leefe Robinson and two other pilots of No. 39 Squadron, he turned northwards, dropping another string of bombs more or less along the line of the Great Eastern Railway in the neighbourhood of Edmonton, Ponders End and Enfield. Leefe Robinson, undeterred by the shells which were bursting round the airship, poured three drums of ammunition into her, first from below, next from the beam and finally from astern. The ship went down in flames and burned for nearly two hours on the ground at Cuffley, south-east of Hatfield. There were no survivors.

Besides costing the Germans the loss of an almost brand-new airship and her entire crew, the raid was extraordinarily ineffective. Not one bomb fell closer to the target area than Schramm's, the damage done by the nearly 500 bombs distributed over East Anglia and the Home Counties was very slight, and altogether only four civilians were killed and twelve injured.

The British attributed this outcome to the understandable reluctance of even the bravest commanders to press home their attacks after seeing what had happened to the SL.11.[50] At least six commanders of naval airships did, in fact, see the SL.11 burning either in the air or on the ground, but it is far from certain that any of them would have reached their objectives even if they had not done so. Peterson, in the L.32, assumed that the ship he saw in flames had come down in the target area, and seeing her may have contributed to his belief that he was making a bombing run 'from the suburb of Kensington towards the City' when in fact he was over Ware, in Hertfordshire. Other commanders had already dropped their bombs in what they thought was the target area, or had given up hope of reaching it. Oberleutnant Kurt Frankenberg, commanding the L.21, admitted that after seeing the SL.11 burn he decided to attack Norwich instead of London, but added that the decisive factor was the weather.[51]

As a result of the loss of the SL.11, the military authorities ruled that no more army airships should be used for raids on Britain. Strasser, refusing to admit defeat, despatched twelve naval airships on 23 September, but only the L.31, L.32 and L.33 approached the London area. The L.30 and eight ships of the L.10 and L.20 classes either did not cross the coast or made only brief flights over the eastern counties.[52]

The results, from the German point of view, were lamentable. The L.33, making her first operational sortie, crossed the English coast at Foulness Point, with the veteran Böcker in command. Böcker made straight for the East End of London, dropping a few bombs on the way to lighten his load. On reaching the target area he dropped bombs at Bow, Bromley-by-Bow and Stratford, but his ship was then hit by anti-aircraft fire and seriously damaged. Losing hydrogen rapidly, he turned for home. Near Chelmsford he was met by Second-Lieutenant A. de B. Brandon of No. 39 Squadron, whose bullets pierced several of his fuel tanks but failed to set the ship on fire. He managed to reach the coast at the mouth of the Blackwater, but recognized that he had no hope of getting home. He turned back with the intention of keeping his ship out of the enemy's hands by ditching her in shallow water, but she stalled and came down in a field at Little Wigborough, south of Colchester. Böcker and his entire crew were captured. They had set fire to the ship with flares, but she had lost so much hydrogen that she did not burn for long. The British were thus presented with a damaged but structurally almost intact Zeppelin, on which they based the design of their rigid airship the R.33.

The L.32, with Peterson in command, fared still worse. After crossing the coast at Dungeness, in Kent, she circled for an hour, presumably with engine trouble. Peterson then set course for London, but after flying over Tunbridge Wells he turned to starboard, aimed seven bombs at a searchlight post near Westerham, and continued northwards over Dartford and Purfleet. For some time the ship was shrouded in mist, but north of the Thames she emerged into clear sky and came under heavy fire from anti-aircraft guns. Peterson dropped the rest of his bombs more or less at random and turned for home, but was held by searchlights and intercepted near Chelmsford by Second-Lieutenant F. Sowrey, like

Robinson and Brandon a pilot of the home defence squadron stationed in Essex. After Sowrey had pumped the best part of three drums of incendiary ammunition into her, the ship caught fire and crashed in flames. Peterson and all his crew were killed.

Mathy, in the L.31, was luckier. After crossing the coast in company with Peterson and ineffectually aiming ten bombs at the Dungeness lighthouse to reduce his load, he flew straight to Tunbridge Wells and thence to London, checking his position from time to time by the light of parachute flares. One of these flares, dropped at Croydon, had the unexpected effect of dazzling gunners and searchlight crews. Helped by the mist, Mathy then flew right across London from south to north without once coming under fire.[53] Most of the bombs he claimed on his return to Ahlhorn to have released over Clapham, Chelsea, Pimlico, the City of London and Islington fell amidst serried rows of houses and shops at Brixton and Streatham.

Even though two of the enemy's most valuable ships had been brought down, the British were not altogether satisfied with their defences. The raid had killed or injured 170 people, most of them victims of bombs dropped by Mathy or Böcker. The majority of the airships which flew over the eastern counties had dropped their bombs harmlessly in open fields or the sea, but nineteen aimed at Nottingham from the L.17 had done a great deal of damage to property, killed three people, and injured many more. Nevertheless, Field-Marshal French had to tell a deputation led by the Mayor of Nottingham that the government could not agree to black out the Midlands by ordering the railway companies to stop all trains and extinguish lights at stations during raids. The experiment had been tried, but had led to so much congestion and such serious delays that the authorities were determined not to repeat it.[54]

Strasser tried three more raids on Britain before the end of the year. On 25 September, barely forty-eight hours after the loss of the L.32 and L.33, he sent Buttlar in the L.30 and Mathy in the L.31 to the southern target area, with orders to make London their primary target, but cautioned them against taking undue risks should clear skies favour the British defences.[55] Seven older ships were despatched to the Midlands, but three turned back and most of the others achieved little. Martin Dietrich, in the L.22, succeeded in bombing Sheffield, but no damage was done to arms factories apart from a small fire, soon put out, which was started in a machine shop at the works of John Brown and Company, the well-known steel and iron firm. Most of Dietrich's bombs fell on cottage property, doing widespread damage and killing or injuring forty-seven people. Buttlar, on reaching the North Foreland and finding the skies clear, turned back without dropping any bombs on land, although he claimed on his return to have attacked Margate and Ramsgate. Mathy, finding similar conditions at Dungeness, made for Portsmouth and flew right over the dockyard, but was dazzled by searchlights and dropped his bombs so wildly that what happened to them remains a mystery to this day. Presumably they fell in the sea.

On 1 October eleven airships were despatched, but only seven crossed the English coast, and only two people were killed or injured by the 200 bombs which they dropped. Only Mathy and Robert Koch got anywhere near London. Koch, in the L.24, set out with the intention of attacking Manchester, but decided to make for London when he found that the wind had carried him further south than he expected. On reaching Hitchin, some thirty miles north of his objective, he was attracted by the lights of an airfield, dropped his entire load, and turned for home. Mathy, still commanding the L.31, was not so lucky. After crossing the coast at Lowestoft he flew straight towards London until he was well past Chelmsford. He then turned to the north-west and made a wide sweep over Hertfordshire so as to approach the target area from the north. Coming under heavy fire from anti-aircraft guns near Cheshunt, he dropped his bombs prematurely and made a right-angle turn to starboard.

Had Mathy held to his original course he might perhaps have reached central London, dropped his bombs and got away before aircraft despatched from airfields in Essex could reach him. As it was, at least three pilots were waiting for him. Second-Lieutenant W. J. Tempest, from North Weald Bassett, spotted an airship coming towards him from a distance of fifteen miles. In the glare of searchlights she looked like 'a small cigar-shaped object'. He closed with her, opened fire just after she dropped her bombs, and saw her 'go red inside like an enormous Chinese lantern'.[56] She shot up about 200 feet and then fell abruptly, narrowly missing Tempest's aircraft. Mathy jumped clear before she struck the ground near Potters Bar. He was still breathing when bystanders reached the spot, but died soon afterwards. The rest of the crew died in the holocaust.

Mathy's death made a profound impression on all ranks of the naval airship division. One petty officer wrote that the life and soul seemed to have gone out of the airship service.[57] But Strasser was not easily discouraged. On 27 November ideal

conditions for a raid on the north and Midlands were predicted. Ten airships, including the newly commissioned L.35 and L.36, were despatched at such short notice that officers celebrating Max Dietrich's birthday with a luncheon party had to throw down their table-napkins and hurry from the mess.[58]

If the experts meant by ideal conditions that the weather would be fine, they were not mistaken. There was some cloud over the North Sea in the afternoon, but by nightfall the skies were clear. There was no moon, but the stars shone brightly.

Two ships, the L.24 and the L.30, turned back with engine trouble. The rest split into two groups. In the north the L.34 and L.35, with Newcastle as their objective, approached the English coast near the mouth of the Tees. They were followed by the L.36, bound for the Firth of Forth. Further south the L.13, L.14, L. 16, L. 21 and L. 22 made for the stretch of coast between Scarborough and the Humber.

The L.34, with Max Dietrich in command, was the first ship of the northern group to cross the coast. She was picked up almost immediately by a searchlight. Dietrich aimed some bombs at the searchlight post and turned to drop the rest of his bombs on West Hartlepool, where fifteen people were killed or injured. Almost at that moment the ship was intercepted by Second-Lieutenant I. V. Pyott of No. 36 Squadron, who had gone up an hour earlier from his base at Seaton Carew to make his second patrol since dusk. Pyott opened fire on her and saw her catch fire and go down into the sea. All that remained of her at dawn was an oily patch on the surface of the water.

The Airship

German naval airship L.31. She took part in more than half a dozen raids on Britain, but was shot down on the night of 1/2 October, 1916. The surface vessel is the battleship Ostfriesland.

Kapitänleutnant Herbert Ehrlich, in the L.35, was about eight miles away when the L.34 caught fire. Realizing that any British pilots who might be about would have no difficulty in seeing his ship silhouetted against the blaze, he turned back and recrossed the coast without dropping any bombs on British soil.

Viktor Schütze, in the L.36, was further north and still some miles out to sea when he saw the whole sky lit up by the burning airship. Skirting the coast, he continued to fly north-westwards for about an hour. At the end of that time he came to the conclusion that the night was too bright for him to stand a chance of getting to the Firth of Forth without being intercepted, especially as he was having trouble with one of his engines. He set course for home after dropping some bombs in the sea to trim his ship.[59]

Of the five ships which approached the coast between Scarborough and the Humber, all crossed it, but the L.13, L.14 and L.22 turned back when engaged by anti-aircraft guns, and the L.22 was found when she reached her base at Nordholz to have about 150 holes in her envelope. The L.16 spent some time over the East and West Ridings of Yorkshire, but the bombs she dropped caused no casualties or damage. The L.22 dropped no bombs, and the casualties inflicted by those dropped by the L.13 and L.14 amounted to two people injured.

Kurt Frankenberg, in the L.21, made a much longer flight over England, from which he was not destined to return. He crossed the coast near Hornsea, went out to sea again when anti-aircraft guns opened fire, but afterwards came back and flew over Leeds and Barnsley, dropping bombs which hit neither of those places. He then spent some hours over Derbyshire and Staffordshire before turning eastwards. He twice managed to shake off pursuing aircraft, but by the time he reached the coast at Great Yarmouth daylight was approaching. There he was engaged by three pilots who opened fire in succession. The ship caught fire and came down about eight miles off Lowestoft. Her destruction was credited to Flight Sub-Lieutenant E. L. Pulling, who was the last to open fire.

Thus at the end of 1916 the British could reasonably claim that they had gained the upper hand, at any rate for the time being. They had brought down seven large rigid airships since the spring, and recent raids had been markedly unsuccessful.

6 Airships in World War I: 1917-18

After gaining access to the Belgian coast in 1914, the Germans were able to send submarines from Ostend and Zeebrugge to attack shipping not only in the North Sea, the Dover Strait and the English Channel but also in the Irish Sea and the channels linking it with the Atlantic. Under international law they were not entitled to sink merchant vessels without prior visit and search and without making provision for the safety of passengers and crews, but they waived this rule when it suited them to do so. Throughout the spring and summer of 1915, and from the early part of 1917 until the war was almost over, they waged unrestricted submarine warfare against British, Allied and neutral vessels trading with United Kingdom ports.

Until 1917 the British tried to meet this threat to their supply lines by sending out ships and aircraft to search for submarines. For this purpose they developed their Sea Scout and Coastal airships and built a chain of airship stations round their coasts. By the end of 1916 some fifty Sea Scouts and about thirty Coastals had been completed, and fifteen airship stations, not all in coastal areas, were in use.*

In 1917 the North Sea airship, which was intended to supersede the Coastal, was brought into service. Airships of this class remained in use until after the war, but the six completed in 1917 suffered from teething troubles which prevented their long endurance from being exploited to the full.[1]

The Vickers rigid airship No. 9, found deficient in lift when tested in 1916 and afterwards modified, was accepted by the naval authorities in the spring of 1917. Her rugged construction and maximum speed of forty-five miles an hour suited the modest role for which she was designed.[2] Based at Howden in Yorkshire, she was used chiefly for mooring trials and the training of crews until, in 1918, the authorities decided to break her up after she had been damaged by a storm. Three more rigid airships, Nos. 23, 24 and 25, were completed in 1917 by Vickers, Beardmore and Armstrong-Whitworth respectively. They were followed early in 1918 by the Vickers-built R.26.

The R.26 was the first ship to bear the prefix R, afterwards borne by all British rigid airships. She was also the last ship of

* These were Kirkwall (Orkney), Longside (Aberdeenshire), East Fortune (Firth of Forth), Howden (Yorkshire), Cranwell (Lincolnshire), Pulham (Norfolk), Wormwood Scrubs (London), Kingsnorth (Kent), Capel (near Folkstone), Polegate (Sussex), Mullion (Cornwall), Pembroke (South Wales), Anglesey, Larne (County Antrim), and Luce Bay (Wigtown). Sub-stations under Mullion were established at Laira (Cornwall) and Bridport (Dorset).

Rigid airship No. 23, designed and constructed by Vickers Ltd and put into commission in 1917 as a training airship

the 23 class. All four ships of this class, although built by three different manufacturers, were based on the No. 9. The R.27 and R.29, which followed the R.26, were built to a different specification and belonged to what was called the 23X class.

From the autumn of 1916, the drawing up of specifications for British manufacturers was strongly influenced by examination of captured German airships. The SL.11, brought down early in September, was the point of departure for the R.31 and R.32, completed in 1918 and 1919 respectively. In the same month, the enforced descent of the L.33 at Little Wigborough gave the British an almost intact product of the Zeppelin factories. After experts had studied her, the authorities invited Armstrong-Whitworth and Beardmore to build similar ships. Vickers, having no shed large enough for the purpose, proposed that they should design and build the largest airship they could accommodate. Their offer was accepted, but it was not until the war was over that Armstrong-Whitworth completed the R.33, Beardmore the R.34 and Vickers the R.80, designed by Barnes Wallis.

In the meantime, ships of the 23 and 23X classes made a few operational sorties over the North Sea, but were used chiefly for training and as experimental craft. The last British rigid airship put into commission before the armistice was the R.31, built like the R.32 by Short Brothers in a shed specially constructed for the purpose at Cardington, in Bedfordshire.

Hunting for submarines with airships,

HMA No. 23 under construction beside the completed No. 9 at Barrow-in-Furness.

flying boats, seaplanes, landplanes and surface vessels did not prove a satisfactory means of checking the expansion of the enemy's underwater fleet. Between the outbreak of war and the end of 1916 the Allies destroyed only forty-six U-boats in all theatres.[3] By the following February eighty-two were operating from bases between the Heligoland Bight and Ostend, three in the Baltic, twenty-four from Pola at the head of the Adriatic, and two in the Black Sea.[4] Their depredations confronted the British with the most serious threat they had faced since the defeat of the Spanish Armada in 1588. So many British, Allied and neutral merchant vessels were sunk by underwater attack in the last few months of 1916 and the early part of 1917 that in April Jellicoe, who had left the Grand Fleet to become First Sea Lord, told the American Admiral William R. Sims that he did not see how Britain could escape defeat if losses continued at the current rate.[5]

Two remedies were proposed. One was to go on using all available warships and aircraft to hunt for submarines in the hope that somehow the situation would right itself. The other was to sail merchant ships in convoy and use warships and aircraft to escort them. Jellicoe favoured the first course, but admitted that it was no more than a palliative. The government insisted on the second. The convoy system was introduced on the Atlantic routes in the late summer of 1917 and was instantly successful. Losses of merchant shipping fell off sharply in September, and the Allies were soon sinking U-boats at the rate of seven a month. In the last twenty-three months of the war they destroyed nearly three times as many as in the whole of the previous twenty-nine.[6]

During the latter part of the war, therefore, Britain's naval airships were used chiefly to escort convoys in home waters and the Western Approaches. Their long endurance made them very suitable for the purpose. In contrast with heavier-than-air machines, they also had the advantage of being able to adjust their speed to that of the ships they were protecting. They did not make nearly as many attacks on submarines as were made by flying boats and seaplanes, but that was only to be expected. Their role was not so much to attack underwater craft as to watch for them and report their whereabouts to the warships and armed auxiliaries which provided surface escort.

The advantages of the convoy system had always been apparent to the French, but it was not until early in 1916 that the French Navy set up an airship service with three Sea Scouts bought from the British. These were afterwards supplemented by two more Sea Scouts, a number of similar craft ordered from Zodiac, and a fleet of larger airships built by Astra-Torres or in the government factory at Chalais-Meudon. In 1916 and 1917 the French resumed control of an airship station at Marquise formerly used by the British and opened other stations at Le Havre, Cherbourg, Brest, Rochefort, Paimboeuf, Arcachon, Aubagne, Oran, Algiers, Bizerta, Ajaccio and Corfu. The French Army continued to maintain an airship division until early in 1917, when its only airship still deemed fit for active service was handed over to the navy in accordance with a decision made in the previous year.[7]

In the United States, reports of the use made by the British of non-rigid airships for maritime reconnaissance and submarine-spotting led the Department of the Navy to make plans in 1916 for the development of an experimental craft. In February of the following year the department ordered sixteen ships. The Goodyear company was invited to build nine of them and to set up a training establishment at Wingfoot Lake. The first of the Goodyear ships made her maiden flight at the end of May, some eight weeks after the United States entered the war. Between that date and the armistice, American airships logged some 400,000 miles of flying from bases on the eastern seaboard of the United States as far north as Chatham, Massachusetts, and as far south as Key West, Florida. An improved non-rigid airship with two engines and a speed of sixty miles an hour was introduced about two months before the end of the war. No American-built airships were sent overseas, but American commanders and crews using Astra-Torres and Zodiac airships supplied by the French made regular patrols from bases in Brittany in the spring, summer and autumn of 1918.

Almost alone among the belligerents, the Italians remained convinced until the end of the war that airships could be usefully employed to give both direct and indirect support to land forces. Their attitude was understandable in view of the difficulty of finding bases for short-range heavier-than-air machines in the mountainous country in which their armies had to fight, but repeated sorties over the enemy's lines cost them fairly heavy losses. The Italian airships were well made, built to high standards, and skilfully handled by commanders and crew whose courage and devotion to duty earned them a high reputation.

In Germany, the military authorities applied themselves during the second half of 1916 to the development of heavier-than-air bombers intended to take the place of airships for raids on Britain. These aircraft were not ready in substantial num-

bers until the early summer of 1917; but the army had ceased to take much interest in airships long before the last of those it had ordered was delivered in the following November. The German Chief of Military Aviation considered that attacks on London by airships had become 'impossible' and that the task must be performed by aeroplanes.[8]

Strasser did not agree. He believed that his airships could still be used over London, but admitted that something would have to be done to make them less vulnerable. One proposal was that, in order to improve their speed, future airships should be fitted with seven or eight engines apiece and that these should be grouped in streamlined gondolas which were then under development but not yet in production. Strasser, feeling that height was more important than speed, argued strongly in favour of the opposite solution at a conference at the Ministry of Marine early in 1917.[9] Everything, he said, must be done to save weight and thus make higher flying possible, even though this might mean that speeds would be reduced and minor structural failures would become more frequent.

Eventually he had his way. At the end of the conference it was agreed that the L.42, which was then approaching completion at Friedrichshafen, should be given five engines instead of six and should have no machine-guns, gun-platforms or sleeping-quarters for her crew. Her girders were to be made lighter, and she was to carry fuel

The second British rigid airship; HMA No. 9, laid down in 1913 but not completed until 1917. A reliable ship, but rather slow.

for thirty hours' flying instead of thirty-six.

On the strength of this decision, Strasser changed the specifications of other airships under construction and due for completion before the new gondolas were ready. He also sanctioned substantial alterations to five ships already completed.* Finally, the undersides of all airships intended for service over Britain were painted black in order to reduce the risk of their being picked up by searchlights.

Strasser was not willing to expose commanders and crews to conditions of which he had no first-hand knowledge. Recognizing that flights over Britain at the altitudes which the new or modified airships were intended to reach might entail hardship as well as danger, he insisted on being taken to the greatest height attainable by the L.42 when carrying ballast equivalent to her normal bomb-load, before launching a new series of raids. Brief tests at heights up to 20,000 feet showed that above 12,000 feet breathing became increasingly diffi-

* The ships affected, other than the L.42, were the L.35, L.36, L.39, L.40 and L.41 (one engine removed) and the L.43, L.45 and L.47 (specifications changed). The L.44 was the first ship with the new gondolas, which were also fitted to the L.48 and later ships, and eventually to all surviving ships in active service.

cult, that water tended to freeze at great heights even when it was mixed with glycerine, and that some men suffered not only from the cold but also from palpitations and dizziness.[10] Satisfied that 'a few whiffs of compressed oxygen' were usually enough to relieve these symptoms, his advisers seem to have made no serious attempt to estimate the effects of prolonged exposure to such conditions, although evidence was available in medical textbooks and reports of polar and mountaineering expeditions. Steps were taken to provide all ranks with fur-lined clothing and bottles of compressed oxygen, but control and wireless cabins and gangways were left unheated. Nor was anything done, until new engines came into service in November, to compensate by forced induction for the loss of power which otherwise afflicts internal combustion engines at high altitudes.

The first high-altitude raid on Britain was planned for the night of 16 March 1917. Strasser's written order directed the L.35, L.39, L.40, L.41 and L.42 to attack London and return by way of Belgium in order to take advantage of a wind expected to blow from the north. Strasser himself, filling a new post as 'Leader of Airships', was to accompany Martin Dietrich in the L.42, leaving Viktor Schütze to control the operation from Nordholz.[11]

The German meteorological service had no station west of Bruges. Hitherto its forecasters had seldom, if ever, been asked to predict conditions above 13,000 feet, and they had no accumulated experience of high-altitude conditions to draw upon. On reaching their operational heights, the airships despatched on 16 March were met by north-westerly winds approaching gale force. All were blown south of their estimated courses. Commanders could not check their positions visually because land and sea were masked by clouds. Direction-finding stations could not do much to help them, because the only stations on the air at the height of the raid were too close together to give accurate fixes of their positions over southern England. In any case little information was received from the stations because, according to German reports, the British jammed their signals continuously throughout the raid.

Failure would therefore have been inevitable even if the efficiency of commanders and crews had not been impaired by the waves of nausea and giddiness and partial losses of consciousness by which survivors of the high-altitude raids afterwards confessed themselves to have been affected. Many of the men were reluctant to use their oxygen bottles, even when they were urged by their officers to do so, for

Detail of engine car of the L.49 – a victim of the 'Silent Raid' of 19/20 October 1917.

fear of seeming to their friends unable or unwilling to endure hardship. Others complained that the oxygen tasted of chemicals and that sucking at the bottles made them feel sick. Few could face solid food. The result was that, after ten or twenty hours in the air, even those who were not more or less incapacitated by frostbite or lack of oxygen became faint from hunger.

Dietrich's experience showed what could happen in such circumstances. Intending to cross the English coast at Orfordness and observing that there was a strong wind on his starboard bow, he made what seemed a generous allowance for it by heading towards Lowestoft. With one engine out of order, he was carried so far south that eventually he found himself within sight of the lighthouse at Ostend. He decided to head northwards, but the wind was now so strong that he was driven stern first in the opposite direction. He then set course for Nordholz, but ended up 250 miles away at Jüterbog. His flight, which never took him within sight of the English coast, had lasted more than twenty-six hours and used up nearly all his fuel.

The other airships succeeded in crossing the English coast, but none of them reached London and none of the bombs they dropped hurt anyone or did more than minor damage. The L.35 (Herbert Ehrlich)

flew briefly over Kent, was blown over France and Belgium, and landed at Dresden with one engine out of action after spending nearly twenty-five hours in the air. The L.39 (Robert Koch) passed over Margate, Ashford, St Leonards, Bexhill and Pevensey, spent many hours over France, and appeared at dawn near Compiègne, where she was shot down by French gunners within sight of the German trenches. The L.40 and the L.41 also made long flights over France after wandering more or less aimlessly over Kent and Sussex, but both managed eventually to reach their base at Ahlhorn. Ehrlich and the commander of the L.40, Erich Sommerfeldt, claimed afterwards to have attacked London, but their bombs fell harmlessly in open country. Hauptmann Kuno Manger, commanding the L.41, reported on his return to base that he had bombed Harwich, but in fact he had dropped his load some seventy miles away near Rye.[12]

In the light of these claims, the results of the raid did not seem to Strasser altogether unsatisfactory. More than two months elapsed before another raid on Britain was attempted, but on 23 April Kapitänleutnant Ludwig Bockholt, in the L.23, relieved the tedium of a routine patrol off the Danish coast by alighting on the water beside a Norwegian schooner bound for West Hartlepool and claiming her and her cargo of pit-props as his lawful prize. Putting a warrant officer and two petty officers aboard her, he sent her to Horn Reefs, where she was met by a destroyer and escorted into the Elbe.[13]

An exploit more to Strasser's taste than this act of bravado followed on 4 May. The L.43 was one of three airships ordered to cover minesweepers in the Heligoland Bight on that day. Her commander,

The Airship

Kapitänleutnant Hermann Kraushaar, saw British light cruisers and destroyers being attacked by U-boats near the Dogger Bank. He dropped bombs which fell so close to some of the ships that bomb-splinters fell aboard the cruiser *Dublin* and some of the destroyers.[14] Although the ships escaped undamaged, this incident helped to bring home to the British the importance of providing not only their heavy ships but also their cruisers and destroyers with effective high-angle guns.

Kraushaar was one of six commanders detailed on 23 May for Strasser's next raid on Britain. The target was London, but a strong south-westerly wind sent all the ships astray. When he crossed the English coast between Felixstowe and Orfordness Kraushaar believed that he was over Harwich. The result was that bombs he thought he was dropping on London fell on fields and villages in Norfolk and Suffolk, killing one man and damaging some cottages. The L.44, with Strasser aboard and Franz Stabbert in command, limped home with only one engine working continuously and another intermittently after making a brief flight over Norfolk. Martin Dietrich, in the L.42, scattered bombs over the East Anglian countryside in the belief that he had reached Sheerness.[15] The commander of the newly commissioned L.47 seems never to have crossed the coast although he claimed to have cruised for more than two hours over England, and bombs dropped from the L.40 and the L.45 fell either in the sea or harmlessly in open fields.

Misleading reports from Kraushaar and Dietrich helped to conceal the full extent of the fiasco from the naval authorities, but the failure of the L.44 to get anywhere near the target area was manifest. Strasser, usually sparing of blame, is said to have become so angry when three of her engines went out of action simultaneously that Stabbert begged him not to shout so loud, 'or the English down below will hear you'.[16] When asked to account for his lack of success, Stabbert could not reply that Strasser was a notorious Jonah and that no commander was ever surprised when things went wrong with an airship in which he was a passenger. He had to content himself with attributing his misadventures to an 'unfortunate coincidence' whose effects were aggravated by the difficulty of navigating an ailing ship with a crew whose faculties were impaired by lack of oxygen and long exposure to sub-zero temperatures. He pointed out that the men could hardly ever be persuaded to use their oxygen bottles until they were already in such poor shape that 'a few whiffs of oxygen' were not nearly enough to revive them.

Aerial view of London showing the R.26 near St Paul's Cathedral. Photograph taken 9 November 1918.

The Kaiser, after studying a report from the Naval Staff, expressed the opinion that airships should no longer be used for raids on London but should be reserved for reconnaissance and co-operation with the High Seas Fleet.[17] When told that the British would move large numbers of troops, guns and aircraft to the Western Front if the raids were discontinued he agreed, however, that further attacks should be made in favourable circumstances.

The general opinion in the naval airship division was that the raids should not be discontinued but that the problem of maintaining alertness and efficiency at high altitudes had to be resolutely tackled. Reports from commanders showed that at heights above 16,000 feet severe headaches, abdominal pains and nausea were common, that men quickly became exhausted by physical labour and that even walking from one end of a ship to the other was an ordeal. Stabbert cited an instance in which men ordered to carry weights forward to trim the L.44 moved so slowly that the ship was endangered. He himself had found that it took him a quarter of an hour to walk 300 feet from the rear to the forward gondola, although he was not carrying anything, and that he arrived exhausted and gasping for air.[18] Furthermore, intense cold and thin air had deleterious effects not only on men but also on machines. The liquid in compasses and other instruments became solid. The water in radiators boiled away, with the result that engines overheated although the air round them was icy cold. When they stopped, they froze and could not be restarted. Control cables became slack because the steel of which they were made contracted at a different rate from that of the duralumin components to which they were hitched. Celluloid windows became so brittle that they sometimes split, admitting blasts of air which made control cars even colder than before.

As a partial remedy for some of these ills, Stabbert proposed that, as far as possible, all heavy work such as hand-pumping of fuel should be completed, and that radiators should be topped up, before ships reached their operational heights. He added that, so far as his own ship was concerned, he intended in future to order his men to start using their oxygen bottles as soon as the ship reached 16,500 feet, even if they felt they could do without them.

Meanwhile the army's heavier-than-air bombers began, on 25 May, a series of daylight raids which culminated on 13 June in an attack on London in which nearly 600 people were killed or injured. It seems likely that the success of this attack was responsible for Strasser's decision to

risk a raid on London during the moonless period in the middle of June instead of waiting for the longer nights of July. He may have feared that if he did not seize his opportunity the permission he had received to continue his raids would be withdrawn and sole responsibility for the bombing of Britain be handed over to the army.

The night chosen was that of 16 June, three nights before the new moon and five before the shortest night. Viktor Schütze, deputizing for Strasser as Leader of Airships, was to take command in the air.

Six airships were detailed for the raid, but the L.46 and L.47 were unable to leave their sheds and the L.44 and L.45 turned back with engine trouble. Schütze's force was thus reduced to Martin Dietrich's L.42 and the newly commissioned L.48, commanded by Kapitänleutnant Franz Eichler and chosen by Schütze as his flagship.

Dietrich sighted the Suffolk coast from a distance of forty miles in broad daylight. He decided to kill time by making for a point on the coast of Kent between Dover and Dungeness before turning inland. He expected to reach it about midnight, but was delayed by a stiff breeze from the south-east and did not arrive there until 2 a.m. Even then he was some miles further north than he supposed. Calculating that he had lost his chance of getting to London and back before daybreak, he dropped bombs at and near Ramsgate in the belief that he was attacking Deal and

A British rigid airship of the 23X Class: the R.29. A step forward from the 23 Class, but still reminiscent of the early Zeppelins.

Dover. By sheer chance, the local naval headquarters were among the buildings hit. The L.42 escaped destruction only because the fracture of a fuel-pipe forced a pilot who had closed with her to break off his attack.

Eichler reached a point about forty miles north-east of Harwich nearly half an hour before midnight, but had trouble with two of his engines and circled for nearly an hour and a half before crossing the coast near Orfordness. He then cruised over Suffolk for another hour, apparently trying to find his bearings. Finally he set course for Harwich, but turned back in face of accurate anti-aircraft fire and was intercepted by Captain R. H. M. S. Saundby of the Royal Flying Corps and Lieutenant H. P. Watkins, an officer of the Canadian Army attached to No. 37 Squadron. The two pilots opened fire simultaneously, but the last burst was fired by Watkins. The ship caught fire and came slowly to earth near Saxmundham. Eichler, Schütze and most of the crew were killed, but a rating named Heinrich Ellerkamm escaped with minor burns by using all his strength to fight his way out of the wreckage. The ship's Executive Officer, Leutnant zur See Mieth, was pulled out of the wrecked wireless cabin with two broken legs by the local policeman.[19] Another rating, Wilhelm Uecker, survived the crash but died of his injuries in the following year.

An odd feature of the raid was the inordinate amount of time wasted by both commanders before they decided to aim bombs at secondary objectives and turn for home. Eichler's record was not altogether reassuring, but Strasser considered him eligible for command, and in any case he had the experienced Schütze to help him.* His attempt to bomb Harwich could have been made at almost any time after 12.30 a.m. By deferring it until daybreak was so near that his ship was visible from the ground without the aid of searchlights, he made disaster almost certain. Dietrich, a seasoned veteran, knew that he could not afford to cross the coast in daylight, but he did not need to wait until 2 a.m. before deciding what to do. At any time after nightfall he could have chosen between heading for London, bombing the nearest East Coast town, and abandoning his mission on the ground that he could not reach the primary target without endangering his ship and that no suitable alternative could

* The L.36, with Eichler in command, was wrecked on 7 February 1917 when she crashed about ninety miles from her base after making a routine patrol. Strasser's report on the findings of the Court of Inquiry was that Eichler had made two errors of judgement but was eligible for command of another airship. The L.48 made her first flight on 22 May and Eichler took command of her on the following day.

be found. As it was, he waited so long that he was very lucky not to suffer the same fate as Eichler. Both commanders took such risks that it seems probable that lack of oxygen and exposure to intense cold impaired their judgement.

The loss of the L.48, with the irreplaceable Schütze aboard her, was the worst blow Strasser had suffered since the death of Mathy. For a day or two he was plunged in gloom. He then rallied and invited his officers to a party at which Dietrich assured him that his ships could still elude the defences by flying higher. On 23 June he urged Scheer not to play into the enemy's hands by countermanding raids on Britain. Nothing, he said, would please the English more than to learn that they had managed to convince the Germans that the raids were not worth making.[20]

This argument helped Scheer to resist demands from the army for a total ban on the production of new airships and the relegation of existing airships to a purely defensive role. Despite an appeal to the Kaiser he was forced, however, to accept restrictions which limited deliveries to one new airship every two months, as compared with the previous average of two ships a month. The airship fleet was to be limited to a total of twenty-five ships in all theatres. Eighteen of the twenty-five would be reserved, in principle, for maritime reconnaissance, but raids on the northern and midland target areas would still be permitted, since these areas could not be reached by the army's heavier-than-air machines.[21]

These restrictions were imposed on 17 August. Four days later Strasser sent eight airships to Britain. Using the L.46 as his flagship, he signalled when the ships were in the air that conditions were favourable for attacks on the midland target area and that commanders were to act accordingly.

Hauptmann Kuno Manger, commanding the L.41, chose Hull as his objective. Flying at a height estimated by the British at 20,000 feet, he crossed the English coast about midnight, but was met by heavy anti-aircraft fire and turned away. His bombs, widely scattered, wrecked a Methodist chapel and damaged other buildings, but no one was killed and only one person was injured.

A number of other commanders claimed on their return to base to have flown over the northern counties and dropped bombs there or attacked shipping off the coast, but no ships were damaged and the British authorities found no craters not attributable to Manger's bombs. Reports which indicated that at least one airship besides the L.41 had passed over places in Yorkshire and Lancashire and that bombs had been heard exploding in the distance

ABOVE: *United States naval airship, c. 1917.*

seemed to have so little substance that they were relegated to a file marked *Hot Air*. It was only when they were compared after the war with reports from German commanders that the British were driven to conclude that a number of airships must in fact have crossed the coast without being spotted by the defences and that some of them could have dropped bombs in places so remote that no trace of them ever came to light.[22]

A feature of the raid which caused the British some uneasiness at the time was the great height at which the airships flew. They knew that, although their defences seemed to have succeeded in spoiling Manger's aim, they had little chance of destroying airships flying at 20,000 feet until new guns and aircraft came into service.

The raid also had disquieting features from the German point of view. Six commanders reported that the liquid in their magnetic compasses froze at sub-zero temperatures. Stabbert added that he also had trouble with other instruments and that his rudder cables became so slack that they jumped off their sheaves.

A graphic account of events in the L.46 was given many years later by her Executive Officer, Richard Frey. He said that many of the crew refused to use their oxygen bottles and that Strasser was among the abstainers. Helmsmen and fitters were incapacitated from time to time

ABOVE: *The last British rigid airship taken into service before the Armistice: the R.31, based substantially on the Schütte-Lanz SL.11.*

by spells of nausea and faintness. The quartermaster became 'completely apathetic'. Strasser retained control of his faculties, but his judgement, Frey thought, might well have been impaired by lack of oxygen. The commanding officer, Kapitänleutnant Heinrich Hollender, went to the other extreme. After taking copious draughts of oxygen 'in order to be alert for any emergency', he showed the classic symptoms of intoxication. When Strasser asked him sharply what was the matter with him, he stood with his hands in his pockets and did not answer. Eventually he allowed himself to be led into the wireless cabin, where he lapsed into a stupor from which he did not fully recover until the ship was on the ground. During a comparatively lucid interval he grumbled at Frey for taking command of the ship on Strasser's orders.[23]

Frey, a young, fit man, rose to the occasion. The ship was brought safely back to base. He often wondered in later years what would have happened if all three occupants of the control cabin had lost consciousness.

A raid on Britain was planned for 12 September, but had to be abandoned. For some days strong winds prevented the airships from leaving their sheds even for routine patrols. In the meantime cylinders of liquid air replaced the much-criticized oxygen bottles. Nothing was done, however, to make control and wireless cabins more comfortable.

At last, on 24 September, eleven ships were despatched with orders to attack

British Coastal airship escorting a convoy, c. 1917.

objectives in the midland target area. One turned back with engine trouble. Eight commanders reported after the raid that they had crossed the English coast, but all bombs dropped on land appeared to the British to come from five ships. Kapitänleutnant Hans Flemming, commanding the L.55, dropped bombs near Skinningrove in the belief that he was attacking Hull. Manger, in the L.41, did attack Hull, but Hollender in the L.46, again with Strasser aboard, mistook the lights of an airfield in Lincolnshire for Grimsby and dropped his bombs on open fields. Prölss, in the L.53, also wasted his bombs on fields, and Ehrlich in the L.35 aimed his at an iron and steel works near Rotherham whose lights were extinguished only just in time to spoil his aim. Very little damage was done even at Hull, and the only casualties were three women injured. The British sent up thirty-seven aircraft, but few of them were capable of climbing to the 16,000 feet or so at which most of the airships flew.

The last raid of the year followed on 19 October, when again eleven airships were despatched. Light to moderate winds at heights up to 10,000 feet promised favourable conditions, but above that height there were strong northerly and north-westerly winds, rising to gale force at 16,000 to 20,000 feet. Some freak of the atmosphere made engines almost inaudible from sea-level, and even the noise of exploding bombs was muffled and seemed far away.

All eleven airships flew over England, but only Buttlar, in the L.54, returned to Germany by the orthodox route across the North Sea. He claimed afterwards that he had crossed the coast 'south of the Humber' and bombed Nottingham and Derby from 21,300 feet.[24] In fact, he approached the coast near Happisburgh in Norfolk but went almost as far south as Harwich before crossing it. He spent only a short time over Britain and his bombs fell harmlessly between Ipswich and Colchester. His height when a British pilot saw his ship near Great Yarmouth on the return flight was estimated at 5,000 feet. It seems clear that Buttlar, who afterwards wrote a book in which he claimed to have enjoyed the war, escaped the gale which was raging at 20,000 feet by flying well below it. Not for the first time, the report he wrote on his return to base was wildly inaccurate.

Two ships returned to Germany by way of Holland. These were the L.46 (Hollender) and the L.47 (Kapitänleutnant Michael von Freudenreich). Hollender spent about twenty minutes over Norfolk and dropped bombs which did negligible damage. Freudenreich flew over the eastern counties for three hours, but he, too, failed to find an objective worth attacking. He dropped seventeen bombs which hurt no one and did no damage.

Four ships landed in Germany after making long and hazardous flights over England and France. Manger, in the L.41, bombed the Austin motor works at Longbridge, in the outskirts of Birmingham, was carried at high speed over the Thames below London, and passed safely over the British trenches at La Bassée in the early hours of 20 October. He was mistaken in thinking that his bombs fell on Manchester, but his twenty-six-hour flight at heights of the order of 16,000 feet was a creditable performance. Oberleutnant Kurt Friemel, in the L.52, also spent twenty-six hours in the air, and he, too, flew at 16,000 feet or so. Blown southwards after crossing the coast a little south of the Wash, he dropped bombs north of London and eventually passed over the French lines near Verdun. He was unable to reach his base at Wittmundhaven but landed safely at Ahlhorn after using up nearly all his fuel. Prölss, in the L.53, followed a similar course and managed to return to Nordholz by way of Nancy. Flemming, in the L.55, also dropped bombs north of London, but was so far out in his reckoning that he believed he had bombed Birmingham, among other places.[25] Supposing himself to be over Dover, he crossed the French lines near Laon in daylight. After climbing to the prodigious height of 24,000 feet he damaged his ship beyond repair by making a rough landing in a wood some 200 miles from his base.

The other four ships never got back to Germany. The L.44 was engaged by French gunners behind the lines after flying over eastern England from the Wash to Folkestone, and crashed in flames. The L.45, dogged by engine trouble and with many of her crew in poor shape, made a fantastic flight from Schleswig-Holstein to the south of France by way of London, where she dropped bombs which caused heavy damage and casualties. Her commander, Kapitänleutnant Waldemar Kolle, succeeded in bringing the ship down near Sisteron and setting fire to her, but two of the crew were lost when a gondola struck the ground as she came down. The L.49 was forced down by French fighters, and the L.50 was last seen disappearing over the Mediterranean after sixteen of her crew of twenty had jumped clear when her commander, Kapitänleutnant Roderich Schwonder, made an abortive attempt to bring her down on French soil. The commander and entire crew of the L.49 were saved, but they were so exhausted by their experiences that their attempt to destroy the ship was unsuccessful. Before dismantling her, the French made notes and drawings which they distributed to their associates and on which the Americans based the design of their post-war rigid airship the *Shenandoah.*

So ended what was sometimes called the Silent Raid. The British believed, wrongly, that the Germans had shut off their engines and allowed their ships to drift before the wind so that they would not be heard. The German commanders would never have tried such a ruse, for experience had taught them that engines which ceased to turn soon froze and could not be restarted.

Neither side could find much cause for satisfaction in the night's events. Apart from the bombing of London, which did not figure in their plans, the Germans had little to show for the loss of five airships and some of their best crews. Nor could the British claim any spectacular return from the seventy-three sorties made by their pilots. The sum of their achievements was that the L.45, when attacked by Second-Lieutenant T. B. Pritchard of No. 39 Squadron, diverged from a course which might have taken her safely back to Germany. Against that modest success they had to set the loss of six aeroplanes and one pilot in accidental crashes, and ninety-one civilian casualties, most of them attributable to the bombs hastily released by Kolle when he found himself over a target he never expected to see. Strasser did his best to explain away the failure of the raid by blaming the weather service and the difficulty his commanders had in obtaining bearings from direction-finding stations. He admitted that height-sickness and errors of judgement on the part of some commanders were also contributory factors.[26]

About a fortnight before the Silent Raid, the Naval Staff in Berlin warned the authorities in German East Africa that an airship carrying supplies might be expected to reach them during the second half of October.

The idea of sending supplies to East Africa by air dated back to 1916, when the former Chief Medical Officer of the small German force there arrived in Germany as an exchanged prisoner of war and suggested that an airship might be used to deliver medical stores of which the troops were in urgent need.[27]

No more was heard of the proposal until, in the early summer of 1917, a joint study by representatives of the Ministry of Marine, the Naval Airship Division and other authorities led to the conclusion that

A French naval airship, c. 1917.

a non-stop flight from Jamboli in Bulgaria to Mahenge in Tanganyika was not out of the question, but that an airship with a capacity of 2,365,000 cubic feet would be needed. The experts arrived at this figure by assuming that sixteen tons of cargo would be carried and that an airship called upon to fly from Jamboli to Mahenge would have to be capable of remaining in the air for four and a half days and covering a distance of 4,350 miles without refuelling.[28]

The capacity of the airships in current production at the Zeppelin factories was 1,977,360 cubic feet. To meet the requirements of the flight to Mahenge, arrangements were made to raise the capacity of the L.57, due for completion in the late summer, to 2,418,700 feet by the addition of two gas-cells which would increase her length from 644 to 743 feet and make her the largest airship yet built. Since there were no reserves of fuel or hydrogen in German East Africa, no return flight would be possible. If the ship reached Mahenge, she would be broken up. Her crew would stay in East Africa until the war was over or they were captured by the enemy.

Command of the L.57 on these terms was scarcely a post which many officers would covet. It went to Ludwig Bockholt, allegedly in Strasser's bad books since he

risked his ship to capture the Norwegian schooner *Royal* in April.*

The ship made her maiden flight at Friedrichshafen on 26 September. After one more trial flight, Bockholt took her to Jüterbog, where the loading of her special cargo of medical and other supplies was completed on 7 October. Although warned that a storm was approaching, he gave orders that she should be prepared that afternoon for a short test-flight which he hoped to complete before the weather broke. By the time she was out of her shed, such a strong cross-wind was blowing that she could not be returned to it. Bockholt decided to ride out the storm in the air and land at Jamboli or elsewhere, but before he was ready to go the ship was flung to the ground by a sudden gust and seriously damaged. He then tried, after all, to return her to the shed, but she broke free, collided with a fence, and burst into flames.

The naval authorities decided within forty-eight hours to modify the L.59, then approaching completion at Staaken, on the same lines as the L.57. The work was done by 25 October, only sixteen days after the order was given.[29]

After studying reports of the disaster to the L.57, Strasser came to the conclusion that Bockholt had done his best and did not deserve to be court-martialled, but that

* See p. 124.

command of the modified L.59 should be entrusted to Herbert Ehrlich, who was to have commanded her in her original form. The Ministry of Marine insisted that the post should go to Bockholt, who had made a good impression by admitting that he had taken a calculated risk with the L.57 so that no time should be wasted. Three tons of medical supplies and twelve tons of weapons, ammunition and spares were stowed aboard the L.59, and Bockholt was given a formal commission to take her to Jamboli in readiness for the flight to East Africa.

Bockholt left Staaken on 3 November and reached Jamboli on the following day. He was then held up for ten days by bad weather. In the meantime the British launched an offensive which soon put most of German East Africa under their control. Moreover, they learned in the first week of November that an attempt to land an airship behind the enemy's lines might be made in the near future, and were ready to give Bockholt a warm reception.[30]

Bockholt made two attempts to fly to Africa about the middle of the month. On each occasion he was forced to jettison so much ballast in order to remain airborne that the flight had to be abandoned.

His third attempt, on 21 November, promised to be more successful. He took off with a light following wind and made good progress. Within a few hours of his departure the German Colonial Office informed the Ministry of Marine that they could no longer take responsibility for the venture, but the wireless transmitter at

British North Sea airship NS.6 over the National Gallery in London, 1918.

Jamboli was unable to get in touch with him. Early on 22 November he crossed the African coast near Mersa Matruh after flying over the western part of Asia Minor and passing close to the eastern extremity of Crete. At nightfall, soon after the crew had sighted a flock of flamingoes, the ship reached the Nile at Wadi Halfa.

From Wadi Halfa Bockholt followed the course of the river as far as Dongola. Thence he continued southwards with the intention of crossing the uplands of Kordofan and passing over the swamps of the Upper Nile. The weather was hot and humid, and it was only by jettisoning ballast and flying nose-up that he was able to maintain a safe height. Having overcome a host of difficulties, he and his crew were looking forward to the successful accomplishment of their mission when they at last received, in the early hours of 23 November, a message of recall transmitted by a powerful station near Berlin. At the same time they learned that the few surviving German troops in East Africa were caught between the British in the north and the Portuguese in the south.

Bitterly disappointed, Bockholt made a wide turn to starboard and headed north from a point almost due west of Khartoum. He passed over the Farafra oasis, already seen on the outward flight, and returned to Bulgaria by a roundabout course which took him over Sollum, Antalya and Constantinople. The ship landed at Jamboli in the early afternoon of 25 November after spending ninety-five hours in the air, covering well over 4,000 miles and consuming about two-thirds of her fuel. Lovers of statistics calculated that, had she headed west instead of south at the outset of her journey, she could have flown non-stop to San Francisco.

The new year began badly for the naval airship division. Strasser was cheered by the arrival of new engines capable of a high output at extreme altitudes and the opening of powerful direction-finding stations at Tondern and Kleve, but for nearly a fortnight at the end of 1917 and the beginning of 1918 his airships were grounded by strong winds.

The weather on Saturday, 5 January, was still bad. Strasser spent the day at Ahlhorn, which had replaced Nordholz as headquarters of the division in the previous summer. There were five airships in the four large sheds at Ahlhorn, but their commanders found little to do apart from setting men to work on routine tasks and discussing future operations. In Sheds I, II and III the L.47, L.58 and L.46 needed little attention beyond the usual topping up with hydrogen, but the crew of the L.51, also in Shed I, were ordered to clean the floors of the engine-gondolas, and in Shed IV civilians from the Schütte-Lanz factory at Mannheim worked throughout the day repairing damage sustained by the SL.20 during a trial flight on 27 December.

In the late afternoon Strasser was talking in his office to Arnold Schütze, commander of the L.58. Both men, chancing to look out of the window at the same moment, saw an orange flame leap towards the sky from Shed I. A few seconds later they heard a series of mighty explosions. Within a minute all four sheds were reduced to skeletons of twisted metal and all five of the ships in them were totally destroyed. Ten naval ratings and four civilians were killed, thirty seriously injured and more than a hundred slightly injured.[31]

Strasser's first thought was that British aircraft had bombed the station. His second was that saboteurs had placed explosive charges in the sheds. A cordon was put round the station, but no saboteurs were caught and no firm evidence of sabotage was ever found. A former petty officer appears to have claimed ten years later that he was paid the equivalent of £100,000 to set fire to the sheds, but there was no confirmation of his story and nothing in the man's record suggests that he ever possessed anything like that sum. According to evidence given at the Court of Inquiry, the first sign of impending disaster noticed by survivors working in Shed I was a noise 'like a motor backfiring'.[32] A glow which seemed to come from underneath the rear gondola of the L.51 was then seen inside the shed. The presumption is that the L.51 caught fire and that the consequent rise in temperature caused hydrogen to escape from the valves of the L.47 and form an explosive mixture with the air inside the shed. The shock-wave caused by the explosion of this mixture would seem to have been responsible for the explosions in the other sheds, the furthest of which was half a mile away.

The cause of the fire underneath the rear gondola of the L.51 remains mysterious. Two men who escaped from the gondola testified that they and their companions did not smoke, strike matches, use inflammable fluids for cleaning or wear nailed boots which might strike sparks from metal parts of the ship. One of them added that, although he could not be sure that the glow he saw from the gondola came from beneath it, he did know that the fire was outside the ship, because his head and hands were scorched when he jumped to the floor of the shed. The Court suggested in its findings that a sheet of asbestos or piece of metal from the roof of the shed

Control gondola of the German naval airship L.54, completed in 1917 and destroyed by British aircraft in her shed at Tondern in 1918.

might have fallen clean through the L.51, destroying one of her fuel tanks, causing sparks to fly between severed wires, and producing the noise heard before the first big explosion. An alternative explanation, which seems more consistent with the evidence of the survivor who jumped through a fire coming from below the ship, is that inflammable material of some kind had collected on the floor of the shed and was ignited by a spark from an unsafe cable. The inspection lamps used by the men in the rear gondola of the L.51 were said to have burnt steadily, but German electrical circuits were notoriously unreliable at a time when the country was desperately short of rubber.

No raids on Britain were attempted for more than two months after the Ahlhorn disaster. At last, on 12 March, five airships were despatched with orders to attack objectives in the midland target area. Strasser led the raid in the L.62. Her commander, Kuno Manger, claimed on his return to base to have attacked Leeds, but the only buildings damaged by his bombs were an inn and some cottages many miles from the town. Michael von Freudenreich, in the newly commissioned L.63, dropped some bombs at Hull, where a few houses were damaged and a woman died of shock. The commanders of the L.53, L.54 and L.61 dropped their bombs either in the sea or on waste land, but claimed to have attacked Hull, Grimsby and an anti-aircraft battery. The British attributed the failure of the raid to low clouds, rain and the great height at which the airships flew.[33]

Strasser despatched three ships on the following day, but recalled them when he found that the wind was shifting to an unfavourable quarter. Martin Dietrich, in the L.42, disobeyed the order and went on to West Hartlepool, where he dropped bombs which wrecked or damaged shops and houses and killed or injured forty-seven people. Strasser was at first extremely angry with him. Afterwards he agreed to pass off the escapade as an attack made at the end of a reconnaissance.[34]

A raid planned for 4 April had to be cancelled because of the weather. On 12 April five airships were despatched with orders to attack objectives in the midland target area. At the last moment Strasser gave commanders the choice of attacking objectives in the southern target area, but added that they were not to bomb London unless he expressly ordered them to do so. Three of the ships made only brief flights over England. Ehrlich, in the L.61, unwittingly flew as far west as Wigan, where he dropped bombs in the belief that he was attacking Sheffield. Manger, in the L.62, reached Coventry and Birmingham, but he failed to hit any major objective at either of those places. He was attacked near Birmingham by Lieutenant C. H. Noble-Campbell of No. 38 Squadron, but his machine-gunners put up such a stout defence that Noble-Campbell was wounded in the head and had to make a forced landing with a damaged aircraft. Twenty-seven people were killed or injured, nearly all of them by bombs from the L.61.

Routine patrols over the Heligoland Bight and towards the Skagerrak, long interrupted by bad weather, were resumed in the spring. They entailed many hours of monotonous flying, but were not always uneventful. On 10 May the L.56, commanded by Kapitänleutnant Walter Zaeschmar, had an encounter near Borkum with a British flying boat piloted by Captains T. H. Pattison and A. H. Munday. On the same day another German airship on reconnaissance, the L.62, blew up mysteriously near Heligoland. The British authorities, on learning of the loss of the L.62, assumed that she was the ship engaged by Pattison and Munday, but the German record shows that they engaged the L.56 and that their attack was unsuccessful.[35]

The Naval Airship Division suffered a further blow on 29 June, when British aircraft from the experimental carrier *Furious* attacked Tondern. The double shed which housed the L.54 and the L.60 was damaged by bombs, and both airships were destroyed. Of the seven British pilots who took part in the attack, four landed in Denmark, one came down in the sea off the Danish coast and was drowned, and two returned to the *Furious* but were unable to land on her flight deck and had to ditch their aircraft. For the rest of the war, Tondern was used only as a standby base to which airships could be diverted in an emergency.

Strasser was consoled to some extent for the Ahlhorn disaster and the loss of the L.54, L.60 and L.62 by the hope that new ships of the L.70 class would confront the British with insoluble problems. The L.70, commissioned on 8 July, was just under 694 feet long, had a capacity of nearly 2,200,000 cubic feet, and was driven by seven Maybach MB IVa engines designed to give a good performance at heights of the order of 20,000 feet. During her trials at Friedrichshafen she attained a maximum speed of eighty-one miles an hour. Strasser, confident that she would be able to outclimb and outdistance any British aircraft, spoke of her to his superiors as the 'final type', but failed to convince them that development of the still larger L.100 could safely be abandoned.

Command of so important a ship might have been expected to go to an officer seasoned by long experience of conditions over Britain. In fact, it went to Kapitänleutnant Johann von Lossnitzer, Strasser's former adjutant. Lossnitzer was well liked by his brother-officers, but his experience of active operations in face of the enemy was confined to eight 'war flights' over the Baltic and two flights over the North Sea in a ship used chiefly as an advanced trainer.[36]

Lossnitzer's first operational flight in command of the L.70 was made on 1 August, when his ship was one of three which were sent to reconnoitre towards the Dogger Bank. Warned that British warships were at sea and had been sighted from a German seaplane, he dropped bombs close to light cruisers and destroyers of Commodore Tyrwhitt's Harwich Force, which he mistook for a battlecruiser accompanied by a destroyer flotilla. Tyrwhitt's comment on the incident was that the German airship commanders seemed to be losing their sense of caution.[37]

Germany was already on the verge of defeat when, four days later, Strasser ordered what proved to be the last raid on Britain. During the early afternoon of 5 August the L.53, L.56, L.63, L.65 and L.70 left Nordholz, Wittmundhaven and Ahlhorn with orders to attack either the southern or the midland target area, but not to bomb London without express authority. Strasser embarked in the L.70,

One of the last airships delivered to the German Army: the LZ.113, photographed in 1917. The influence of Schütte-Lanz on Zeppelin design is noticeable in the closer approach to a streamlined shape.

but he told his commanders that they were to maintain 'careful wireless discipline' and that operations would be controlled from Nordholz. Nevertheless he broke wireless silence to transmit an eleventh-hour order to all airships to attack in accordance with a prearranged plan.[38]

With what seems extraordinary lack of caution, the ships approached the English coast in conditions which made it very unlikely that they would escape detection. The L.53, L.65 and L.70 were seen at 8.10 p.m. from the Leman Tail light vessel, about forty miles from the Norfolk coast. Fifty minutes later the L.56 and L.63 were heard closer to the coast and further south. The sky was overcast and rain was falling intermittently, but visibility above the clouds was very good. Major Egbert Cadbury, flying with Captain R. Leckie as gunner and observer in a DH. 4 two-seater with a maximum speed of more than 120 miles an hour and a service ceiling of 22,000 feet, left Great Yarmouth at 9.5 p.m. He soon sighted all three of the ships which had been seen earlier, and had no difficulty in closing with the L.70, which was flying slowly westwards at 17,000 feet. A burst from Leckie's gun started a fire which ran the whole length of the ship. Within a minute or two she plunged, a blazing mass, into the sea. Cadbury then attacked the L.65, but the gun jammed and Leckie was unable to free it.

On seeing the L.70 in flames, the surviving commanders judged, correctly, that they had been given a misleading forecast of conditions over England, and soon turned for home. Some of them claimed on arrival that they had attacked places near the coast, but no bombs fell on land.

The death of Peter Strasser in action came as a fitting end to an offensive of which he had been the guiding spirit. Since the outbreak of war, German naval airships had taken part in more than forty raids on Britain and had devoted to the purpose rather less than a fifth of their total effort in all theatres.[39] Reconnaissance of the Heligoland Bight had always been their main task in terms of the number of sorties given to it, but they had also paid some attention to operations against the Russian Baltic Fleet and its bases. In addition a few sorties over the Mediterranean had been made from Jamboli or elsewhere. The army's airships had taken part in some seventeen raids on Britain and had also attacked objectives as far apart as Paris, Warsaw, Bucharest and Salonika. About two hundred tons of bombs dropped from airships had fallen on British soil and had killed or injured nearly 2,000 people since the war began.

Whether the raids on Britain were worth

making from the German point of view will always be a controversial question. The British official historian of the war in the air came to the conclusion that they were, if only because they led the British to divert to home defence resources which might otherwise have been used on the Western Front. Although this was also Strasser's view, the precise effect of the diversion on Britain's fortunes remains hard to judge. At any rate in the latter part of the war, aircraft, guns and searchlights would have had to be kept at home anyway to deal with heavier-than-air bombers. Britain's output of war material was at times adversely affected by absenteeism resulting from air attacks, but only for brief periods.

On the debit side of the account, Germany's investment in large rigid airships for naval and military use proved a fairly expensive business. Of seventy rigid airships used by the navy, fifty-two were destroyed or forced down by enemy action, accidentally destroyed or otherwise lost. A further six were written off before the date of the armistice as obsolete or surplus to requirements, so that only twelve remained in commission when hostilities were suspended. The army began the war with seven rigid airships and commissioned another thirty-seven before deciding to cut its losses. Of the total of forty-four, only two were still extant at the date of the armistice, and these had been laid up for many months after serving under naval control on the Baltic Front. To these material losses must be added the odium which the Germans incurred by repeatedly dropping bombs which damaged private property and killed civilians. As a persistent advocate of raids on Britain by lighter-than-air machines, Strasser cannot be acquitted of all blame for allowing a situation to arise in which his commanders and crews were execrated as Huns and baby-killers. He saw for himself that commanders had great difficulty in finding, let alone accurately bombing, legitimate objectives. Yet he repeatedly urged the continuance of an offensive which was bound to lead to a great many indiscriminate attacks. The number of civilians killed by bombs dropped from airships would, indeed, have been considerably higher than it was had not commanders often dumped their loads in the sea or on open fields while claiming to be attacking built-up areas.

Strasser's death was not quite the end of the Naval Airship Division. His successor, Kapitänleutnant Paul Werther, submitted proposals for a new generation of airships capable of carrying a two and a half ton bomb-load to 26,000 feet or more.[40] He was warned that henceforth most maritime

Postscript to war: the L.65 sabotaged at Nordholz to prevent the government from surrendering her to the victorious allies.

reconnaissance would be done by heavier-than-air machines, but no formal decision to suspend attacks on Britain seems to have been recorded. The order for the L.100 was cancelled early in October, but plans were made to complete ships of the L.70 class up to the L.73 or even the L.74. In the outcome, only the L.71 was ready in time to be commissioned before the war was over.

In the meantime a few more reconnaissance flights were made. Eduard Prölss was reconnoitring the Heligoland Bight in the L.53 on 11 August when he made contact with the Harwich Force and was shot down off Terschelling by Lieutenant S. D. Culley, the pilot of an aircraft launched as an experiment from a lighter towed by a destroyer.

The last reconnaissance flights of the war by rigid airships were ordered on 12 October. The L.63 and the L.65 left Ahlhorn and Nordholz that afternoon to cover a minesweeping operation planned for the following day, but poor visibility caused both commanders to turn back before nightfall.

In the meantime the German imperial government, soon to be swept away by internal and external pressures, had opened negotiations for an armistice. While the negotiations were in progress, naval ratings who claimed to be acting on behalf of Sailors' Councils akin to those established in Soviet Russia rebelled against their officers and seized the bases of the High Seas Fleet. Eventually they gained control of the Naval Airship Division's operational bases in north-west Germany. They did no harm to the surviving airships, but the gas-bags of some ships not already laid up were deflated.

Clause XXVII of the armistice agreement between Germany and the Allied and Associated Powers provided that all German naval aircraft should be immobilized at bases to be specified by the Allies and the United States of America. When the agreement was signed, the navy still had a dozen airships on its books. The oldest was the L.14, the newest the L.71. The L.72 was almost ready for delivery, but work on her was stopped and the manufacturers claimed that she was still their property. Two army airships, the LZ.113 and the LZ.120, still survived.

Under the terms of the Treaty of Versailles, first formally presented to the Germans in draft form on 7 May 1919, Germany was forbidden to maintain naval or military air forces and was called upon to accept restrictions which threatened her aircraft industry with extinction. Incensed by these proposals, Right Wing opponents of the Republican régime broke into the sheds at Nordholz and Wittmundhaven

and wrecked the L.14, L.42, L.52, L.56, L.63 and L.65 in order to prevent the government from surrendering them to the Allied and Associated Powers. The Allies, affronted by this gesture and by the scuttling of German warships interned at Scapa Flow, seized the rest of Germany's naval and military airships, including the L.72. They insisted that the *Bodensee* and the *Nordstern*, built by the Zeppelin company since the armistice for commercial use, should also be surrendered to them.

The Allies then parcelled out the surrendered airships among themselves. Britain received the L.64 and the L.71; France the L.72, the LZ.113 and the *Nordstern*; Italy the L.61, the LZ.120 and the *Bodensee*. The SL.22, commissioned in the summer of 1918 despite complaints from Strasser that she was already out of date, was broken up and her parts distributed among the victorious powers. The L.30, allotted to the Belgians, was also broken up because her new owners had no use for her as a complete ship, and the L.37 was dismantled for shipment to Japan. The L.72 was renamed the *Dixmude*, the *Nordstern* the *Méditerranée*, the *Bodensee* the *Esperia*.

The surrendered ships did not prove as valuable to their new owners as perhaps they hoped. The *Dixmude* made a record-breaking non-stop flight of nearly five days over the Sahara in 1923, but was lost with all hands while flying from the south of France to Algeria later in the year. The French and the Italians were not prepared, in face of such setbacks, to spend the large sums needed to develop the rigid airship as a long-range transport aircraft. The British were; but they had already sent a rigid airship across the Atlantic and back by the time the L.64 and the L.71 were delivered to them in the summer of 1920. It is fair to say that, on the whole, they owed less to their acquisition of these ships than to their capture of the L.33 in 1916.

7 The post-War Years

Ferdinand von Zeppelin died on 8 March 1917 at the age of seventy-nine. He had ceased to believe that airships could play a decisive part in the war, but left his successors with a robust faith in their future as commercial aircraft.

Soon after the armistice, the directors of the Zeppelin company considered a proposal that the L.72 should be sent across the Atlantic to prove that airships could link Germany with the United States.[1] Such a flight was out of the question as long as Germany was still technically at war with the Allied and Associated Powers, and even when the peace treaties were signed and ratified some time might elapse before it could be expected to do more good than harm. Largely on Eckener's advice, the firm decided to shelve the project and build two ships suitable for flights between German cities and later between European capitals.

The *Bodensee*, completed in the late summer of 1919, was faster and more comfortable, but no larger, than the airships of 1914. Between the last week in September and the end of the year she carried about 2,300 passengers and thirty-five tons of mail and freight on the Berlin-Friedrichshafen route.[2] She also made two experimental flights to Stockholm.

The *Nordstern*, slightly larger than the *Bodensee*, was designed with an eye to regular flights between Germany and the Scandinavian countries. Unfortunately for Eckener's plans, the firm was not allowed to keep her. In the summer of 1920 the Allies insisted that she and the *Bodensee*, as well as the L.72, should be surrendered to them. Eckener and his colleagues might have faced a future devoted to the making of pots and pans if they hadn't managed to obtain an order which would keep them in business as manufacturers of airships.

An answer to their problem was found as an indirect consequence of the refusal of the United States Senate to ratify the Treaty of Versailles. To put a formal end to hostilities between Germany and the United States, a separate treaty had to be negotiated. Diplomatic contacts in an atmosphere less frigid than that of 1919 gave the Germans an opportunity of ventilating a proposal that the relatively small sum due to the United States as compensation for war damage might be remitted in the form of an airship to be built by the Zeppelin company and paid for by the state. The Americans were building a rigid airship of their own, and had also ordered one from Britain. Nevertheless they were willing to accept, in lieu of gold, an airship capable of crossing the Atlantic from east to west, and if necessary to meet the difference between its cost and the amount due to them.

The experts calculated that a ship with a capacity of 2,500,000 cubic feet would be needed. Under the terms of the armistice and the peace treaties, as interpreted by the Allied Council of Ambassadors, no ship with a capacity of more than 1,100,000 cubic feet could be built in Germany. But the Allies agreed, after some debate, to waive this restriction. Towards the end of 1921 the company received authority to begin work on a ship with a capacity of 2,542,320 cubic feet, a length of 656 feet, and the works designation LZ.126.[3]

In Britain, the R.31 made her maiden flight about three months before the armistice. Built by Short Brothers but designed by a team of naval architects which included a Swiss who had worked for Schütte-Lanz, she had a capacity of 1,547,000 cubic feet, a length of 615 feet, and a wooden framework. Powered at first by six and later by five Rolls-Royce Eagle engines, she proved about as fast as the substantially larger German airships of the L.57 class. But her life was destined to be short. On 6 November 1918 she left Cardington to fly to the naval airship station at East Fortune. During the flight her joints were seen to be coming apart. She was diverted to Howden, put into a

ABOVE: *The R.34; first airship to cross the Atlantic and first aircraft of any kind to make the two-way crossing.*

shed whose roof had been destroyed by fire, and there irreparably damaged by heavy rain.[4]

The R.32, completed about twelve months after the R.31 and built by the same manufacturer to substantially the same design, was more successful. After serving for the first year of her life as an experimental craft, she was used to train crews of the United States Navy attached for the purpose to the Royal Air Force. In 1921 she again provided valuable experimental data by being intentionally tested to destruction.

Both the R.33 and the R.34 were delivered in 1919. Except for their engines, they were essentially copies of the L.33. After taking part in fleet exercises and making a number of goodwill flights to continental Europe, the R.33 was used in 1921 at Pulham and Howden to test the theory that a 643-foot-long rigid airship could not only remain moored to a mast for long periods in all kinds of weather, but could also be brought to the mast in winds too strong for any large airship to be safely walked into a shed. The advantages of this method were convincingly shown when the R.33, after flying from Croydon in pouring rain, was successfully attached to the mast at Pulham in a wind rising in gusts to gale force.[5]

In the summer of 1919 her competitor, the R.34, broke a number of records by flying from Scotland to the United States and back to England. Two British airmen, John Alcock and Arthur Whitten Brown, had already crossed the Atlantic in a modified heavier-than-air bomber, but they flew from west to east. The R.34 was the first airship to make a transatlantic flight, the first aircraft of any kind to cross from

Display outside the Marconi Company's office during the R.34's transatlantic flight.

east to west, and the first aircraft of any kind to make the double crossing. These were considerable feats for an airship which was admittedly underpowered and whose gross lift was only sixty tons. A great deal was due to the skill of her captain, Major G. H. Scott, and his readiness to take calculated risks in order to show that commercial airship flights across the Atlantic were not beyond the bounds of possibility.

Carrying thirty legitimate travellers in addition to a trespassing kitten, a stowaway and twenty tons of fuel, oil, ballast, food and drinking water, the R.34 left East Fortune early on 2 July. Flying nose-up to gain aerodynamic lift, she made fairly good progress until she was off the coast of Nova Scotia, where she met stormy weather. For a time she seemed so likely to run out of fuel that Scott thought of trying an emergency landing in Massachusetts. Eventually the weather improved and she was able to make Montauk Point. Four and a half days after leaving East Fortune, she landed at Roosevelt Field, Long Island, with only enough fuel left for another forty minutes' flying. The stowaway, an airman named Ballantyne, was sent home by sea, but the authorities took a lenient view of his escapade and he afterwards reached commissioned rank.[6]

The return flight began on 10 July. Most of it was made with one engine out of order, but favourable winds enabled Scott to reach Pulham in just over three days. The R.34 survived until early in 1921, when she flew into a hillside in Yorkshire. Her crew managed to get her back to Howden, but she was there irreparably damaged by gusts of wind before she could be housed.

The R.80, ordered in 1917 and completed in 1920, differed from most rigid airships conceived during the war in being built, like the Vickers airship No. 9, to an original design. She was not a copy of the L.33, like the R.33 and R.34, or based on the SL.11 like the R.31 and R.32. She was 534 feet long, with a capacity of 1,250,000 cubic feet and a good streamlined shape. Four Wolseley-Maybach engines gave her a theoretical range of nearly 4,000 miles at sixty-five miles an hour or 6,400 miles at fifty miles an hour.[7] She was designed for wartime use and was armed, but seemed to her manufacturers likely to make a suitable prototype for commercial airships. During her lifetime Vickers put forward proposals for a transatlantic airship service, but at first gained no support for them.[8] She was used to a limited extent for experimental work and training, but the authorities did not exploit her capabilities as thoroughly as Vickers would have liked.

Other British rigid airships under con-

struction or projected at the time of the armistice included the R.35, R.36, R.37, R.38, R.39 and R.40. The first and the two last were never built. The R.36, based essentially on the German L.48, was constructed by Beardmore and delivered to Pulham in May 1921. She had a capacity of 2,101,000 cubic feet and was powered by four Sunbeam Cossack engines. She was used for a variety of purposes, including traffic control, but had rather a chequered career. In August 1921 she overshot the mast at Pulham and was damaged. She was then hastily walked into a shed occupied by the surrendered L.64, which had to be sacrificed to make room for her.

The R.37, similar to the R.36, was built under contract by Short Brothers, who had almost completed her when, in 1921, work on her was stopped. She was dismantled in 1924.

The R.38 was laid down in 1918 in response to a demand from the Admiralty for an airship capable of patrolling for three days over an area 300 miles from her base and cruising or hovering in strong winds for a further twenty-four hours after her return. She was to have been built by Short Brothers at Cardington, but after the armistice the government responded to a complaint from the firm that they were losing money on airships by announcing that it proposed to use its powers under the Defence of the Realm Act to nationalize Cardington, and that the R.38 would be completed by the Royal Airship Works which would then be created. She was designed by a team drawn from the Royal Corps of Naval Constructors, but working under the Director of Airship Construction. The leader of the team, Constructor-Commander C. I. R. Campbell, was appointed manager of the Royal Airship Works when Cardington was nationalized. These arrangements proved unfortunate, since they had the effect of

The R.101 at Cardington mooring mast October 1929, with rollers being used to steady her without preventing her from turning her nose to the wind.

The R.80, ordered during the First World War but completed in 1920. Not a copy of a Zeppelin or a Schütte-Lanz, but built to an original design.

making Campbell and his staff sole judges of their own work so far as the design of the R.38 was concerned.

The ship was completed in the summer of 1921. She was 699 feet long and had a capacity of 2,724,000 cubic feet and a disposable lift of nearly forty-six tons. Her six Sunbeam Cossack engines gave her a maximum speed of seventy-one miles an hour, but they were heavier than the engines first envisaged, and her structure was not strengthened to compensate for the added weight. No longer needed by the Admiralty, she was intended for sale to the United States Navy and was given American naval markings and the American naval designation ZR–II. The Americans were told by the Air Ministry that she could be taken across the Atlantic after she had done fifty hours' flying, but the British officer in charge of flying trials, Flight Lieutenant J. E. M. Pritchard, was of the opinion that she ought first to do 150 hours' flying, including fifty hours in the hands of an American crew.[9]

The R.38 first flew on the night of 23–24

June 1921, when she spent about seven hours in the air and was found difficult to control at the moderate speed of thirty-eight knots, or roughly forty-five miles an hour. A second trial five nights later revealed weaknesses in her fins and showed that she was still rather unmanageable at moderate to high speeds, despite modifications made after her first flight. During her third flight, in the middle of July, some of her transverse girders gave way after her speed had been increased to fifty knots. Pritchard, who attended the trials as official representative of the Air Ministry and seized the elevator wheel at a critical moment during the third flight, pressed for a thorough inspection before she flew again. He also proposed that future trials should be made at a height of not less than 7,000 feet in order to reduce the strains imposed on the ship during turning movements.

On 23 August the ship left Howden for her fourth flight. She was to have moored that night at Pulham, but was overtaken by darkness and poor visibility when still some fifteen miles away. Her captain, Flight Lieutenant A. H. Wann, was not sure of his exact position. He decided to spend the night over the North Sea. When daylight returned he pushed the ship to her maximum speed of sixty-two knots before attempting a series of tight turns at fifty-four and a half knots. While carrying out these manoeuvres at a height of 2,500 feet, she broke in two and fell into the Humber. Wann was one of five survivors, but was too badly injured to appear before the Court of Inquiry which sat at the end of August and early in September. Forty-four lives were lost.

A technical sub-committee of the government's Aeronautical Research Committee afterwards reviewed the findings of the Court of Inquiry, interviewed Wann and considered other evidence. The sub-committee found that the ship had broken up because her structure was subjected to strains it was not strong enough to bear, but that Wann's use of the controls was legitimate.[10] Campbell and his helpers were criticized for leaving aerodynamic forces out of account when they formulated their design, but were given credit for trying to obtain data which would have enabled them to calculate the likely stresses on the ship more accurately than they succeeded in doing. The design ought, it was suggested, to have been submitted to expert scrutiny before the ship was built.

How far these strictures were deserved is hard to say. Having lost his life in the crash, Campbell was not in a position to remind the sub-committee that he could not have found experts competent to pass

The R.38. Intended at first for the Admiralty and later for sale to the United States Navy as the ZR-II. Wrecked during a trial flight over the Humber in 1921.

judgement on his design unless he had been allowed to go outside official circles and consult independent designers such as Wallis and Pratt. From the spring of 1920 he was burdened with administrative tasks which gave him little opportunity of catching up with recent research. Had he been working for a commercial firm, this would not have happened, and he would have had a chance of correcting his errors when the ship was handed back to the manufacturers for modification, as doubtless she would have been after the second or third trial. He was not responsible for the decision to hasten the trials. It was his misfortune that Pritchard's recommendation that the ship should not be flown again until she had been thoroughly examined reached the Air Ministry at a moment when the head of the relevant department was away, when the Americans were pressing for early delivery, and when the Royal Air Force was anxious to be done with airships and concentrate on heavier-than-air machines.

When the R.38 was lost, the government had already agreed that the Air Ministry's airship section should be disbanded as soon as this last ship was off their hands. During the next few months the airship stations were placed on a care and maintenance basis, the designers at Cardington reverted to the Royal Corps of Naval Constructors, and officers and men not needed for care and maintenance were posted to other jobs. A government spokesman explained in the House of Lords that none of this need affect the development of airships for commercial use. The fact remains that more than ten years elapsed between the first and second crossings of the Atlantic by a British airship.

In France, the loss of the *Dixmude* in 1923 was decisive. Why the *Dixmude* foundered off the coast of Sicily with more than fifty men aboard her when she had already been reported over Algeria was never satisfactorily explained; but she was known to have diverged from her course in an unsuccessful attempt to dodge a storm, and the presumption was that she had succumbed to stresses she was not strong enough to bear.* A plan to use the *Méditerranée* for passenger services to Algeria was abandoned, and no more was heard of projected flights from French West Africa to Brazil. The *Méditerranée* survived until 1925, and was then abandoned. The French Navy's interest in airships lapsed a few years later, when three non-rigid ships still in its possession

* The fate of the *Dixmude* remained mysterious until, shortly after her disappearance, the body of her commander was found floating in the water. The remains of her hull were discovered by chance about ten years later.

The first American-built rigid airship: the ZR-I, or Shenandoah, *completed in 1923 and based substantially on the wartime Zeppelin L.49.*

became obsolete and were taken out of service.

The Italians ended the war with a reputation for building pressure airships of impressive size and performance. Shortly before the armistice the British bought from them a semi-rigid airship with a capacity of 441,000 cubic feet and a speed of fifty-one miles an hour.[11] Known to her purchasers as the SR.1, she was flown by Captain George Meager from Rome to Kingsnorth in three days, including brief stops at Aubagne, Saint Cyr and an emergency landing ground in the valley of the Rhône.[12] After making a number of demonstration flights in connection with the peace celebrations and the issue of Victory Bonds, she was taken out of service in the autumn of 1919.

In 1921 a large semi-rigid airship built under contract in Italy for export to the United States was shipped across the Atlantic in sections and erected at Langley Field. Named the *Roma*, she made her first flight in the United States on 15 November. With two of her six Italian engines replaced by more powerful engines built in the United States, she flew on 21 December from Langley Field to Washington.[13] Two months later, while undergoing high-speed tests at what seems the dangerously low altitude of 1,000 feet, she began to break up in the air, went out of control and crashed into a hillside. This was not the fault of her designer, who could not be expected to foresee that her purchasers would subject her structure to strains it was not meant to bear by installing more powerful engines than those specified.

No steps were taken to develop rigid airships in the United States until the late summer of 1919, when the Secretary of the Navy sanctioned the building of a ship based on the plans and drawings circulated among the Allied and Associated Powers after the enforced descent of the L.49 in 1917. In the meantime a plan was made to beat the British in the race to be first across the Atlantic by using a Goodyear non-rigid airship, the C-5, to make the flight from west to east with the help of the prevailing wind. On 14 and 15 May the C-5 flew from Montauk, Long Island, to St John's, Newfoundland, covering a distance of more than a thousand miles in just under twenty-six hours. A few days later she was blown from her moorings by a gale and lost at sea with no one aboard her.

The rigid airship ordered in 1919 was completed in the late summer of 1923 at Lakehurst, New Jersey, and inflated with helium, then unobtainable in commercial quantities outside the United States. She bore the service designation ZR-1 but was named the *Shenandoah*. After making her

maiden flight on 4 September she flew in just under two days from Lakehurst to St Louis and back under the command of Commander F. R. McCrary of the United States Navy.

Mooring trials were then carried out at a mast specially built for the *Shenandoah* at Lakehurst. On 16 January 1924 she was torn from the mast by a sudden gale. A skeleton crew and an acting commander, Lieutenant-Commander M. R. Pierce, were aboard her at the time. By promptly dropping ballast, they managed to lift her above a line of trees towards which she was drifting.[14] But their troubles were not over. She was down at the nose, two of her gas-bags were damaged, and she was not under power. Pierce succeeded in starting her engines and getting her on an even keel by shifting ballast, but meanwhile she was carried every moment further from the mast. It was only after nearly nine hours that he was able to bring her safely home.

In the following October, after the damage had been repaired, the *Shenandoah* made a long and roundabout flight to the West Coast and back in the hands of a new skipper, Commander Zachary Lansdowne. Leaving Lakehurst on 7 October, she reached Seattle by way of Illinois, New Mexico, Arizona and California. She returned on 26 October after covering more than 9,000 miles.

Meanwhile the finishing touches were put to the LZ.126 at Friedrichshafen. In the last week of September 1924, she showed her paces by flying to Malmö and back at an average speed of well over sixty miles an hour.

Some Germans, fearing that the LZ.126 might be the last big airship Germany was allowed to build, were bitterly opposed to

her leaving the country for the far side of the Atlantic. But their fears were groundless. In the following year the Locarno treaties removed all restrictions on the manufacture of civil aircraft in Germany. In any case there was no substance in complaints that the LZ.126 was to be sent to the United States because hatred of Germany still lingered in the breasts of her former enemies. No one had forced the Germans to build an airship for the Americans. They had volunteered to do so in order to provide revenue for the Zeppelin company and employment for its workpeople.

Hugo Eckener, undeterred by threats of sabotage and even assassination, made arrangements to take the ship to Lakehurst while the *Shenandoah* was away. Leaving Friedrichshafen on 13 October, she completed the 5,000-mile journey by way of the Azores and Massachusetts in eighty-one hours.

Soon after her arrival, the hydrogen was removed from her gas-bags and replaced by helium. The *Shenandoah* had to be deflated for the purpose, since there was not enough helium in the United States, or indeed anywhere, to fill two large airships. Bearing the service designation ZR-III, she flew a few weeks later to an airfield near Washington to be named the *Los Angeles* at a ceremony whose climax was marked by the release of white doves as

The ZR-III, or Los Angeles. *Built in Germany as the LZ.126 and flown to the United States in 1924.*

emblems of the concord established between Germany and the United States. She was so named, according to the Secretary of the Navy, 'because she has come to us from overseas like an angel of peace'.[15]

But the *Los Angeles* was not destined to cement the bonds of friendship between nations as a passenger and freight-carrying airship on commercial routes. Until her withdrawal from service in 1932 she was used for a variety of purposes, including scientific research, the taking up and launching of landplanes or seaplanes in mid-air, and experiments with aircraft carriers. But she remained essentially a naval airship, whose primary function in wartime would be co-operation with the fleet. Her 331 flights included visits to Panama and Cuba; but she could not be used to show the flag in European countries, since the helium that would be needed to top her up after long flights was not available in Europe.

The *Shenandoah* was not permanently pushed into the background by the arrival of the LZ.126. In 1925 she covered about 28,000 miles before making what was destined to be her last sortie. Still commanded by Zachary Lansdowne, she left Lakehurst on 2 September for the Middle West. Soon after she had run into a strong headwind over Ohio early on 3 September, her coxswain reported that she was rising and that he could not keep her down. Lansdowne put her nose hard down and opened up her engines to full speed, but she rose about 4,000 feet in a few minutes, and gas had to be valved off before her ascent could be checked at 6,200 feet. The loss of gas having made her heavy, she then began to fall so rapidly that Lansdowne jettisoned all his remaining ballast in order to avert a crash. After she had fallen about 2,800 feet in two minutes, she was whirled upwards by a violent up-current. Foreseeing that she would start to fall again as soon as its force was spent, Lansdowne ordered the crew to prepare to jettison fuel tanks and heavy equipment. His Executive Officer, Lieutenant-Commander Charles E. Rosendahl, climbed from the control car into the keel so as to be ready to supervise these measures when the moment came.

Almost immediately after this, there was a sharp rending sound as the control car parted company with the keel. For a time the car hung suspended by the cables connecting it with various parts of the ship. When these gave way it plunged to the ground, carrying eight men to their deaths.

Looking aft along the keel, Rosendahl was confronted with an even more awe-inspiring spectacle. The whole of the after portion of the ship, some hundreds of feet in length, had broken away from the 200-foot bow section and was receding into space.

Happily, the consequences in terms of lives lost were not quite as calamitous as might have been expected. There was enough helium in the gas-bags of the after portion of the ship to cause it to act as a free balloon. Twenty-two men stepped out of it when eventually it reached the ground. Three had been killed when two engine gondolas were wrenched away from it, three flung out of the ship when she broke in two. The only fatal casualties were these six men and the eight occupants of the control car.

The bow section rose to a height of 10,000 feet before Rosendahl and his companions were able to check its ascent by valving gas. They then succeeded, by throwing out heavy objects, in preventing it from falling too fast. It came gently to earth, and all seven men were saved.

Before a guard could be mounted, souvenir hunters had removed so much of the wreckage that the work of the government's investigators was seriously hampered. Experts concluded from what remained that the ship had broken up because she was not strong enough to withstand the strains imposed on her by vertical currents.[16]

The fate of the *Shenandoah*, following the loss of the *Dixmude* and the R.38, convinced many members of the public that airships were inherently unsafe and hence not suitable for commercial use. This was an understandable conclusion, but not necessarily a sound one. The *Dixmude* was a war-time airship in which strength had been sacrificed to lightness. The *Shenandoah* was a copy of such an airship. The R.38 was in a different category; but she, too, had been designed in the first instance to meet war-time needs. The loss of these three ships did not prove that manufacturers with the resources available in Britain and the United States in time of peace could not build sound commercial airships.

8 New Horizons

During the early post-war years, British statesmen were sometimes asked why they spent a good deal of the taxpayer's money on the Royal Air Force and very little of it on civil aviation. Part of their answer was that the nation would not thank them for giving small airlines large subsidies to facilitate travel between London and Paris by British and foreign businessmen and pleasure-seekers. Air services which brought the capitals of the self-governing Dominions closer to Westminster would, they implied and sometimes said, be a different matter.

In the summer of 1921 an Imperial Conference was held in London. A. H. Ashbolt, Agent-General for Tasmania, proposed while the conference was sitting that an imperial air company should be formed to link the British Isles with India, Australia, New Zealand and South Africa. Six airships were to be acquired and adapted for the carriage of passengers and mail.[1]

A committee was appointed to look into his proposal and any similar proposals. The committee reported favourably on Ashbolt's scheme, but none of the self-governing Dominions or the Crown Colonies, except Australia, was willing to contribute to the cost of it.[2] The loss of the R.38 suggested, too, that existing British airships, built as they were to wartime standards, might not be very suitable for the purpose Ashbolt had in view.

A rather different scheme was proposed in the following year by Commander C. Dennistoun Burney (afterwards Sir Dennistoun Burney) with support from Vickers and the Shell Petroleum Company. During the war Burney had invented the paravane, a device which saved many ships from being sunk by mines. He had offered his invention to the naval authorities, who told him that they were not interested in its application to merchant vessels and that he was free to exploit its commercial possibilities. The result was that, having come to a mutually satisfactory arrangement with Vickers, he found himself at the end of the war with a comfortable income and a reputation for combining inventive skill with commercial acumen.

Burney had never seen an airship when the hope of doing something to help his country out of the post-war depression led him to address himself to the problem of imperial communications and come to the conclusion that possibly airships might provide an answer.[3] Before submitting his scheme to the authorities, he consulted Hugo Eckener as well as the directors of Vickers and Shell. He also recruited a team of experts consisting of Barnes Wallis, J. E. Temple and P. L. Teed. Wallis and Temple were, next to H. B. Pratt, the leading

Dr Hugo Eckener.

British authorities on airships; Teed was a distinguished metallurgist who had worked with Wallis during the war. Pratt was not a member of the team, but agreed to act as adviser.

The gist of the Burney scheme, in its original form, was that an organization should be set up to take over the Air Ministry's airships and associated plant and bases, build five new airships, and operate frequent and regular passenger services to India. Later, more ships would be built and flights to India on alternate days would be supplemented by weekly flights to Australia. A company with a nominal capital of £4,000,000 would raise £3,400,000 by the issue of debentures and ordinary shares, and the governments of the United Kingdom, India and Australia would be asked to co-operate in guaranteeing the interest on the debentures for the first ten years and a dividend of six per cent on the ordinary shares from the second to the tenth year.

Burney pointed out that regular flights would have to be started as soon as possible so that profits could be earned, and that therefore experimental airships which might need nursing in the early stages would not do. To ensure a supply of suitable airships, he and his associates concluded with Eckener in the early summer of 1923 a tentative agreement for the

Model of airship to be used for transatlantic passenger service proposed by Vickers soon after the armistice.

establishment in England of a subsidiary of the Zeppelin organization.[4] The arrangement contemplated was that there should be a British and a German construction company, both with factories in Britain, and a British and a German holding company, linked by an agreement to pool information and exchange licences. There would also be two companies operating services. Finally, there would be a link with the Goodyear company if plans for the establishment of a Goodyear-Zeppelin corporation in the United States bore fruit.

The commercial advantages of an arrangement such as this were obvious. On the one hand, it would enable the Germans to build in Britain much larger airships than they were allowed by the Council of Ambassadors to build in Germany. On the other, it would give the British the benefit of co-operation with an organization which had proved its ability to build airships quickly and economically and to run commercial airship services. From a military point of view, international agreements between firms associated with the manufacture of arms were always suspect. But such arrangements were common in peace-time, and objections to them were often more fanciful than real.

The scheme was first formally submitted to the authorities in the spring of 1922, while Lloyd George's post-war coalition government was still in office and before the agreement with Eckener had been concluded. The Admiralty, believing that modern airships which could be used for maritime reconnaissance in time of war would be a national asset, gave it a favourable reception. The Air Ministry found fault with some aspects of the scheme, but withdrew its objections after changes had been made and the number of airships to be provided in the first instance had been raised from five to six. Other bodies which reported favourably on the scheme included the Committee of Imperial Defence and a committee invited to consider how the mail service to the Far East and Australia could best be accelerated.

But governments were to come and go before anything was settled. Towards the end of 1922 Lloyd George was hurled from power. Bonar Law, the next Prime Minister, fell mortally ill and was succeeded after a few months of office by Stanley Baldwin. It was not until the late summer of 1923 that the Secretary of State for Air in Baldwin's government, Sir Samuel Hoare, told the House of Commons that the government had decided, in principle, to accept Burney's offer to run a passenger and mail service to India with six airships. He added that the

ships should have considerable strategic value and that the Air Ministry would be able to charter them for manoeuvres and training.

Hoare also said that the details of a contract between the government and the Burney group would be settled by the Treasury. But the months went by, and no contract followed. The only positive step taken during the rest of the year was the formation by Vickers of a subsidiary company, the Airship Guarantee Company, to deal with the matter. Meanwhile the Air Ministry made it clear that, although they were willing to do business with Burney and his associates, they were not prepared to hand over their surviving airships, plant and bases without a *quid pro quo*, or to grant unrestricted access to information gathered by their meteorological service. Howden was sold early in 1924 to a firm which proposed to demolish it, and had afterwards to be bought back by the Airship Guarantee Company for £61,000.[5]

Not surprisingly, anxiety was felt about the future of Cardington. In reply to a question in the House of Commons, Hoare told the Member of Parliament for Bedford on 21 January that Cardington would be reopened and used to build airships for the Burney group as soon as the legal formalities which had held up the contract were settled.

Only a few hours later, the government was defeated in the House of Commons and forced to resign. On the following day a Labour government came to office under the leadership of Ramsay MacDonald, who was at one time regarded as a dangerous fellow-traveller but afterwards reviled by his fellow-Socialists as a crypto-Tory. Sir Samuel Hoare was succeeded as Secretary of State for Air by Brigadier-General C. B. Thomson, a retired army officer who had

Early experiment with a mooring mast mounted on land at Barrow-in-Furness.

thrice offered himself without success for election to the House of Commons. To qualify him for admittance to the councils of the nation, Thomson was given a barony and chose the title of Lord Thomson of Cardington.

The new government had no clear majority in the House of Commons and depended on Liberal support to maintain it in office. Ramsay MacDonald was therefore in no position to carry through the programme of nationalization to which his political philosophy inclined him. Rumours that he intended, none the less, to put a spoke in the capitalist wheel by repudiating the Burney scheme elicited a denial that the government was contemplating an announcement to that effect. The Member for Bedford, dissatisfied with this reply, said pointedly that he hoped Thomson's choice of title did not mean that the government was thinking of building airships.

The rumours proved well founded. In the course of the annual debate on the Air Estimates on 14 May, MacDonald announced that the government had decided to reject the Burney scheme on the ground that it would create a virtual monopoly and that some of its technical and financial provisions were unsatisfactory. Cardington was to remain government property. The Air Ministry was to undertake a comprehensive programme of research and development, build a 5,000,000-cubic-foot airship, and establish an airship terminus in India and an intermediate base in Egypt. As a consolation prize, the Airship Guarantee Company was to be offered a contract to build a second airship for £350,000, and an option to buy it back for £150,000 when an airship service to India was shown to be feasible. About £1,000,000 was to be spent on the government's airship, but this figure would include the cost of the research and development programme.

As the government's critics pointed out, a serious objection to this scheme was that it would provide only two airships instead of six. Moreover, only one of them would be available for commercial use. The Air Ministry intended, when their ship had been proved capable of carrying passengers and mail to India and back, to use her for lifting troops or aircraft, or in case of need for maritime reconnaissance.

An even weightier objection to the new scheme was that it forced the Air Ministry to compete with private enterprise for the services of the few men qualified by experience to design such an airship as the government had in mind. Since the Royal Corps of Naval Constructors had ceased in 1921 to concern itself with airships and capable designers in the private sector

The Air Ministry's R.101 – rival of the R.100.

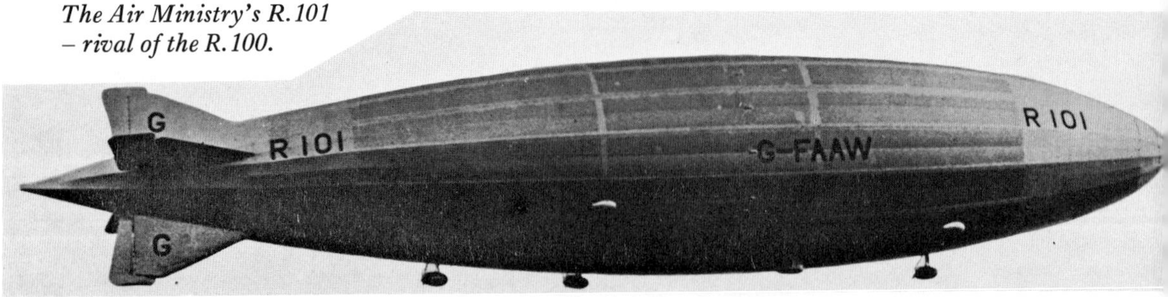

were not likely to give up their jobs to become temporary civil servants without pension rights, the race was lost by the Air Ministry before it began. The post of Chief Designer of their ship went to Lieutenant-Colonel V. C. Richmond, a builder of docks who had become interested in airships during the First World War and had made himself an authority on the 'dopes' or varnishes applied to the envelopes of blimps. An able engineer who was willing to take advice, Richmond might have produced a successful design had he been free to follow a well-trodden path. As things were, he was more hampered than helped by the elaborate programme of preliminary research to which the government was committed, and was forced to work in a blaze of publicity which made it difficult for him to reject innovations of which accounts had already been given to Paraliament and the press. When he found, for example, that the diesel engines he at first proposed to use were likely to give trouble, he was not allowed to replace them by well-tried petrol engines.[6]

The Air Ministry began by reopening Cardington and enlarging the shed in which they proposed to build their ship, already called the R.101. The R.33 was reconditioned for experimental use, and on 2 April 1925 was flown from Cardington to Pulham. On 14 April she was torn from the mast at Pulham by a storm, and blown with a damaged nose over the North Sea. But she had a crew as well as food and fuel aboard her at the time, and was successfully brought back by Squadron Leader R. S. Booth. While the damage was being repaired, arrangements were made to recondition the R.36. The R.33 next flew on 5 October, when experiments were made to determine the stresses imposed on her envelope and hull by turning movements akin to those which had wrecked the R.38. Practically the whole of the design staff of the R.101 were aboard her, but the designers of the rival airship were not represented, although it was generally understood that the experiments were meant to provide data for the benefit of the Airship Guarantee Company as well as the Air Ministry.[7]

During the rest of the year, and again in the following year, the R.33 was used to try out methods of releasing and recovering heavier-than-air machines.[8] Towards the end of 1926, after more than £70,000 had been spent on her, she was found to be in poor condition and was taken out of service. The R.80 was scrapped in 1924 and was not used to provide data for the designers of the new ships, although she was the Air Ministry's only streamlined ship and cost less to maintain than the R.33 and the R.36.[9]

LEFT: *Close-up of point of attachment of the envelope of airship to head of mooring post. Great difficulty was experienced in making a connection which should afford no 'play' yet would allow rotary movement without causing the envelope to chafe through.*

BELOW: *The R.33 moored to the 100-foot mast at Pulham, Norfolk.*

Dr (afterwards Sir) Barnes Wallis.

OPPOSITE: *The R.100 moored at Cardington.*

A contract to build the rival airship, soon to be known as the R.100, was given to the Airship Guarantee Company on 24 October 1924. Of the contract price of £350,000, £50,000 was regarded by the Air Ministry as a capital grant to offset the expense to which the company was put as a result of the sale of Howden. Wallis and his team began work in 1924 at Vickers House in London, moved later to premises owned by Vickers at Crayford in Kent, and eventually went to Howden. N. S. Norway, better known as the novelist Nevil Shute, joined the team after work had begun and was employed as Chief Calculator. Unlike their opposite numbers at Cardington, the designers of the R.100 were seldom embarrassed by premature disclosures to the press about their activities, and were free to change their minds and correct their mistakes as they went along. They considered the merits and shortcomings of diesel engines and then came to the conclusion that experimental kerosene-hydrogen engines would be better, but in the end used reconditioned Rolls-Royce Condor aero-engines which proved very satisfactory. They made good progress in 1924 and 1925, but work on the R.100 was much hampered between 1926 and 1928 by industrial disputes.

In the meantime estimates of the weight and lift of the R.101 convinced the Air Ministry that she would not be able to carry the hundred passengers or two hundred troops they had hoped to put aboard her, and that therefore accommodation for only fifty passengers and ten tons of mail should be provided. In 1927 the Airship Guarantee Company was informed that the R.100 would not be required to fly to India and back before acceptance but would be expected to fly to Canada and back.[10] The reason given was that her petrol engines were not suitable for use in the tropics, but many people found this explanation unconvincing. They believed that the true reason was that the Air Ministry wanted their own ship to be the first to fly to India.

When Burney propounded his scheme in 1922, he looked forward to having the Zeppelin company as a partner, not a rival. By 1926 the situation was quite different. Freed by the Locarno treaties from the shackles of Versailles, Eckener and his colleagues were able to raise by public subscription a large sum to be spent on the construction of a civil airship in Germany. The ship had to be long and slim because the only big shed still standing at Friedrichshafen was not tall enough to hold a broad-beamed ship. The Zeppelin company's veteran Chief Constructor, Ludwig Dürr, designed a cigar-shaped 3,700,000-cubic-foot ship 776 feet long,

with a maximum diameter of roughly 100 feet. She received the works designation LZ.127 and was expected to attain a maximum speed of the order of eighty miles an hour.

No attempt was made in the United States to compete with Britain and Germany in the development of civil airships, but in 1926 Congress authorized the construction of two 6,500,000-cubic-foot ships for the Department of the Navy. Invitations to tender, issued after elaborate specifications had been drawn up by the naval authorities, brought no less than thirty-seven different designs, all of which were carefully scrutinized by the navy's experts and considered at various levels. All this took so long that no order was placed until October 1928, when the contract for both ships was awarded to the Goodyear company. Wind-tunnel tests were then made to determine the best shape for the enormous shed in which the ships would be built. A turtle-backed structure covering more than eight acres was completed in time for the first ship, the ZRS-4 or *Akron*, to be laid down in the early winter of 1929.

In Continental Europe outside Germany, interest in airships was revived in 1925 by a two-day Mediterranean cruise made by the *Esperia* and an Italian-built semi-rigid airship designed by General Umberto Nobile and known as the N.1. Nobile was an aeronautical engineer with academic qualifications who set little store

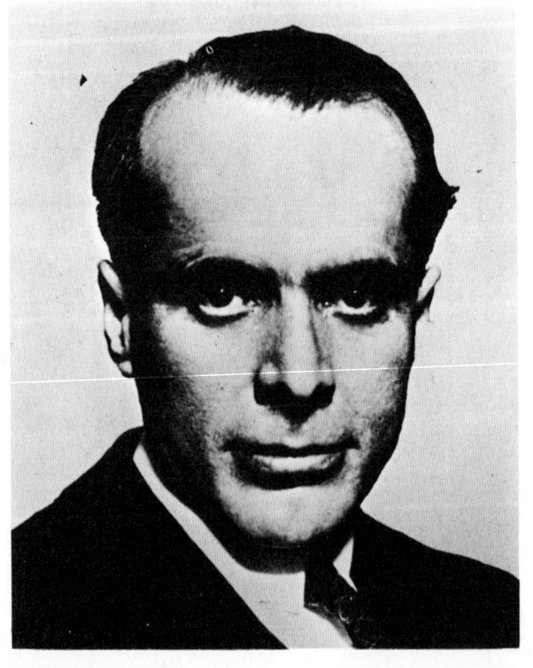

RIGHT: *General Umberto Nobile, c. 1926.*
BELOW: *General Nobile's N.1* (Norge) *of 1925.*

by his military rank. The N.1's feat aroused the interest of the Norwegian explorer Roald Amundsen. On learning that the ship was for sale, he decided to buy her and use her for polar exploration. The money was provided by Lincoln Ellsworth, an American who had financed the second of two attempts by Amundsen to reach the North Pole in a heavier-than-air machine.[11]

In the following March the N.1 was formally handed over to Amundsen and named the *Norge*. Nobile agreed to fly Amundsen to the North Pole in her on the understanding that he was to have sole command of the ship but that Amundsen would exercise a general supervision over the enterprise as a whole. Her passenger accommodation was modified to save weight and provide space for additional fuel.

The *Norge* was not particularly impressive in appearance. Only 350 feet long but broad in the beam, she held 653,000 cubic feet of hydrogen. But her three Maybach engines gave her a good turn of speed, and she proved exceptionally reliable. Amundsen's luck did not fail him when he chose her to take him and his companions over Arctic ice-floes.

With twenty-one men aboard her, the *Norge* left Italy on 10 April 1926 and arrived next day at Pulham, where Nobile was allowed to park her beside the R.33. On 13 April she took off for Leningrad, where she touched down on 15 April after pausing briefly at Oslo. Bad weather in the far north kept her at Leningrad until 5 May, when she took off on a two-stage flight to Spitzbergen by way of Varanger Fjord and the North Cape.

Nobile reached King's Bay, Spitzbergen, on 7 May and was joined there by Amundsen. He found Commander Richard Byrd, of the United States Navy, preparing with his co-pilot, Floyd Bennett, to beat him and his companions in the race to be first over the North Pole. In the early hours of 9 May, before Amundsen and Nobile were ready to start, Byrd and Bennett took off from King's Bay in a Fokker monoplane. They returned sixteen hours later with the news that they had flown to the North Pole and back.

It remained for Amundsen and Nobile to cap this feat by traversing the polar ice-cap and landing on the far side of it.[12] Now with sixteen men aboard her, the *Norge* left King's Bay about 10 a.m. on 11 May and made straight for the pole. Hjalmar Riiser-Larsen, a Norwegian aeronaut who had received part of his training in Italy and had introduced Amundsen to Nobile, acted as navigator. In the early afternoon he announced that the ship was approaching the North Pole, and shortly afterwards that she had reached it. Norwegian, Italian and

American flags were thrown out, handshakes were exchanged. A wirelessed announcement brought a stream of congratulatory messages from the outside world.

But the ship and her crew were still far from their destination. Nobile continued across the polar ice-cap towards the North Polar Basin and Alaska. Unable, even on rare occasions when the ship was not flying through dense fog, to distinguish landmarks in the waste of snow and ice beneath him, he had to rely on his instruments, Larsen's calculations and an airman's instinct to take him in the right direction. The cold was intense. A layer of ice covered exposed metal parts of the ship. From time to time lumps of it fell off under the influence of heat generated by the engines. Some struck the airscrews and broke with explosive force into fragments which were hurled against the lower part of the envelope, tearing holes in the fabric which had to be hastily patched by the crew.

After some hours visibility improved. At 6.45 a.m. on 13 May land was sighted on the port bow. Larsen announced that the ship was approaching Point Barrow and that Nome lay ahead and slightly to starboard. During the morning she passed over a settlement identified as Wainwright, a place which Amundsen and another member of the crew had visited in 1922.

In the early hours of 14 May the ship was still going strong, but all aboard her were desperately tired and some had almost reached the limits of their endurance. A dense fog forced Nobile to fly high, since he knew that mountainous country lay beneath him. Above the fog a strong headwind was blowing. Not even Larsen was sure of the ship's whereabouts, but occasional glimpses of coastline showed that she was close to the Bering Strait and in danger of being carried out to sea. Amundsen and Nobile agreed that they must land at the first opportunity.

The opportunity came when they saw houses and men. The question was whether they could bring the ship down safely without a ground crew. The fog had melted away, but a wind approaching gale force was blowing. Nobile headed into it and dropped almost to ground level. Spectators seized ropes thrown to them, but Nobile feared that the ship would be torn from their grasp as soon as she lost steerage way. As if by a miracle, the wind died down at the last moment, and the landing was smooth. A crew on the verge of collapse staggered from the ship after being continuously on duty for sixty-nine and a half hours and travelling 3,300 miles without a break. They found that they had reacher Teller, a small township on an inlet of the Bering Strait about fifty miles north-west of Nome.

The flight made Nobile a hero in his own country. The rest of the world, it seemed, could not hear enough of Amundsen. An unedifying dispute broke out as to which of the two men was chiefly responsible for the success of the expedition. Many years later, General Nobile, while giving generous praise to Larsen for his navigation, made it clear that he regarded the successful completion of the trans-polar flight as largely due to five Italian members of the crew.

Soon after his arrival at Teller, and well before he fell out with Amundsen, Nobile decided to mount an airborne polar expedition of his own. A fund was raised in Milan, his native city, and a successor to the *Norge* was built. Named the *Italia*, she was very similar to her forerunner in appearance and characteristics

The *Italia* reached King's Bay, Spitzbergen, on 6 May 1928, after skirting the Julian Alps and flying across Central Europe and the Barents Sea in three stages. She was met by her base ship, the *Città di Milano*, the Norwegian whaler *Hobby* and an eight-man handling party from a mountain regiment of the Italian Army. She was moored to a mast on arrival, but later in the day was wheeled into a roofless shed.[13]

Nobile was aiming at much more than a flight over the polar ice-cap. He hoped to make an aerial survey of Severnaya Zemlya, fly over parts of Greenland hitherto unexplored, and visit the North Pole at least twice for the purpose of disembarking and re-embarking a party of explorers qualified to make a scientific examination of the polar region. For that reason, equipment carried in the *Italia* included sledges, snowshoes, skis, sleeping bags, specially made boots, gloves, helmets and other clothing, a windproof tent, and an inflatable rubber vessel described as a raft and distinct from the rubber dinghies which were also carried. The raft was intended to be lowered, with men and equipment aboard it, either on water or on snow or ice.

Nobile left King's Bay early on 11 May with the intention of flying over Severnaya Zemlya, but bad weather forced him to turn back later in the day. The ship was then immobilized for the best part of four days by snow which settled on top of her hull and turned to a sheet of ice.

By noon on 15 May the weather was good enough for a fresh attempt. The *Italia* left King's Bay at 1 p.m. She returned at 10.20 a.m. on 18 May from a sortie comparable with the *Norge*'s epic flight from King's Bay to Teller. Nobile had every reason to be pleased with a ship which had carried him and his companions for sixty-nine hours over pack-ice and

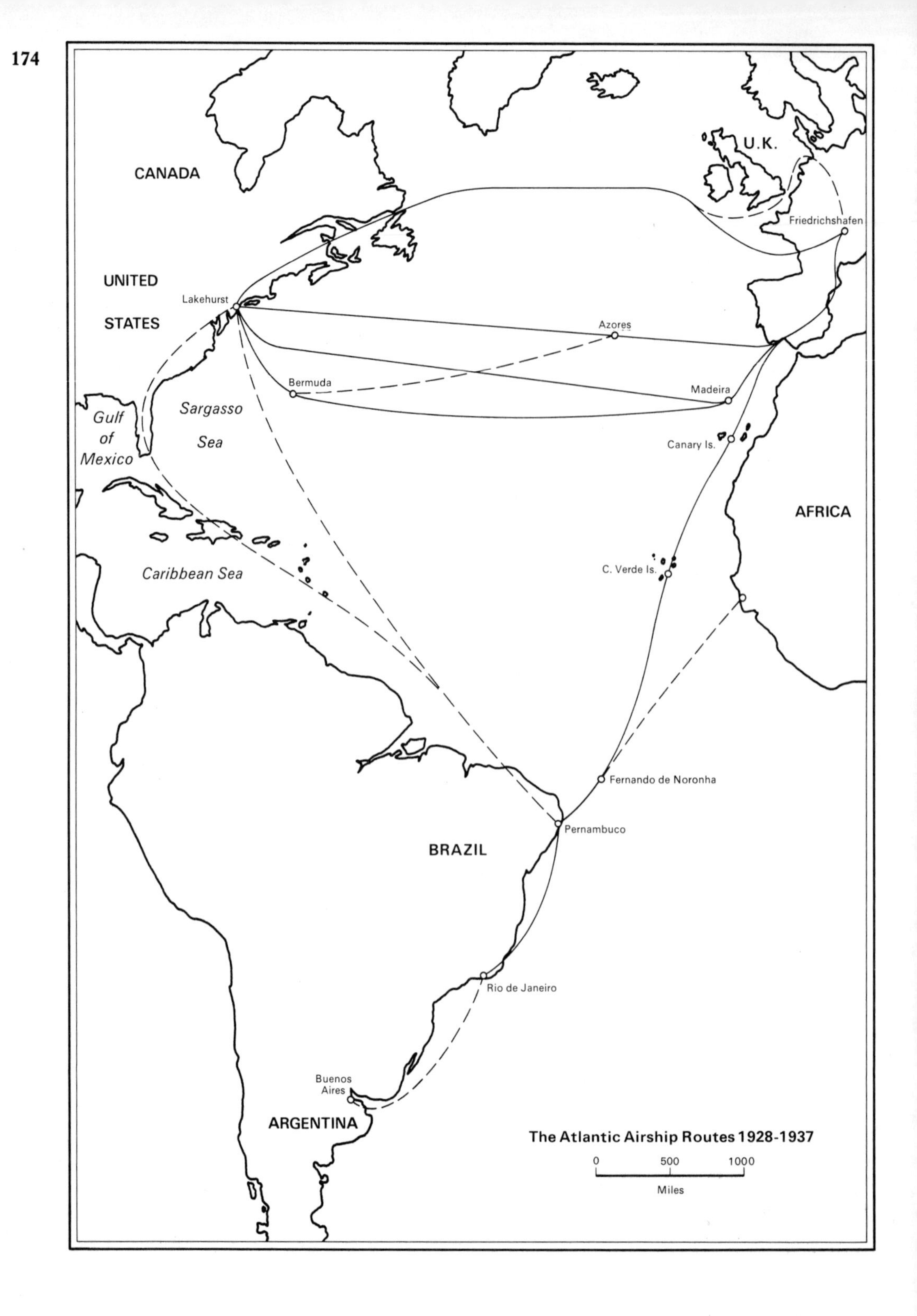

The Atlantic Airship Routes 1928-1937

enabled them to see and photograph parts of the earth's surface of which only vague and incomplete descriptions had been published.

The next few days were devoted to preparations for the polar flight. By 23 May the ship was ready. She left King's Bay at 4.28 a.m., carrying enough fuel for a flight of at least 4,000 miles and the ship's company detailed in Table 7.

Nobile did not make straight for the North Pole, as he had done in 1926, but headed for Greenland. The ship soon ran into fog, but visibility improved in the afternoon, and about 6 p.m. the north-eastern extremity of Greenland was sighted. Nobile continued on a north-westerly course as far as the 27th meridian west of Greenwich, and then turned north along it. At 10.30 p.m. Zappi reported that the ship was dead on course. With a following wind, she took about two hours to cover the last 125 miles.[14] Soon after midnight the estimated position of the pole was reached, and Nobile threw out an Italian flag in which was wrapped a cross blessed by the Pope.

The outward flight, with favourable winds, had taken about twenty hours. Expecting a strong headwind on the return flight, Nobile decided, after despatching messages to the Pope, the King of Italy and Mussolini, to postpone the lowering of the raft with its party of explorers until his next visit. At 2.20 a.m. on 24 May he headed south along the 25th meridian west of Greenwich. If the wind continued to blow from the south, he could expect to strike the north coast of Spitzbergen not far from the meridian of King's Bay.

Once again, the ship ran into a belt of fog. For eight hours she cruised above it, using only two of her three engines to save fuel. At the end of that time Nobile came down to 900 feet to make observations which showed that the ship was making only about twenty miles an hour over the ground. They also showed that the wind was now blowing not from the south but from the south-west. What they did not show was that the change had occurred many hours earlier and that consequently the ship was far to the east of her intended course.

In the light of these observations, Nobile ordered Arduino to bring the third engine into use. During the rest of her flight the ship was noticeably unsteady. Besides pitching and yawing, she vibrated. Alessandrini, the Foreman Rigger, asked that her speed should be reduced to lessen the risk of damage to her forward bracing. Nobile thought it better to push on as rapidly as possible. Despite the crew's attempts to carry out his orders, the ship made slow progress. For hours on end she flew blindly through fog or blizzards, and her uneven motion made it difficult for the helmsman to maintain a constant heading. Like the *Norge*'s, the crew had to repair rents torn in the *Italia*'s envelope by lumps of ice which her airscrews hurled against it.

At 7 a.m. on 25 May there was still no land in sight, although the ship had been heading more or less south for more than twenty-eight hours. Nobile, not yet aware of the full extent of the leeway he had made since leaving the North Pole, was forced to recognize that he must be far off course. For the moment, at any rate, he and his officers had no means of discovering their whereabouts. All they could see was pack-ice below them and dense cloud above. They succeeded in making wireless contact with King's Bay, but their position could not be fixed by a bearing from a single station.

About two and a half hours later the coxswain shouted that the elevator wheel was jammed. With all three engines shut off on Nobile's orders, the ship sank to 200 feet above the inhospitable surface of the frozen sea.

She then began to rise again. Nobile ordered Cecioni to dismantle the elevator mechanism. While he was doing so, the ship continued to rise, and at 2,700 feet she emerged into brilliant sunshine. Zappi and Mariano seized the opportunity of taking a reading on the sun, but from this they estimated, incorrectly, that the *Italia* was only 180 miles from King's Bay and should be home by 4 p.m.

By 9.55 a.m. the wheel was free. Nobile then went below cloud and resumed his flight with two engines running. About half an hour later, Cecioni startled him by calling out that the ship was down by the stern. She was then flying at 600 feet and losing height at the rate of more than a hundred feet a minute. Nobile told Arduino to start the third engine, but the ship continued to fall and he saw that a crash was imminent. He ordered emergency measures, including the stopping of all three engines to reduce the risk of fire. An attempt to lighten the ship by throwing out the ballast chain failed for lack of time, and at 10.33 a.m. the control cabin came into violent contact with the jagged surface of the pack-ice. Pomella was killed and Nobile, Zappi, Mariano, Viglieri, Biagi, Cecioni, Trojani, Malmgren, Behounek and the dog Titina were thrown out. Relieved of their weight, the ship shot into the air and was seen no more. Arduino, Caratti, Ciocca, Alessandrini, Pontremoli and Lago went with her. They, too, were never seen again.

Of the ten survivors, only Titina was quite unhurt. Nobile had a broken leg and other injuries, including a damaged arm. Cecioni, too, had a broken leg. Zappi was so badly bruised that at first he could hardly move, but he made a good recovery. Mariano, Viglieri, Biagi, Trojani, Malmgren and Behounek were bruised and shaken, but not incapacitated. From the jetsam scattered on the pack-ice they recovered the tent intended for the three or four explorers who were to have disembarked at the North Pole. In the hope of making it clearly visible from the air, they afterwards coloured it red with dye extracted from marker-bombs carried in the airship as a means of checking her ground speed. Their first thought was to get Nobile, Cecioni and Zappi under cover; but all nine men and the dog had eventually to crowd into the tent for lack of other shelter.

The survivors had about two and a half hundredweight of food, including pemmican, chocolate, malted milk tablets, some sugar and butter, a small quantity of cheese and a tin of meat extract. They provided themselves with water for drinking by melting snow and ice, but not pack-ice, which yielded only undrinkable brine. Apart from the food, their most important asset was a radio transmitter and receiver, fortunately in working order. Biagi sent his first distress signal within two and a half hours of the accident; but it was not picked up by the *Città di Milano*, which was transmitting press reports at the time. Throughout the greater part of the long search that followed, the tent was believed to be much further west than it was.

No rescue party having arrived by the end of the fifth day, Malmgren, Zappi and Mariano set out on 30 May to trek southwards in search of help. After wandering over the pack-ice for three or four days they walked into a blizzard. At the end of another ten days or so, Malmgren was in such a bad state that he begged Zappi and Mariano to leave him to die. Reluctant to abandon him but mindful of their promise to do their best for the men in the tent, they stayed in the neighbourhood for another twenty-four hours in the hope that he might recover and join them.

Soon afterwards, Mariano was stricken with snowblindness and screamed in agony, but was able to continue with bandaged eyes. An aircraft flew over the men about the end of the third week in June, but the pilot did not see them. Afterwards they heard other aircraft. They staggered on until 27 June, when Mariano was lamed by a fall. The two men then sat down to await their fate.

Meanwhile the party in the tent lived in daily hope of rescue. Biagi's radio watch paid a dividend on 6 June, when he learned that one of his distress signals had been picked up by an amateur listener at Archangel. On the following day a message transmitted from Rome told him that the *Città di Milano* was now receiving his signals and was trying to locate the tent. By 8 June he was in constant two-way communication with her.

But still no help arrived. Behounek saw an aircraft approach the tent on 17 June, but it turned away. On the same day a French flying boat, in which Roald Amundsen had embarked with the intention of expunging the memory of his quarrel with Nobile by taking part in an attempt to save his life, arrived at Tromsö after flying from Normandy by way of Bergen. Manned by a French crew, the aircraft left Tromsö for Spitzbergen on 18 June but never arrived. It was last seen heading north across the Barents Sea from the North Cape.

On 19 June the occupants of the tent saw a number of aircraft, but they too turned away. Among them was an Italian flying boat piloted by Major Umberto Maddalena of the Regia Aeronautica. Maddalena returned on the following day, accompanied by another Italian flying boat, and Biagi was able to make radio contact with him. His plane was not equipped to land on ice, but he dropped supplies, including food, boots, sleeping bags and smoke signals. Further supplies, dropped from two aircraft arrived in the course of the next day or two.

A bold attempt at rescue was made by Captain Gennaro Sora, commanding officer of the *Italia*'s handling party. Accompanied by two civilian volunteers, Sora disembarked on 18 June at the northern extremity of North East Land. Equipped with a sledge drawn by nine huskies and laden with provisions and medical supplies, the three men set out across the pack ice in what they hoped was the direction of the tent. One of the volunteers had to give up after a few days and agreed to make his own way back to base; Sora and the other volunteer, a Dutchman named Van Dongen, went on and were overtaken by a series of calamities which included the loss of a great part of their provisions when the sledge fell through the ice. By 4 July only two huskies were still alive and Van Dongen was ill, unable to move, and at times delirious.

In the meantime Maddalena's arrival encouraged the occupants of the tent to hope that suitable aircraft would soon arrive to take them to safety. Nobile made up his mind that if only one man could be carried at a time Cecioni should go first and Behounek next. He himself would wait until the end.

On 23 June two aircraft approached the tent and one of them, fitted with skids, landed on the ice. The youthful pilot introduced himself as Lieutenant Einar-Paal Lundborg of the Swedish Air Force and said that he had come to rescue General Nobile. When Nobile pointed out that Cecioni needed medical attention and should have priority, he replied that he had orders to rescue General Nobile and no one else. Eventually Nobile gave in and departed with Titina.

Lundborg returned to the tent about six hours later, but misjudged his approach and made a bad landing which overturned his aircraft. He was forced to remain at the tent until, on 6 July, another Swedish pilot arrived to take him away.

By that date at least three different groups of men were in need of help. These were Cecioni, Viglieri, Trojani, Behounek and Biagi at the tent; Zappi and Mariano somewhere to the south of it; and Sora and Van Doren, somewhere between the tent and North East Land. In addition the fate of the six men carried away when the airship struck the ice was still unknown.

On 8 July Boris Chukhnovsky, the pilot of an aircraft co-operating with the Russian ice-breaker *Krassin*, began a systematic reconnaissance of the area. He followed up a preliminary survey on that day by setting out on 10 July to see what could be done to rescue the five men at the tent. Chance led him to spot Zappi and Mariano, but he then flew into fog and made an emergency landing which damaged his aircraft. He and his co-pilot, observer, mechanic and photographer were unhurt, and his radio transmitter still worked. He was unable to say exactly where he had landed, but transmitted an accurate account of the whereabouts of Zappi and Mariano.

The *Krassin*, already on her way to the tent, continued her slow voyage through the pack-ice in the light of this information. In the course of the next forty-eight hours members of her crew saw a man who turned out to be Zappi, and afterwards two men who were rightly thought to be Sora and Van Dongen. Her master decided to push on to the tent and then return to pick up the other men. He reached the tent on 12 July. Zappi and Mariano, the latter in poor shape, were duly picked up on that day, and Sora and Van Dongen were rescued on the same day by Swedish and Finnish airmen. On 15 July the master of the *Krassin* completed a highly successful mission by embarking Chukhnovsky and his crew and lashing their aircraft to his ship.

With the exception of Malmgren, all the men who emerged alive from the *Italia* on 25 May survived the hardships to which they were exposed while awaiting rescue. In the long run the greatest sufferer was

General Nobile. Besides receiving injuries which caused him pain and discomfort long after his broken leg was healed, he was so harshly criticized for allowing himself to be rescued first that he resigned his commission in the Italian Army and accepted an appointment in Russia. Later he returned to Italy to take up an academic post.

It is easy to say, and natural to feel, that Nobile ought to have insisted on staying at the tent until the end. It is not so easy to see what useful purpose would have been served by his doing so in the circumstances in which he was placed by Lundborg's refusal to depart from the letter of his instructions. Had Nobile refused to leave the tent on 23 May, Lundborg would not have rescued Cecioni, for he would do nothing without a specific order. When Nobile agreed to go, he did his best for his men by putting himself in a position to insist, when he reached King's Bay, that Lundborg should be sent back to fetch Cecioni. He could not foresee that Lundborg would crash his aircraft and bring the rescue operation to a standstill until another suitable aircraft was found. In doing his best for his men at the risk of having his motives questioned, he acted honourably. A less imaginative man would doubtless have made the opposite decision. He would thereby have escaped criticism, but Cecioni would not have been rescued any earlier.

9 The intercontinental airship: 1928-30

When Umberto Nobile startled the world by crashing the *Italia*, six years had elapsed since Commander Burney offered to carry passengers and mails to India within four years if he received authority to go ahead. Meanwhile the lead once held by the British had been thrown away. In the summer of 1928 the R.100 and the R.101, ordered only towards the end of 1924, were still unfinished. Their German rival, the LZ.127, was almost ready for her maiden flight.

It was 8 July 1928 when Boris Chukhnovsky began his search for the red tent. This was also the ninetieth anniversary of the birth of Ferdinand von Zeppelin, and the day when his married daughter broke a bottle of champagne over the bows of the LZ.127 and named her the *Graf Zeppelin*.

On 18 September the *Graf Zeppelin* made the first of half a dozen trial flights. Eckener used these flights to show her to as many as possible of the people whose money had helped to build her. One of them, begun on 2 October, was intended to take her over Berlin, but heavy rain was falling there that day. Eckener set course for Flushing, spent the night cruising over the North Sea after passing within sight of Lowestoft and Great Yarmouth, and took in Hamburg as well as Berlin on the return flight.

A fast, handy ship designed to carry enough fuel for flights of 6,000 miles or more, the *Graf Zeppelin* differed from the ships planned by the British in providing accommodation for only about twenty passengers, or up to thirty with some sacrifice of comfort. In any case, with only one ship her owners could not hope to run frequent and regular intercontinental services on the lines of the Burney scheme. Eckener is said to have told his intimates that he was not in favour of building more or larger airships until a demand for long-range passenger services was definitely shown to exist. In the meantime he would do his best to create such a demand by using the *Graf Zeppelin* for a series of spectacular demonstration flights. A good showman whose bluff manner hid considerable astuteness, he foresaw no great difficulty in financing such excursions as long as airships capable of intercontinental flight were still a novelty.

Early on Thursday, 11 October 1928, the *Graf Zeppelin* left Friedrichshafen on her first flight to the United States.[1] She carried sixty-three people and a miscellaneous cargo of freight and mail, including more than 60,000 letters and parcels specially franked for the occasion. Eckener chose a route which took him down the valley of the Rhône, across the Gulf of Lions to Barcelona, and thence by

Chart room of Graf Zeppelin.

way of Malaga and Gibraltar to the Azores, where he set course for Bermuda.

On Saturday 13 October, the ship was struck in mid-Atlantic by a violent squall. Her frame escaped damage, but fabric torn from her port fin threatened to jam her elevators, and her speed had to be reduced while volunteers poised precariously above an angry sea made a temporary repair. Eckener raised excitement in the United States to fever pitch by asking the navy to stand by and then keeping wireless silence for many hours. After flying through another storm near Bermuda, he reached Lakehurst, New Jersey, on Monday 15 October, to find 250 journalists, a handling party of approximately 400 sailors, and at least 20,000 impatient sightseers awaiting his arrival. The flight from Friedrichshafen had taken an unconscionably long time, but such relief was felt at the ship's safe arrival that criticism was stifled.

The return flight, begun in the small hours of 29 October, was quicker, but the *Graf Zeppelin*'s passengers can scarcely have received the impression that the airship had already become a serious rival to the ocean liner. After twice running into unpredicted storms, the ship was blown far off course while flying through a dense fog. The weather was cold and the passengers' quarters were inadequately heated.[2] Eckener completed a somewhat hazardous crossing of the North Atlantic by reaching the French coast near the mouth of the Loire, and early on 1 November disembarked his passengers and a much publicized stowaway at Friedrichshafen. His cargo included more than a hundred thousand letters and parcels.

The *Graf Zeppelin*'s next trip to the United States was due in the middle of May 1929. In the meantime Eckener busied himself with preparations for a round-the-world flight. The American newspaper proprietor William Randolph Hearst agreed to finance the project, stipulating that the flight should begin and end in the United States. Eckener also found time to take a party of influential guests on a three-day cruise over France, Italy, Greece and Palestine. On his return he had to answer complaints from the French government that he had flown over the Schneider arms factory at Le Creusot and the naval base at Toulon.

The transatlantic flight projected for the middle of May was ill-fated from the outset. The advertised date of departure was 14 May. When the day arrived, passengers who had paid £400 for their tickets had to be told that the ship could not leave because her permit to fly over French territory had not arrived. When it did arrive, it was found to stipulate that the frontier

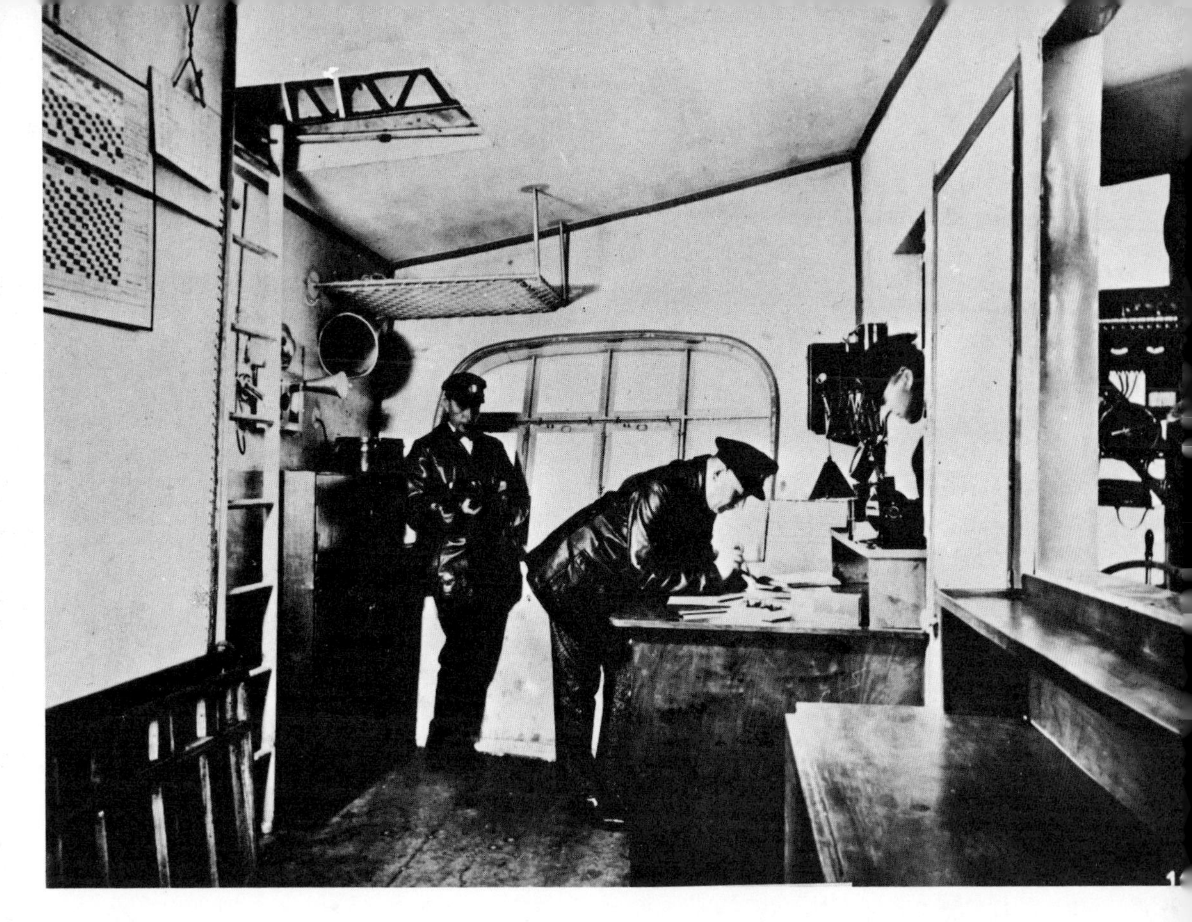

should be crossed between 7 and 9 a.m. and that prior notice should be given to various authorities. The outcome was that the passengers had to be asked to put up with a further delay so that an early start could be made on 16 May.

The ship left Friedrichshafen at 6 a.m., carrying eighteen passengers and a cargo which included 'a playful female gorilla named Susie'.[3] A forty-five-mile-an-hour mistral – the north wind described in Provençal legend and song as 'the wind that drives men mad' – bowled her down the valley of the Rhône at such a spanking pace that she reached the Mediterranean by midday. Soon afterwards, one engine stopped. Eckener decided to carry on, but gave the order to turn back when another engine failed.

The time was now 6 p.m. With her air speed reduced to fifty-five miles an hour, the ship made fairly good progress until she arrived over the Gulf of Lions and was met by the wind that had helped her in the morning. Between midnight and 8 a.m. on 17 May, when she reached the mouth of the Rhône, she covered about 200 miles at an average speed over the ground of twenty-five miles an hour.

From that point she faced the full force of a wind now blowing in gusts at speeds up to fifty miles an hour. At times her ground speed fell to little more than five miles an hour. Profiting by slightly better conditions after midday, by 2 p.m. she succeeded in battling her way to a point near Valence, about a hundred miles up the valley. Once at Valence, Eckener would be

able to choose between making his way home by the valley of the Isère and the Swiss lakes or continuing northwards in the teeth of a wind which could be expected to die away when the funnel between the Maritime Alps and the mountains of central France was left behind.

At that stage, two more engines went out of action in swift succession. With only one still working, the ship would undoubtedly be blown down the valley of the Rhône and out to sea if Eckener tried to maintain his northerly heading.

This calamity was not altogether unforeseen. The breakdown of the engine first affected had been traced to modifications made shortly before the flight began.[4] Since these modifications had been made to four of the engines but not the fifth, the situation in which Eckener found himself in the early afternoon was more disagreeable than unexpected.

The ship had just passed the entrance to the valley of the Drôme, which runs more or less at right angles to the valley of the Rhône and joins it about twelve miles below Valence. Eckener hoped to find there a sheltered place where an emergency landing might be made, but soon gave up the attempt. Lifted by a providential upcurrent above the hills on the left bank of the Drôme, the ship continued to drift southwards.

In these dire circumstances, Eckener had no choice but to brush aside hard feelings arising from the tardy arrival of his permit, and accept help from the French. In the light of reports that the *Graf Zeppelin* had been seen almost motionless over a small town near Nîmes in the morning and was obviously in trouble, the French authorities offered facilities for her to land either at Orly, near Paris, or at the airship base near Toulon from which the *Dixmude* had made her last sortie in 1923.

Orly was as unattainable as Friedrichshafen. Cuers-Pierrefeu, the airship base near Toulon, was downwind from the valley of the Drôme and could be reached without great difficulty even by an airship with only one engine working. Arriving as night was falling, the *Graf Zeppelin* was hauled down by French sailors and walked into one of two sheds brought from Düsseldorf after the armistice. She returned to Friedrichshafen on 23 May.

Some commentators concluded from this experience that airships were too unreliable to be suitable for intercontinental flight. Others regarded the landing at Cuers-Pierrefeu as proof that, given a good commander, an airship could do almost anything. A point not always grasped was that the *Graf Zeppelin* would never have been in any serious danger if Eckener had felt free to take her to the nearest airship base as soon as he found that the mistral was too much for him. The captain of an ocean liner, confronted with a situation comparable with that which faced Eckener at 8 a.m. on 17 May, would surely not have hesitated to make for the nearest convenient port. But he would have had the advantage over Eckener of possessing a full set of charts and sailing directions, and of knowing exactly what he had to do in order to comply with international regulations.

At the beginning of August Eckener

A two-berth cabin on the Graf Zeppelin.

took the *Graf Zeppelin* to Lakehurst to prepare for the first stage of her round-the-world flight. The journey was completed without incident in four days. Eckener and his crew received the same tumultuous welcome from the Americans as had greeted them the previous October.

The round-the-world flight was to be accomplished in four stages. The ship was first to fly from Lakehurst to Friedrichshafen. The next stage, beginning at Friedrichshafen and ending at Tokyo, would provide some scientific justification for the voyage by taking passengers over parts of Siberia little known to geographers. A long flight over the Pacific would then carry the ship to Los Angeles. Finally, she was to fly from Los Angeles to Lakehurst, avoiding the Rocky Mountains by passing through the gap between the Colorado Plateau and the Sierra Madre.

In the early hours of 8 August the *Graf Zeppelin* left Lakehurst for Friedrichshafen, carrying in addition to her passengers and crew a cargo which included a Boston terrier and a live alligator. The flight was completed in just over fifty-five hours, and was without incident except that Eckener celebrated his sixty-first birthday in mid-Atlantic and received a testimonial from the passengers.

At Friedrichshafen a representative of the Soviet government joined the ship. Among the sixty-one persons aboard her when she left for Tokyo early on 15 August were six Japanese, a Frenchman, a Spaniard, a Swiss and two American naval officers who took a professional interest in the flight.[5] One of the two was Charles E. Rosendahl, now commander of the *Los Angeles*. Britain and the British Commonwealth were represented by the explorer Sir Hubert Wilkins and Lady Drummond-Hay, an enthusiastic air traveller who had made the round trip to the United States and back in the *Graf Zeppelin* in 1928.

Eckener was urged to gratify the Soviet authorities by flying over Moscow, but insisted that his route must be determined by the weather. Much to their indignation, he followed a course which took him well north of the capital and brought him to the West Siberian Plain by way of Vologda and Perm. Crossing the huge marshes south of the Gulf of Ob occupied the whole of the second night. On 17 August he reached the Yenisei and headed across the Central Siberian Plateau towards the Lena river. He had hoped to show his passengers the vast crater made by the famous meteorite which fell in Siberia in 1908, but neither he nor the Soviet representative knew its exact whereabouts, and he failed to find it.

Early on the following day the ship reached Yakutsk. Now an important centre linked by frequent air services with the Lena goldfields and with the air route from European Russia to the Far East, in 1929 the town was known to Western Europeans chiefly as a place to which political exiles had been sent in Tsarist days and as the site of prisoner-of-war camps during the First World War. Before heading across wild country towards Ayan, on the Sea of Okhotsk, Eckener dropped a wreath in memory of German prisoners who had failed to return.[6]

The next 500 miles caused Eckener more anxiety than almost any other part of the trip. Between him and the Sea of Okhotsk lay the mountains of the Jugjur Range. Much less formidable than the main ridge of the Stavonoi Range, of which they are an offshoot, they were none the less a source of worry to an aeronaut distrustful of his maps and determined not to waste hydrogen by flying higher than was strictly necessary. Hard put to find the pass traversed by the track linking Ayan with Yakutsk, he had to climb to 5,000 feet or more before the mountains fell away and he saw the Pacific at his feet.

From Ayan, a flight of some 1,500 miles on a southerly course brought Eckener to his destination. By the afternoon of 19 August he was over Honshu. In order to take advantage of ideal conditions expected towards sunset, he cruised over Tokyo and Yokohama for a couple of hours before going in to land at the Japanese Navy's air station at Kasumigaura. Soon after 6 p.m. by local time, or 10 a.m. by Central European time, the ship was safely housed in a shed brought from Jüterbog as part of the spoils of war. Her flight from Friedrichshafen had taken almost exactly four days and six hours. At a time when long-distance air travel in heavier-than-air machines was still an affair of cramped limbs, splitting headaches and tedious nights in draughty rest-houses or primitive hotels, her passengers had travelled in considerable comfort. Well fed and well supplied with drinks, though not allowed to smoke, they were not confined to their seats but were free to walk about quarters so well insulated from the noise and vibration of the ship's engines that they hardly knew she was moving until they glanced at the landscape passing beneath them at seventy miles an hour.

In Japan, not yet committed to courses which afterwards estranged her from the West, Eckener and his European and American passengers were received as honoured emissaries from countries with which the framers of Japanese policy were still eager to cultivate good relations. So many gifts were showered on them that some had to be packed up and sent by sea.

The *Graf Zeppelin*'s departure from

Kasumigaura was scheduled for the early morning of 22 August. As she was being walked out of the shed, one of her gondolas struck the floor and was damaged. Eighteen officers and ratings of the Japanese Navy who considered themselves responsible for the accident were so upset that they are said to have pledged themselves to commit suicide if she failed to reach the United States.

With the damaged gondola repaired, the ship departed at 3 p.m. on 23 August. The weather during the next few days was not uniformly good. In other respects the flight across the Pacific was uneventful, except that Eckener suffered from indigestion and other ailments attributed to over-indulgence in unfamiliar food during his four days in Japan.

Having gained a day by crossing the international dateline but lost seven hours by continuing her eastward progress, the ship was over San Francisco by the afternoon of 25 August. At one time Eckener had thought of making San Francisco his next stop after Tokyo, but ultimately Mines Field, Los Angeles, had been chosen as a more suitable staging-post because of its relative freedom from fog. A handling party of sailors and marines stood by to moor the ship to a sixty-foot mast brought from San Diego in sections and re-erected in Mines Field.

Eckener reached Los Angeles about 1 a.m. on 26 August, but stood off for some hours in order to approach the mast in daylight. When he came in at 5 a.m., he found that the air just above the ground, instead of being warmer than at 1,500 feet, was eleven degrees colder.[7] To bring the ship down to sixty feet, he had to valve off a good deal of hydrogen.

Eckener knew that such inversions were not uncommon on the west coast of the United States, and that taking off in an inversion could be hazardous. On more than one occasion an airship correctly ballasted for conditions at ground level had been known to make an apparently successful take-off, only to fall like a stone on reaching a layer of warm air a few hundred feet above the earth and becoming relatively less buoyant.

The *Graf Zeppelin* left Mines Field for Lakehurst shortly before 1 a.m. on 27 August. Barely an hour before she was due to start, Eckener learned that she was heavy at the mast, although all the hydrogen provided by the American naval authorities for topping up had been pumped into her. To lighten her, ballast and provisions had to be unloaded and some of the crew left behind to complete the journey by rail. Even then, she rose scarcely at all when Eckener gave the order to cast off. To avert a collision with power

cables at the edge of the field, her coxswain had to put her nose up so sharply that her tail scored a furrow in the ground. He then reversed the wheel, so that her tail went up and she jumped the cables like a horse clearing a fence.

The ship then climbed to a safe height with all five engines at full power. She went on to complete a successful flight to Lakehurst by way of San Diego and El Paso, arriving at 6.40 p.m. on 29 August. Her circumnavigation of the globe had taken just over three weeks, including stops at Friedrichshafen, Tokyo and Los Angeles.

At the beginning of September the *Graf Zeppelin*'s First Officer, Ernst Lehmann, took her back to Friedrichshafen, leaving Eckener to discuss plans for the future with friends and associates in the United States. Among the projects he had in mind was a flight from Germany to Brazil in the spring or early summer of the following year. The company's policy was still to use the *Graf Zeppelin* mainly for exhibition flights until the time seemed ripe for regular passenger services across the North and South Atlantic.

Only a few weeks later, a spectacular fall in prices on the New York Stock Exchange launched an economic landslide which was to put millions of people out of work and flood the world's markets with raw materials and manufactured goods which no one could afford to buy. On the eve of this calamity, the two large British airships ordered in 1924 were at last completed.

On 12 October the R.101 was walked from her shed and hitched to the mast at Cardington in readiness for her maiden flight. By that time, pre-flight trials had shown that she was not likely to live up to claims made for her by government spokesmen. Her engines could not be run at high speeds without setting up unacceptable vibrations, and they could not, therefore, be made to develop their full power. Her disposable lift at normal temperature and pressure was only about thirty-five tons, as compared with the sixty-four tons specified for the R.100 and the seventy-five tons predicted for the R.101 in 1924. Since atmospheric conditions in India would lop eleven tons from her gross lift, this meant that, at best, she would be able to carry barely enough fuel for a two-stage flight from Cardington to Karachi by way of Ismailia.[8] In the light of these figures Wing Commander R. B. B. Colmore, the Director of Airship Development, recommended that no flight to India should be attempted before the following March. In the meantime the ship should be given another six tons of lift by the removal of reefing girders and the letting out of her gas-bag wiring, so that more hydrogen could be pumped into her. After the flight, her capacity should be increased by the insertion of an additional bay amidships, so that still more lift would be obtained.

Between 14 October and 18 November, the R.101 made seven trial flights. These were to have included a forty-eight-hour endurance test, but she returned to the mast after less than thirty-one hours. No speed trials were completed, because one of her engines cut out at a crucial moment. With four engines running, she attained an airspeed of sixty-three miles an hour on one leg of a triangular course.[9]

While moored to the mast on 11 November, the R.101 rode out a storm at least as violent as that which damaged and nearly wrecked the R.33 in 1925. She withstood winds which rose to a speed of more than eighty miles an hour in gusts, but rolled considerably. Her coxswain reported that every time she rolled her valves opened and most of her gas-bags shifted. In the light of this experience her valves were lightly adjusted, and projections which threatened to chafe her gas-bags were padded.

Since a Labour government had come to office in the previous June, it fell to Lord Thomson to decide what should be done with the R.101 after she returned to her shed at the end of November in order to leave the mast clear for the R.100. He accepted most of Colmore's recommendations, but stipulated that the additional bay should be inserted before, not after, the flight to India, and that the flight should take place not later than the end of September 1930.[10]

The R.100 proved by far the better ship. Her unladen weight exceeded the contract figure by fifteen tons, but her maximum speed of eighty-one miles an hour was eleven miles an hour above the contract speed. Her disposable lift worked out at

The R.100 under construction at Howden.

The Graf Zeppelin
at Recife (*Pernambuco*).

fifty-one tons with ninety-five per cent pure hydrogen in her gasbags, or fifty-four tons with ninety-seven per cent pure hydrogen.[11]

Between 16 December 1929 and 29 January 1930 the R.100 made five trial flights, including one of nearly fifty-five hours. She proved fast, handy, stable and reliable. Wrinkles appeared in her cover at high speeds, but they had no adverse effect on her performance and disappeared when her speed was reduced to the seventy miles an hour stipulated in the company's contract. A more serious shortcoming was that a good deal of water found its way into her envelope in wet weather. For fear that this might cause rapid deterioration of her gas-bags, arrangements were made to waterproof the upper part of the envelope in the course of minor modifications carried out between February and April. The trouble was never entirely cured, but the gas-bags seemed to stand up well to repeated wettings.

Meanwhile a start was made with Colmore's first-stage modifications to the R.101. A preliminary examination of her gas-bags showed that all were holed and that one had more than a hundred holes. The holes were repaired, and the modifications were allowed to go forward despite the obvious risk that the gas-bags would become even more susceptible to damage by chafing when their wiring was let out.

Just after the middle of May, when the R.101 was grounded and the R.100 preparing for her sixth flight, the *Graf Zeppelin* again stole the limelight by beginning an impressive crossing of the South Atlantic. Her flight was financed largely by the issue of postage stamps eagerly bought up by the world's stamp collectors. Leaving Friedrichshafen on 18 May, Eckener made a two-stage flight to Pernambuco by way of Seville, flew thence to Rio de Janeiro, and completed a spectacular outward journey by making a non-stop flight from Pernambuco to Lakehurst, omitting a scheduled stop at Havana for fear of running into stormy weather there. On 7 June the *Graf Zeppelin* reached Friedrichshafen after stopping to disembark passengers at Seville and flying through a hailstorm which nearly beat her to the ground. The whole trip had taken just over three weeks, including two stops at Seville, two at Pernambuco and one each at Lakehurst and Rio de Janeiro.

On 21 and 22 May, while the *Graf Zeppelin* was over the South Atlantic, the R.100 made a twenty-three-hour flight over London, the North Sea, the north of England and the Midlands to test the effects of the modifications made since January and to try out her wireless equipment. The flight was uneventful except that the airship's pointed tail, which was more ornamental

than useful, collapsed when her engines were run at full speed. To save expense, she flew thereafter with a rounded tail.

On 23 June the R.101 was brought out of her shed for the first time since the previous November. Soon after she was moored to the mast, a huge rent appeared in her cover. This was followed on 24 June by a smaller rent. The damage was repaired in time for a short trial flight on 26 June, and on 27 June the ship made a twelve-hour flight intended as a rehearsal for her appearance at the Royal Air Force Display at Hendon on the following day.

Her performance on 27 June was far from reassuring. She pitched a good deal and gave the impression of being very heavy on her elevators.[12] Her crew had to jettison no less than nine tons of ballast, although she did not fly at heights which ought to have caused her to lose much hydrogen by valving if her valves were working properly.

Early on the following day she left Cardington to fly to London and cruise over the Thames Estuary until the time came for her to appear at Hendon. All went reasonably well until, in the late afternoon, she was flying over Bedfordshire on her way home. She then began to behave so oddly that the very experienced Captain George Meager, who was acting as her First Officer and was in charge of the control room at the time, felt frightened in an airship for the first time in his life.[13] After passing Luton, she went into a series of short, sharp dives from which her coxswain, his face streaming with sweat, was able to extricate her only by exerting all his strength. Meager, thoroughly alarmed by the coxswain's remark that 'it was as much as he could do to hold her up',

The LZ.127 (Graf Zeppelin) *of 1928. The most successful passenger airship yet built, but slimmer than her designer could have wished.*

released about a ton of ballast. She then became steadier, but something like another ten tons of ballast and fuel had to be jettisoned before she was brought to the mast.

When the flight was over, Meager told his superior officer that he would not fly again in the R.101 unless expressly ordered to do so, but would stick to his own ship, the R.100. In the light of subsequent events, he came to the conclusion that the R.101 might well have crashed on her way back from Hendon if he had not released ballast when he did.[14]

On 29 June the R.101 was walked into her shed so that the R.100 could use the mast until she left for the round trip to Canada which was needed to complete her acceptance trials. Before the flight could be made, a date which suited the Canadian authorities had to be chosen, and the R.100 had to make one more twenty-four-hour flight to test her cover once again and make further experiments with her wireless equipment. As things turned out, a combination of bad weather at home and elections in Canada prevented her from starting her transatlantic flight until almost the end of July.

In the meantime, a thorough inspection of the R.101's gas-bags showed that they were again holed and that evidently the padding intended to prevent chafing had proved ineffective. After anxious debate, the authorities at Cardington came to the conclusion that the only remedy open to them was to use more padding. They seem not to have foreseen that no opportunity of giving this expedient a thorough test would arise before the ship left for India.

The next step was to lengthen her by inserting the additional bay. This was held up by an order from the Air Member for Supply and Research, Air Vice-Marshal Sir

A contemporary drawing of the saloon of the R.100.

John Higgins, that she must be kept in one piece until he was sure that the R.100 would be able to go to Canada and that the R.101 would not have to go in her stead. It was not until 21 July that Higgins obtained from Thomson a ruling which allowed him to cancel his standfast order and tell Colmore to go ahead.[15] Since the job had to be completed by 22 September if Thomson's deadline for the flight to India was to be met, this meant that Colmore would have only nine weeks in which to transform an unsound ship into a sound one by slicing her in two, inserting an additional gas-bag designed to hold as much hydrogen as an early Zeppelin, and stitching her up again. It also meant that when the work was done he would have barely a week in which to satisfy himself by practical trials that the ship was fit to fly from Cardington to Ismailia and from Ismailia to Karachi.

10 The intercontinental airship: 1930-37

On 26 July 1930 the R.100 completed a twenty-four hour flight over England, Wales and the Channel Islands, mostly in rain and cloud. Three days later she began the first Atlantic crossing made by a British airship since 1919.

The 700-foot-long ship left Cardington for Montreal at 2.48 a.m. by Greenwich Mean Time on 29 July, carrying thirty-six tons of petrol and oil and five and a half tons of ballast in addition to seven passengers, six officers, thirteen engineers, twelve riggers, three wireless operators, a chief steward, a chef and two assistant stewards. She also carried 500 gallons of drinking water and about a ton of provisions. She was still the property of the Airship Guarantee Company, but the flight, like her seven trial flights, was organized by the Air Ministry and her crew were paid by the state. They wore for the occasion a special uniform, bought by themselves except for caps and cap-badges drawn from government stores.

The captain of the ship was Squadron Leader R. S. Booth, but he had with him Colmore as a passenger and Major G. H. Scott, Assistant Director of Airship Development (Flying), as a supernumerary member of the crew. Scott was an aeronaut of vast experience who had helped to make history by taking the R.34 to the United States and back eleven years earlier, but for Booth to have at his elbow a counsellor who was both senior to him and inclined to take chances was not an unmixed advantage.

The R.100 made a fast and easy crossing of the Atlantic from the north-west corner of Ireland to Belle Isle, off the coast of Labrador. The rest of the flight was not quite so trouble-free. On 31 July Booth was persuaded, against his better judgement, to put on speed in an attempt to reach Montreal before nightfall. The ship was thrown almost on her beam ends by a sudden squall while flying at seventy knots over the St Lawrence, and he had to slow down while rents in the fabric of three of her fins were repaired. A few hours later she was hit by another squall, which lifted her in a nose-down attitude from 1,200 to 3,000 feet in about a minute. Almost immediately afterwards, a second gust carried her to 5,000 feet. This time no harm was done, except that a drum of highly inflammable varnish was knocked over and a meal about to be served was sent flying.

Not noticeably affected by the damage to her fins, the ship arrived over Montreal in the early hours of 1 August. Booth cruised about for some hours, and at dawn came in to moor at St Hubert airport. At 5.37 a.m. by local time, or 9.37 a.m. by Greenwich Mean Time, the ship was safely secured to the mast erected there for the

purpose. She arrived with 1,500 gallons of petrol left after covering about 4,000 miles in just under seventy-nine hours.[1]

Except for an 800-mile round trip to Ottawa, Toronto and Niagara Falls on 10 and 11 August, the R.100 stayed at Montreal until 13 August. She made the return flight to Cardington in fifty-seven hours thirty-six minutes, covering about 3,400 miles and arriving with fuel tanks still one-third full.[2] At one point Booth had to seize the elevator wheel from an inexperienced rigger who brought the ship down to 500 feet and very nearly ditched her.

When the R.100 returned to England, the R.101 was still in two pieces at Cardington. All concerned were working at high pressure to complete her reconstruction by 22 September so that she would be able to carry the Secretary of State to India about the end of the month. Despite efforts which brought some of them to the verge of exhaustion, the best they could manage was to have her ready to fly as soon after 25 September as she could be walked out of her shed. Even on the most hopeful calculation, this was too late for her to be despatched by 30 September. Eventually her departure was fixed for Saturday 4 October, with the proviso that she must first be pronounced fit to go.

ABOVE: *The R.100 moored at St Hubert Airport after flying from Cardington to Montreal.*

Meanwhile two members of the government's Airworthiness of Airships Panel, Professor L. Bairstow and Professor A. J. Sutton Pippard, examined data supplied to them for the purpose of calculating whether she was theoretically sound. They were surprised by the extent to which she differed from the original conception, as a result not only of the insertion of the new bay, but also of other changes made since she first flew.[3] However, on 26 September Professor Bairstow said that a permit to fly should be issued so that she could be tried out in the air. Whether she should be granted a Certificate of Airworthiness – without which she could not be allowed to fly over foreign countries – was another matter.

About this time it was said that because of financial stringency arising from the Wall Street crash the government intended to keep either the R.100 or the R.101, but not both. It was even hinted that the Royal Airship Works might close down, or its activities be severely restricted, should the R.101 fail to live up to the claims made for her. In that case men employed at Cardington on a temporary basis might be thrown out of work at a moment when jobs were almost impossible to find. These reports were only rumours; but they could have been true. Thus the fear that subordinates might suffer hardship if the ship did not leave for India on time was added to the powerful motives the officers responsible for the Air Ministry's airship programme already had for wishing to get her certified as fit to go.

It happened that about the middle of September Sir John Higgins completed his tour of duty as Air Member for Supply and Research. He was succeeded by Air Vice-Marshal H. T. C. Dowding, afterwards Sir Hugh and later Lord Dowding. Dowding knew nothing about airships and had never been in one. Before he had time to read more than a tiny fraction of the thousands of minutes, memoranda and reports about the R.101 in the Air Ministry's files, the question of granting her a Certificate of Airworthiness came up for decision. The Airworthiness of Airships Panel existed for the purpose of making recommendations about such matters, and there was also an Aeronautical Inspection Department attached to Dowding's organization. But Dowding was not in a position to interpret the findings of these bodies without guidance from his adviser on airships, and in any case the Airworthiness of Airships Panel had not yet had time to make a full report on the R.101 in her modified state.

Dowding's adviser on airships was Wing Commander Colmore. Colmore told him that the loss of the R.38 had led to the conclusion that an airship ought to do 150 hours' flying before attempting an intercontinental flight. Since the R.101 had already done 102 hours' flying but had not completed her forty-eight-hour endurance test or her high-speed trials, it had been agreed in principle before Higgins left the department that she should be deemed fit to go to India if she did both in the course of a single flight after the modifications begun in July were completed.

What Colmore did not add, or at any rate failed to make clear to Dowding, was that most of the R.101's flying had been done in 1929, before her gas-bags were let out. She was then a notably stable ship, although rather slow and sluggish. In 1930, after her gas-bags were let out, she had made only two flights of more than a few hours, and had behaved badly on both of them.

In the light of subsequent events, Dowding came to the conclusion that he ought to have insisted on prolonged trials of the R.101 in her new form before she was allowed to leave for India. At the time, the proposal that she should bring her flying time up to 150 hours by making a forty-eight-hour flight, during which her speed could be tested, seemed to him quite reasonable. The only difficulty was that a forty-eight-hour flight could not be fitted into the few days still available. He then settled for a twenty-four-hour flight, but found that even this was hard to arrange. He was determined to travel in the ship and see for himself how she behaved, but would miss an important engagement if she left at the time proposed and returned twenty-four hours later. He asked whether lopping six or seven hours off the flight would do any harm. Colmore said that, on the contrary, it would give everyone more time to prepare for the flight to India.

The outcome was an agreeable excursion which told Dowding scarcely anything about the fitness of the ship for the purpose in view. It lasted less than seventeen hours, so it fell short of being an endurance test by thirty-one hours. One engine developed a minor fault, so no high-speed trials were attempted. The flight was made in calm weather, mostly at night, so no light was thrown on the ship's behaviour in bumpy, stormy or sultry conditions. Since there was nothing to make her roll or pitch, her officers had no means of judging whether the faults noticed on her last two flights had been cured. An experienced pilot of heavier-than-air machines, Dowding was favourably impressed by the smoothness of her motion, but he paid more heed to what Richmond and Colmore thought than to his own feelings. They seemed satisfied that the addition of the new bay had made her a better ship.

The ship returned to the mast on 2 October. Later in the day Dowding and Colmore reported to Thomson. As they were going into Thomson's room, Dowding said to Colmore: 'You are my adviser. Whatever line you take, I shall back you up.'[4]

In the meantime Bairstow and Pippard had sent an interim report to the effect that, although they had still not been given time to draw up a full report on the R.101 as she now was, they were satisfied that her structure and aerodynamic design conformed with the requirements laid down. An inspector from the Aeronautical Inspection Department strongly opposed the issue of a Certificate of Airworthiness, but his objections were based on detailed criticisms of gas-bags and of measures taken to prevent surging and chafing. Colmore seemed confident that the faults he mentioned could and would be put right by the time the ship was due to leave.

Dowding came to the conclusion that a Certificate of Airworthiness should be prepared, but that a further inspection of the ship should be made before it was handed over. Accordingly, a certificate was drawn up later in the day and signed by the Deputy-Director of Civil Aviation. It was handed to the captain of the ship on 4 October, after two inspectors had spent about two hours examining her.[5]

U.S.S. Akron *built by the Goodyear Zeppelin Corporation, 1931.*

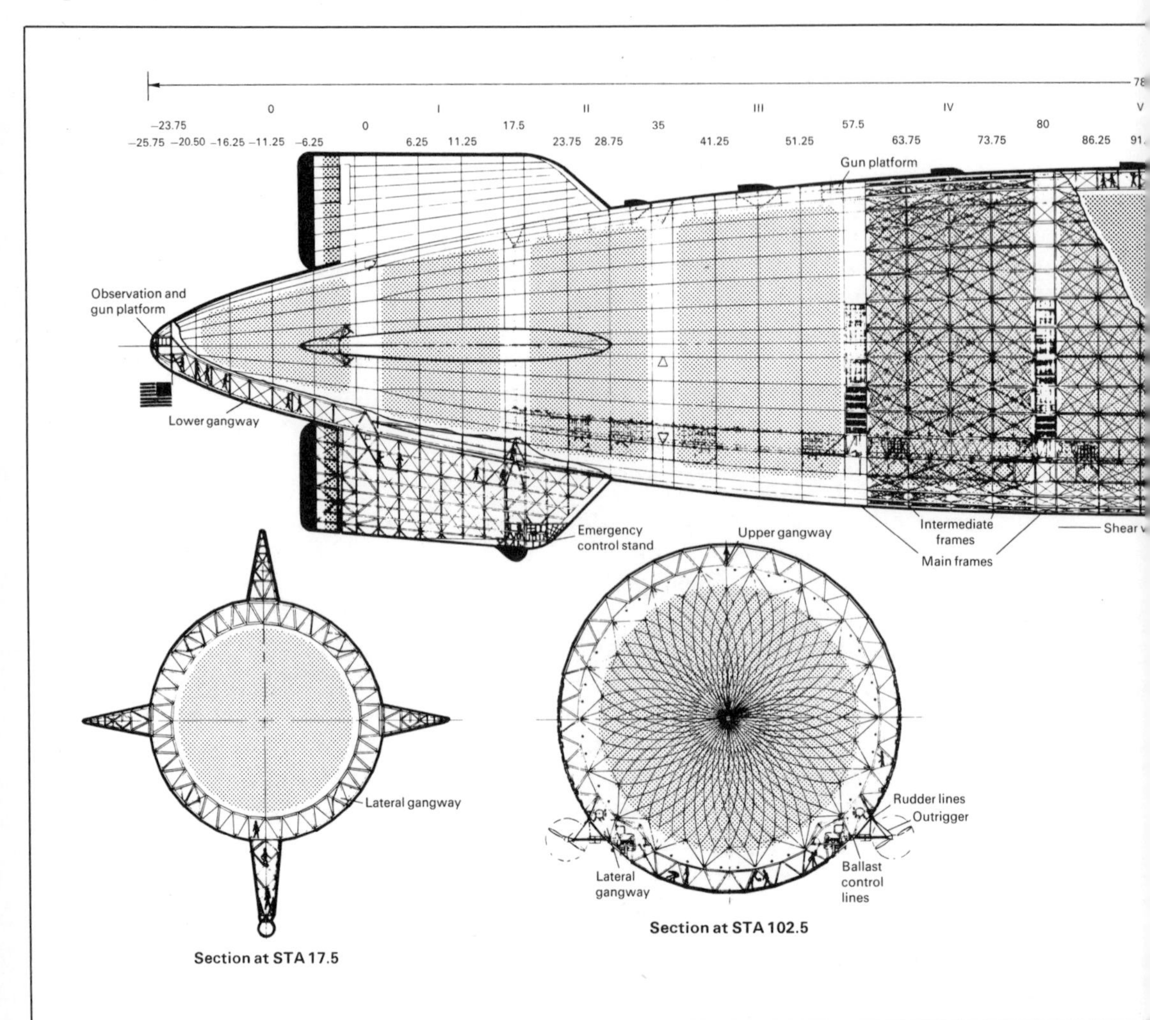

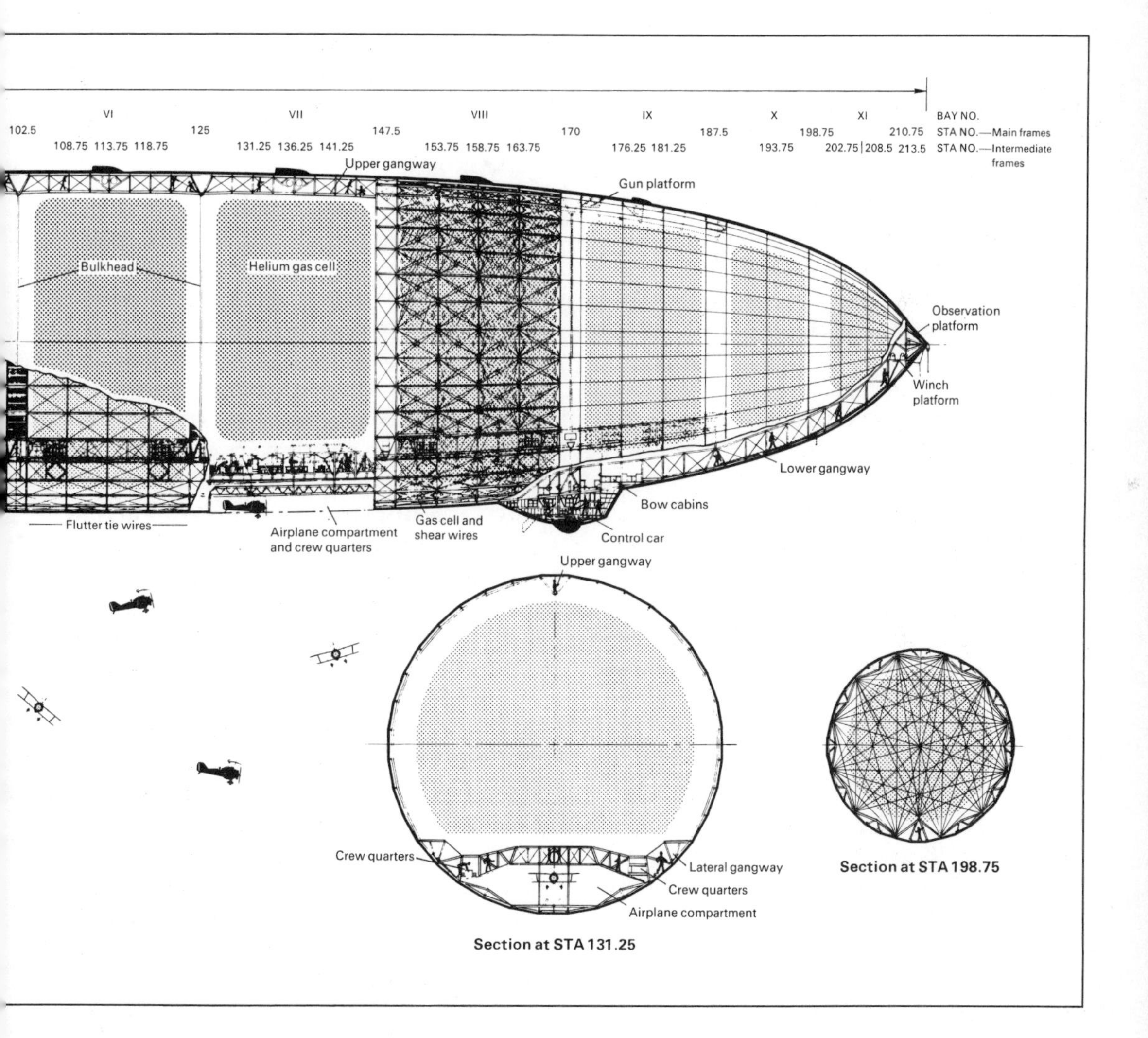
VI
VII
VIII
IX
X
XI
BAY NO.
102.5
125
147.5
170
187.5
198.75
210.75
STA NO.—Main frames
108.75 113.75 118.75
131.25 136.25 141.25
153.75 158.75 163.75
176.25 181.25
193.75
202.75 208.5 213.5
STA NO.—Intermediate frames
Upper gangway
Gun platform
Bulkhead
Helium gas cell
Observation platform
Winch platform
Lower gangway
Bow cabins
Control car
Flutter tie wires
Airplane compartment and crew quarters
Gas cell and shear wires
Upper gangway
Crew quarters
Lateral gangway
Crew quarters
Airplane compartment
Section at STA 131.25
Section at STA 198.75

To meet the objection that the R.101 had not passed her high-speed trials, Dowding proposed that trials should be made soon after she left Cardington for India, and that she should turn back if the results were unsatisfactory. This was a proposal he was almost bound to make without, one is forced to conclude, much expectation that it would be taken seriously. The captain of a ship carrying distinguished passengers on a long voyage was not very likely to turn aside from his route in order to carry out high-speed trials over a measured course, or to be influenced by the results if he did. As things turned out, conditions while the R.101 was over England on 4 October were quite unsuitable for such a test.

Dowding said many years later that he was not pressed in any way by Thomson to sanction the issue of a Certificate of Airworthiness.[6] He felt at all times that he was perfectly free to make his own decision. He agreed that the certificate should be issued, with the proviso that a further examination of the ship should be made first, because he was satisfied that Colmore thought the ship airworthy and that the further examination would take care of the points raised by the inspector. He himself had no expert knowledge, and he had had no time during his fortnight at the Air Ministry to digest the man-high pile of documents which appeared when he called for the files on the subject. In these circumstances he had no choice but to rely on Colmore, who was the expert appointed to advise him and was willing to back his faith in the ship by travelling to India in her.

On the day of his interview with Dowding and Colmore, Thomson was visited by the Director of Civil Aviation, Sir Sefton Brancker. Brancker was not an authority on airships, and his job did not often bring him into contact with the Secretary of State. But he was a good listener, to whom people were willing to talk about their problems because, although not particularly discreet where his own affairs were concerned, he was rightly judged too honourable and too good-natured a man to betray a confidence or make capital of other people's troubles. He had decided to see Thomson because he knew that officers who had flown in the R.101 since her gasbags were let out had no confidence in her. Moreover, from the moment when he received an invitation to accompany Thomson and Colmore to India in the R.101, he had felt that there was something chimerical about the project. He did not believe that she would reach Karachi. Still worse, he had a hunch, a presentiment – he hardly knew what to call it – that the flight, if it did come off, would be the end of him.[7]

Brancker was not alone in thinking that the R.101 would not reach Karachi. The Editor of *The Aeroplane* doubted whether she would get beyond Ismailia.[8] Squadron Leader Booth, who had stood in for her First Officer during her rehearsal for the Hendon Display, was not convinced that she would get that far.[9] Even Colmore had suggested that additional masts should be provided at Baghdad or Basra and at Athens or Malta.[10] The French government had not been asked to provide facilities for emergency landings at Orly or Cuers-Pierrefeu, but inquiries had been made about facilties for topping up there.[11] Furthermore, it was known that even if the ship did reach Karachi she would not be able to carry enough fuel to make the return journey except in favourable conditions.[12]

Brancker could not tell the Secretary of State for Air that death waited for him on the road to Karachi. He did say that the wisdom of sending the modified R.101 on a long voyage without adequate trials was questioned in some circles. Thomson replied that if Brancker wanted to back out of the trip plenty of men would be glad to take his place.

This was unwise. The fact that Brancker was an enthusiastic pilot of heavier-than-air machines although he was too short-sighted to see the ground when he landed in itself argued a certain courage. Apart from that, by taking part in many hazardous flights Brancker had shown that he was brave to the point of foolhardiness. Thomson, like Brancker, had been a soldier. He ought to have known that Brancker's visit was not likely to have been prompted merely by regard for his own safety. When he snubbed the transparently sincere though perhaps not very astute Director of Civil Aviation, Thomson brushed aside a warning which could have saved his own life and the lives of forty-seven other men.

The crew of the R.101 devoted Friday, 3 October, to eleventh-hour preparations which gave some of them little time for sleep that night and continued throughout the greater part of the following day. Thomson, Brancker and Colmore, too, were busy. Unlike Thomson, his manservant, and the ship's officers, Brancker did not take out a special life insurance for the trip, although he felt more strongly than ever after his interview with Thomson that he had little chance of coming out of the ship alive.

Next morning the weather was good enough for Brancker to be flown by a friend to Norwich in the morning and afterwards back to Bedfordshire. But the barometer was falling and the outlook was unpromising. On the way to Cardington in the late

The burnt-out remains of the R.101 after she had crashed near Beauvais during the first stage of her projected flight from Cardington to Karachi.

afternoon, Brancker asked the friend who was driving him to take some roses to the woman pilot Amy Johnson, who was ill in a nursing home.

The R.101 left Cardington in dismal weather at 6.36 p.m., carrying a crew of forty-two and twenty-five tons of heavy oil for her diesel engines. After embarking her twelve passengers and their luggage, which included a case of champagne brought by Thomson, she had to drop four tons of ballast before she could leave the mast. Flight Lieutenant H. C. Irwin was Captain of the ship, but the ubiquitous Scott was present and made most of the decisions. It was Scott who decided that the flight should begin although the experts predicted unfavourable weather along the route. Irwin had drawn up in the summer a programme of trial flights to be undertaken after the new bay was inserted and before the ship left for India, but his proposals had been turned down.

The direct route from Cardington to Ismailia would have taken the R.101 right across the Alps. Despite the claims by Thomson and others that airships would soon be able to carry huge loads over lofty mountain ranges, Scott and Irwin had no intention of attempting such a feat. They could reach the Mediterranean from Cardington without climbing to uneconomic heights either by flying down the valleys of the Saône and Rhône or by skirting the mountains of central France on the west and passing through the gap between the Cévennes and the Pyrenees.

The ship moved off slowly, flying well below clouds which came down to 1,500 feet, and pitching and rolling in a gusty wind. She was soon soaked by heavy rain which added several tons to her weight. At 8.21 p.m., when she was over London, Irwin signalled that he proposed to make for the Mediterranean by the westerly route, passing over Paris, Tours, Toulouse and Narbonne. This route, chosen in preference to the easterly route because the valleys of the Saône and Rhône had a reputation for sudden storms, would add many miles to the distance he had to cover, and he would have to fly in the teeth of a strong south-westerly wind to reach Tours from Paris.

With one engine temporarily out of action, the ship passed over Hastings at 9.35 p.m. She was then flying at 1,000 feet or less, but Irwin signalled that he would gain height gradually in order to clear the high ground ahead of him.

The sixty-mile crossing from Hastings to the mouth of the Somme took 111 minutes, and the ship seemed to some of those aboard her not much more than her own length above the water. She flew so low over Saint Valéry-sur-Somme that eyewit-

nesses felt sure she was trying to land. She seemed to the inhabitants of Quesnoy, a few miles further on, to be only just above their roof-tops. But Irwin, apparently, was undismayed. He knew the ship was heavy, but had been told she could carry up to sixteen tons above her disposable lift by relying on her engines. He signalled that his 'distinguished passengers', having sighted the French coast, had gone to bed after eating an excellent supper and smoking a 'final cigar' in the gas-proof room provided for the purpose.

Scott, too, retired about midnight. Irwin remained at his post until the watch was changed at 2 a.m., when he went to get some rest after handing over to the Officer of the Watch. At 1.52 a.m., Le Bourget gave the ship's position as one kilometre north of Beauvais. Her indicated height was 1,000 feet above sea level, but at 1 a.m. she had seemed to observers at Poix airfield to be only 300 feet above the ground. A forty-mile-an-hour wind, rising in gusts to fifty miles an hour or more, was blowing from the south-west, but veering and backing between west and south.

Some families at Cardington sat up late that night. Among households still astir well after midnight was that of Lieutenant-Commander Noël Atherstone, First Officer of the R.101. In the early hours of 5 October, Atherstone's familiar knock was heard at the front door. Atherstone's dog Timmy, an Alsatian renowned for his fierceness, ran to the door. The door was opened. No one was there. The knock was repeated at the back door. Again, the door was opened and no one was there.[13]

At 2 a.m., as the watch was being changed, the ship passed over Beauvais, heading towards the 750-foot-high limestone ridge which lies south-west of the town. Before reaching it she dived to earth, came to rest in a field 425 feet above sea-level and burst into flames. Eight men scrambled from the blazing wreckage, but two of them died soon afterwards. The survivors testified that they heard the engine telegraphs signalling either 'Half Speed' or 'Slow' immediately before the crash. The ship's elevators were found in the full-up position and her rudder was amidships. Her girders were twisted and broken, although she was said to have been moving at only five miles an hour when she hit the ground.

The cause of the accident was never established beyond question. A Committee of Preliminary Investigation interrogated eyewitnesses, and a Court of Inquiry held many sittings and issued a lengthy report. The Court advanced the theory that the ship dived because one or more of her forward gas-bags became deflated and the gas rushed to her tail, causing her nose to

Court of Inquiry into the loss of the R.101, held in the Great Hall of the Institute of Civil Engineers at Westminster. Centre, the Attorney-General, Sir William Jowett, reads his opening speech; right, the Chairman, Sir John Simon, sits flanked by two assessors (one barely visible).

tip downwards. But there was no real evidence to support this belief, and experts from the National Physical Laboratory and the Airworthiness of Airships Panel testified that the ship would not have nose-dived if her forward gas-bags had collapsed, but would have settled tail-first. Many years later, one of two assessors who sat with the chairman confessed that the Court never did find out what happened.[14]

This does not mean that the loss of the R.101 was unaccountable in the sense that no one could think of reasons why she should have crashed. On the contrary, the difficulty was to know which of her many shortcomings was the effective cause of the disaster.

The Court had some difficulty in establishing the exact sequence of events immediately before the crash, but the bulk of the evidence suggested that the ship first went into a dive from which her height-coxswain succeeded in pulling her out, and that this was followed by a second dive from which he could not save her. This interpretation was challenged by E. F. Spanner, a former member of the Royal Corps of Naval Constructors and a persistent critic of the Air Ministry's airship programme. Spanner pointed out that one witness who had a particularly good view of the R.101's descent saw only a single dive. Spanner believed that the R.101 broke up in the air when her elevators were moved abruptly to the full-up position, much as the R.38 had done when thrown into an abrupt turn. But the experts who checked Richmond's calculations testified that the R.101 was structurally much stronger than the R.38. It seems likely that the damage to her girders, which figured prominently in Spanner's argument, was caused by fire after she hit the ground.

At the time of the accident the R.101 was flying at an altitude which gave her little margin of safety. She was approaching a ridge from the lee side and was therefore likely to be struck at any moment by a down current. The wind was strong, changeable and gusty. Her crew was relatively inexperienced.[15] She had no forward ballast releasable from her control car, having used it all up before she left Cardington. During her last flight before the new bay was inserted, when she did have ballast which could be released from her control car, her acting First Officer had released about a ton of it at a crucial moment because she was so heavy on her elevators that her height-coxswain found her almost uncontrollable. In the light of these considerations, it seems unnecessary to postulate a structural weakness of which there is no real evidence.

If the R.101 crashed because she was in a vulnerable position and heavy on her

The United States Navy's ZRS-4 (Akron) *on her maiden flight, 23 September 1931.*

elevators, it remains to ask why she flew so low and what made her so heavy. Was her crew deceived by an inaccurate altimeter into believing she was higher than she was? No one knows, but the *Graf Zeppelin*'s altimeter is said to have given a false reading that night.[16] Again, it is impossible to offer more than a tentative explanation of the heaviness noticed towards the end of each of her last two flights before she was carved up. The most plausible theory is that, after the wiring of her gas-bags was let out, lateral and fore-and-aft surging of her bags made her unsteady in rough or bumpy weather, with the result that she pumped out gas through her lightly set valves whenever she met such conditions. The weather was rough throughout her flight from Cardington to Beauvais. If she lost gas continuously, the wonder is not that she crashed but that she got as far as she did.

To the day of his death, Lord Dowding deplored the fact that the R.101 had no bow elevators like those fitted to some early Zeppelins.[17] Whether bow elevators would have saved her from crashing near Beauvais is a matter for conjecture. It seems fairly certain that, in the conditions prevailing at the time, she would in any case have run out of fuel well short of Ismailia. She might conceivably have got as far as Cuers-Pierrefeu, or have made an emergency landing at Narbonne.

Contrary to popular belief, the government did not decide immediately after the loss of the R.101 that no more of the taxpayers' money should be spent on airships. A plan to spend £400,000 on minor improvements to the R.100 and on a new ship, the R.102, was laid before Parliament in the spring of 1931. It was turned down later in the year on financial grounds. A committee which reported adversely on the scheme from the financial point of view stated that it did so partly because the public would insist on the use of helium instead of hydrogen, and that this would be expensive. The government announced in the following September that, because it was forced by a world-wide slump to make cuts in public expenditure, henceforth no more would be spent on the airship programme than was needed to keep the authorities abreast of developments.

After some argument, the government accepted the R.100 and agreed to pay the balance of her contract price. She was said to have cost the nation £363,000, but the manufacturers spent considerably more on her. Eventually she was sold for scrap after her engines and gas-bags had been removed. Her remains were torn apart and squashed flat by a streamroller.

The Zeppelin company thus became the sole organizer of passenger flights by inter-

continental airships. After Hitler came to power the company was, however, forced to accept a substantial measure of state control.

The two monster airships built for the United States Navy were intercontinental airships in size and performance, but they were not used commercially and they could not make long flights to places where helium was not available for topping up. The *Akron* was completed in the late summer of 1931 and made her maiden flight on 23 September. Her gross lift was 193 tons and her disposable lift about eighty tons. She was designed to carry five fighter aircraft which could be released and recovered in flight. In the early winter of 1931 she made a ten-hour flight with the record number of 270 people aboard her. A theoretical range of more than 10,000 miles and a maximum speed of more than eighty miles an hour made her very suitable for maritime reconnaissance on a grand scale, but her officers complained that in practice the amount of flying they could do was limited by the need to conserve helium, and that this made it difficult for them to learn to handle her in all kinds of weather.

On 4 April 1933 the *Akron* left Lakehurst to take part in some naval manoeuvres in the Atlantic. She carried a crew of seventy-six in addition to the Chief of the Bureau of Aeronautics, Admiral William A. Moffett. A storm was sighted to the south, but her captain, Commander F. C. McCord, decided to carry on in the hope that he could outdistance the storm by a change of course. The storm caught up with her while she was flying at an indicated height of 1,600 feet. After coping for an hour and a half with heavy rain and strong winds, she was struck by a squall and fell rapidly, but recovered after ballast had been dropped. She returned to her former height and was then struck by another squall. She fell at a rate estimated at fourteen feet a second, her elevator cables parted, and she struck the water in a tail-down attitude and soon broke up. Only three of her crew were rescued.

A Board of Inquiry came to the conclusion that the ship was in good shape when she left Lakehurst, and attributed the

disaster to errors of judgement by her captain. McCord, it was said, ought to have flown away from the storm instead of trying to outdistance it. No correction had been made to the ship's altimeter to compensate for the drop in pressure caused by the storm, and in consequence her altitude at the crucial time had been over-estimated by something like 600 feet. A subsequent examination of the wreckage showed that her structure was sound, although this, it would seem, can scarcely have applied to her elevator cables.

In these depressing circumstances the *Akron*'s sister ship, the ZRS.5 or *Macon*, made her maiden flight on 21 April 1933. With a maximum speed of eighty-five miles an hour, she was about four miles an hour faster than the *Akron*. After completing her acceptance trials she was commissioned in the following June, under the command of Commander H. Dressel, USN. Based at Sunnyvale, California, she proved so useful to the Pacific Fleet that demands for her removal from service for a thorough overhaul in the fall of 1934 were resisted. Even when damage to some of her girders during a flight from California to the West Indies led the Department of the Navy to order modified girders, she was kept in commission and the new girders were installed piecemeal as they arrived.

The work had not yet been completed when the *Macon* left Sunnyvale on 11 February 1935 to take part in naval manoeuvres in the Pacific. After contending with winds up to gale force for twenty-four hours, she ran into turbulent air off Point Sur during the return flight. She fell about 1,000 feet, one of her fins and part of

The United States Navy's ZRS-5 (Macon) *under construction at Akron, Ohio. The completed airship was almost identical in appearance with the* Akron.

her hull broke away, and three of her gasbags collapsed. Commander Dressel had been succeeded as captain of the ship by Commander Wiley, one of the survivors of the *Akron* disaster. After an unsuccessful attempt to regain an even keel by dropping ballast, Wiley saved most of his crew, but not his ship, by making an emergency landing on the surface of the water. One man jumped out of the ship as she was descending and was killed, and another failed to return after going back to the wreck to search for his belongings, but eighty-three were saved. The United States Navy was thus left with only the German-built *Los Angeles* still extant, though no longer in commission.

The history of the *Akron* and the *Macon* suggests that, admirable in conception though these handsome airships were, their designers were less successful than Barnes Wallis and Ludwig Dürr in finding the right combination of power, strength and lightness. However that may be, by 1935 the day of the giant rigid airship as an instrument of maritime reconnaissance was felt to have passed. The future of naval aviation lay, in the opinion of most strategists of the day, with carrier-borne and shore-based landplanes and large flying boats.

Continuing her series of spectacular exhibition flights, the *Graf Zeppelin* flew in the summer of 1931 from Friedrichshafen to Leningrad and went on to make an aerial survey of Severnaya Zemlya and Franz Josef Land. A rendezvous in Arctic waters with a submarine carrying Sir Hubert Wilkins was planned, but Wilkins was unable to complete the project. The *Graf Zeppelin* carried a team of geographers, meteorologists and physicists drawn from several nations, and her exploit was of genuine scientific interest. Leaving Leningrad on 26 July, she made a successful descent on the following day beside the Russian ice-breaker *Malygin*, but Eckener soon took off again for fear that floating ice might damage her. She returned to Leningrad on 30 July and flew to Berlin on the same day.

Other flights by the *Graf Zeppelin* in 1931 included a tour of the British Isles. In the course of the year she made more than seventy flights, carried about 2,000 passengers and travelled some 73,000 miles,[18] including three round trips to Brazil.

In 1932 the *Graf Zeppelin* made nine round trips to South America, beginning in April with a remarkable flight from Friedrichshafen to Pernambuco in sixty-one hours. Another nine followed in 1933. In October Eckener took his ship to the United States for the first time since 1930, flying her from Friedrichshafen to Chicago

The longest airship yet built: the Zeppelin Company's 804-foot-long LZ.129 (Hindenburg) *of 1936.*

in four stages, with stops at Pernambuco, Miami and Akron. After visiting the exhibition at Chicago which was the advertised attraction for his passengers, he flew her back to Freidrichshafen by way of Akron and Seville.

During the next two years the *Graf Zeppelin* continued to be employed on the South Atlantic route during the spring, summer and autumn months, but plans for regular passenger services across the North Atlantic made slow progress. When the *Graf Zeppelin* completed her hundred and eighth crossing of the South Atlantic towards the end of 1935, she had still made only seven crossings of the North Atlantic. Plans had been made to build a new ship, the LZ.128, as a sister ship to the *Graf Zeppelin*, but work on her was stopped when the bigger and faster LZ.129 was laid down in 1934. On the assumption that the LZ.129 would be in service by 1936, ten round trips to the United States were planned for that year.

The LZ.129, named at Eckener's suggestion the *Hindenburg*, duly made her maiden flight in the early spring of 1936. More than 800 feet long and driven by four 1,100-horsepower Daimler diesel engines, she was designed to carry fifty passengers, but was afterwards modified to carry seventy or more. Her gas-bags were intended to hold some 7,000,000 cubic feet of helium, but had to be filled with hydrogen since the United States government was not prepared to part with helium to fill a ship which might be used for warlike purposes. A further setback for Eckener was the German government's decision in 1935 that henceforth passenger services should be organized by the state and that the Zeppelin company's role should be limited to the building of airships for delivery to a nationalized operating company.

The *Hindenburg*'s first flight from Friedrichshafen to Rio de Janeiro was due to begin on 31 March 1936. Much to Eckener's indignation, she and the *Graf Zeppelin* were used between 26 and 29 March to drop electoral leaflets over Germany on Hitler's behalf. Even so, she departed for South America on the appointed day, with Ernst Lehmann in command. One of her engines broke down over the Atlantic, but it was repaired on her arrival, and on 6 April she set out to return to Friedrichshafen. Two of her engines were out of action for forty-two hours on the homeward flight, but she arrived safely on 10 April. She was then taken out of service for three weeks while her engines were overhauled at the Daimler factory.

Her next intercontinental flight, begun on 6 May, took her from Friedrichshafen

to Lakehurst in just under sixty-two hours. Once again, Ernst Lehmann was in command. The return flight was completed in just under forty-three hours. In the course of the year she made ten round trips to the United States and seven to Brazil. The *Graf Zeppelin* made seventy-three flights in 1936 and brought her total since 1928 to well over 500 flights.

During the winter of 1936–7 long-term plans were made for transatlantic passenger services by two German-built and two American-built airships. Eighteen round trips between Frankfurt and Lakehurst by the *Hindenburg*, and fifteen between Frankfurt or Friedrichshafen and Rio de Janeiro by the *Graf Zeppelin* were scheduled for 1937. In addition a new ship, the LZ.130, was advertised as due to leave either Frankfurt or Friedrichshafen for Rio de Janeiro on 27 October and to make the return flight at the beginning of November. The return fare to Lakehurst varied from 720 to 1,350 dollars, according to the time of year and whether the traveller wanted only a single berth or a whole cabin to himself. The single fare to Rio de Janeiro was 1,500 Reichsmarks for a berth in a two-berth cabin or 2,200 Reichsmarks for a single cabin.

The 1937 season began in March with the first of the *Graf Zeppelin*'s scheduled flights to Rio de Janeiro by way of Pernambuco. The *Hindenburg*'s first flight to Lakehurst was not due until May. She left Frankfurt at 8.15 p.m. on 3 May, carrying thirty-six passengers and a crew of sixty-one. Nearly half her berths were empty, but she was booked almost to capacity for the return flight. Max Pruss was in command, but Ernst Lehmann, now head of the government-sponsored corporation responsible to the Air Ministry for organizing the flights, had decided almost at the last moment to go with him. One of his motives, although by

no means the only one, was that a warning that an attempt might be made to destroy the ship had been passed to his office by the German Ambassador in Washington.[19] Such warnings were not uncommon, and were usually regarded as the work of cranks. A time bomb had, however, once been discovered in the *Graf Zeppelin*, and an attempt had been made in 1931 to sabotage the *Akron*. Lehmann knew that the *Hindenburg* was regarded in some quarters as a symbol of National Socialist power and ruthlessness.

Forbidden for political reasons to fly over France or Britain, Pruss reached the North Atlantic by way of Flushing, the Dover Strait and the English Channel. By the early hours of Tuesday 4 May he had cleared the Channel and was south of the Old Head of Kinsale.

Pruss was due at Lakehurst on 6 May. His estimated time of arrival was 8 a.m. Delayed by headwinds, he arrived eight hours late. He had then to wait for a storm to blow itself out before he could approach the mast. Some two hours after his arrival Commander Rosendahl, now Commandant of Lakehurst, advised him by radio that the weather was improving, and at 7.10 p.m. he ordered the crew to their landing stations. A few minutes earlier the *Hindenburg*'s Chief Rigger, Ludwig Knorr, had told another member of the crew that something about No. 4 gas-bag, near the tail, made him think it might be leaking, but before he could make a close inspection he had to go to his landing station at the other end of the ship.

About ten minutes were needed to trim the ship for her final approach to the mast.

Drawing of the Hindenburg, *showing constructional details. With modern materials and methods of construction, larger and stronger airships could be built with far less expenditure of man-hours.*

At 3.00 p.m., 6 May 1937, Manhattan had its last look at luxurious lighter-than-air transport (Hindenburg). *The May sun would soon be obscured by thunderstorms, and the schuduled landing would be delayed.*

By 7.20 p.m. she was dead level and in perfect balance. A few minutes later, when her forward landing lines were out and she was about 200 feet from the mast, several members of her crew heard a sound which one of them compared with the firing of 'a small gun or rifle' and another with the pop heard when the burner of a gas stove is ignited. Her Chief Engineer saw, near the centre of No. 4 gas-bag, a sudden, intense glow.

Within a few seconds, the whole of the after-part of the ship was a mass of flames. As the fire swept forward, she came slowly to the ground in a tail-down attitude. Flames poured from her nose 'like fire out of a volcano'.[20] The sight was so terrible that a radio commentator who was giving an eyewitness account became incoherent and had to break off his narrative. Miraculously, sixty-two of the ninety-seven people aboard the ship survived the holocaust. Lehmann came out of the wreckage alive but died on the following day. Pruss was badly burnt but made a wonderful recovery.

Eckener's first thought when he heard the news was that the ship had been sabotaged. Later he came to the conclusion that a gas-bag near the tail, possibly damaged by a bracing-wire which could have broken as the ship turned sharply into the wind during her final approach to the mast, must have developed a leak and that escaping gas must have been ignited by static electricity. This was accepted as a likely explanation by the American Board of Inquiry, but it was pure hypothesis. There was no evidence that a bracing-wire did break, and an expert witness testified at the inquiry that static electricity could not have caused the fire.[21] Ludwig Knorr died without saying what he thought was wrong with No. 4 gas-bag, but it cannot have been anything very serious or he would have raised the alarm instead of merely making a casual remark about the matter. Surviving members of the crew were confident that no substantial escape of gas could have occurred without their knowledge and that any gas which did escape from a gas-bag near the tail would have blown away. Sabotage remains a possibility, but the ship was so much behind schedule that a time-bomb would presumably have been intended to explode after passengers and crew had left the ship.

Whatever its cause, the destruction of the *Hindenburg* put an end to intercontinental flights by hydrogen-filled airships. The *Graf Zeppelin* was grounded while Eckener and others tried to persuade the American authorities to release supplies of helium so that transatlantic services could be resumed. The United States government was willing to authorize the export

ABOVE: *Inside the* Hindenburg. *Through open windows, cruising along at forty knots, passengers could hear dogs barking at them just 500 feet below.*

of helium for commercial airships, but insisted on safeguards against its use for military purposes. This proviso enabled opponents of the sale of helium to Germany to spin out their opposition until the project lapsed.

The LZ.130, a second *Graf Zeppelin* intended to carry thirty passengers, was completed in 1938 but was destined never to fly to the United States. In the summer of 1939 she cruised over the North Sea and in British territorial waters to pick up and analyse radar transmissions. The British sent fighters to look at her on one or two occasions, but did not molest her. Both the original *Graf Zeppelin* and her namesake were dismantled during the Second World War. The LZ.131, intended as a super-*Hindenburg*, was laid down in 1938 but never completed.

ABOVE: *The* Hindenburg *disaster. In May 1937 the airship was destroyed by fire after an Atlantic crossing.*

11 Yesterday and tomorrow

By the end of the third decade of the twentieth century, most European strategists were convinced that airships would play, at most, only a very small part in any future war between European powers. Naval, military and air historians pointed out that during the First World War Germany's large rigid airships had proved unsuccessful in a tactical role and less accurate than heavier-than-air machines when used as long-range bombers, while at sea they had failed to provide a satisfactory substitute for cruisers because their attempts to reconnoitre the approaches to the Heligoland Bight had been repeatedly frustrated by the weather. Small pressure airships had proved useful for convoy escort and as submarine spotters, but after the middle of the nineteen-twenties no European government contemplated using them for such purposes in a future war. The British continued for some years to believe that large rigid airships might still have some value as troop-carriers or, in some circumstances, for maritime reconnaissance. But their faith in lighter-than-air machines did not long survive the loss of the R.101 and the financial and economic setbacks of the early nineteen-thirties.

That American strategists saw the future of the airship in a different light is not surprising. Separated by vast expanses of salt water from any potential enemy, the United States might conceivably be attacked by a European power or combination of powers, but was more likely to find herself at war with Japan. In either case she would be free to use airships for submarine-spotting, convoy escort or strategic reconnaissance at ranges up to hundreds or even thousands of miles from her shores without risking their destruction by hostile aircraft, unless these were carrier-borne.

The United States would, however, be handicapped in a war with Japan by the exposed position of her interests and possessions in the Far East and the Western Pacific, her lack of a first-class naval base west of Pearl Harbor in the Hawaiian Islands, and the fact that the League of Nations had granted mandates for the former German colonies in the Pacific north of the equator to Japan. As soon as possible after the outbreak of war the Americans would aim, therefore, at capturing bases in the mandated islands from which a force could be sent to relieve the Philippines and from which their armed forces could strike at the Japanese fleet and, if the need arose, at Japan itself. Ten large rigid airships, of which the ships ordered from the Goodyear-Zeppelin Corporation in 1928 would be prototypes, were to be provided to scout ahead of a surface fleet advancing westwards from Pearl Harbor for the purpose. Each airship would carry small heavier-than-air machines which could be launched and recovered in flight, but whether these were to be used to protect her against hostile aircraft or to extend the area reconnoitred in a given time was a controversial issue.

The *Akron* was commissioned at Lakehurst in the last week of October, 1931. The naval authorities had drawn up a programme by which she was to go to the West Coast in the following January and fly thence to Ewa, near Pearl Harbor, where a mast that was to have been used by the *Shenandoah* in 1924 would be made ready for her. She was then to take part in a series of naval manoeuvres, culminating in tactical exercises connected with the concentration of the fleet on the West Coast.[1]

Recognizing at the last moment that this was more than a newly commissioned airship could be expected to undertake, the authorities cancelled the visit to Ewa and reduced the *Akron*'s role to participation in one exercise in March. As things turned out, an accident to her tail during preparations for a demonstration flight made even this impossible. The *Akron* spent most of her seventeen months' service at Lakehurst, making only one visit to the West Coast in the spring and early summer of 1932. During those seventeen months she had three different commanders. She took part in only two fleet exercises, and on both occasions was without her heavier-than-air machines. Her performance during these exercises, although not brilliant, was creditable, but it did not throw much light on her ability to carry out the task for which she was intended.

The *Macon*, on the other hand, took part in fleet exercises on at least nine occasions during her twenty months of service and carried up to four aircraft at a time.[2] But she was repeatedly misemployed in a tactical role, and she crashed a few months before she was due to take part in large-scale manoeuvres in the Central Pacific which would have provided a fair test of her capabilities.

Both ships, in short, were given too much to do. Instead of being treated as experimental prototypes, instead of being nursed through their teething troubles and then thoroughly tested in the role for which they were designed, they were forced to undertake a variety of tasks for which they were not suited.

Contrary to popular belief, the naval authorities did not immediately after the loss of the *Macon* lose interest in large rigid airships. Detailed proposals were made for new ships, including a trainer to replace the *Los Angeles* and a 9,500,000-

cubic-foot ship designed by Charles P. Burgess of the Bureau of Aeronautics and intended to carry nine dive bombers.[3] These and other proposals were sympathetically considered by the General Board of the Navy, but the loss of the *Akron* and the *Macon* before they had had a chance of giving a convincing demonstration of their worth put a powerful lever into the hands of men who objected to airships on principle or because they resented any diversion of funds from the acquisition of surface warships and heavier-than-air machines. The issue degenerated into an unedifying controversy which dragged on until 1940. By that time there was such an urgent demand for heavier-than-air machines that a decision in favour of the large rigid airship was not to be expected.

When the *Macon* was lost, the only naval airships still formally in commission were the blimps J-4, G-1 and K-1 and a small metal-clad pressure airship, or 'tin blimp', the ZMC-2, which was intended as a scaled-down prototype of a new generation of large airships. There was also the *Los Angeles*, but officially she was not in commission, although she was used occasionally for mooring trials and continued to fly from time to time until 1938. The most modern of these ships was the K-1, built in 1931 as an experimental craft, but the G-1, completed as a commercial aircraft in 1929, had only just been acquired by the navy. The United States Army had four blimps which were used for coast defence.

The navy acquired no more airships until 1937, when the army relinquished its responsibility for off-shore patrols, disbanded its airship service, and handed over

The 200,000-cubic-foot metalclad ZMC-2 of 1929, showing interior during course of construction. Intended as the scaled-down prototype of a new generation of large metal airships, and seen by some designers today as forty years ahead of her time.

its surviving blimps. Two of these, the TC-13 and TC-14, were commissioned after some delay as naval airships. In the same year the navy began to expand its lighter-than-air fleet by buying more commercial blimps for use as trainers, and in 1938 Goodyear produced in collaboration with the Naval Aircraft Factory a 404,000-cubic-foot experimental blimp, the K-2, with four 550-horse-power engines driving tractor airscrews.[4]

In the summer of 1940, with war with Germany in the offing, Congress sanctioned a programme of naval expansion which included forty-eight blimps, but there were still only ten in service when dire events in the Far East brought the United States into the war some eighteen months later. About 150 were built during the next three years and used for off-shore patrols and convoy escort from bases in the Continental United States, the West Indies, Brazil and French Morocco. The great majority of the blimps used during the Second World War were K-class ships, developed by Goodyear from the K-2 but fitted with a variety of engines.

At the end of the Second World War the United States naval authorities claimed that, from start to finish, no merchant vessel sailing in a convoy whose escort included a blimp was ever sunk by a submarine. So far as is known, no submarines were directly destroyed by blimps, but German submarine commanders have stated that the deterrent effect of these small airships was substantial. One blimp, the K-47, was brought down by return fire from a submarine which she attacked off the coast of Florida on 18 July 1943, but the submarine is said to have been sunk later in the day by surface warships. One member of the crew of the blimp was killed by a shark, and the rest were rescued.

Remarkable feats performed by K-class blimps during the Second World War included the first transatlantic flights by pressure airships. In the early summer of 1944 six blimps of Blimp Squadron Fourteen flew from Weeksville, North Carolina, to Port Lyautey, in Morocco, by way of Newfoundland and the Azores, completing the 3,145-mile journey in eighty hours, including stops totalling twenty-two hours. In the following spring six blimps of the same squadron made a still faster crossing by way of Bermuda. The flight from Bermuda to the Azores, a distance of 1,881 miles, was the longest over water made up to that time by a pressure airship, and was completed in less than thirty hours.

Other airships used by the United States Navy on active service during the war included a few blimps of the M class, introduced in 1943. More than twenty of

Lighter-than-air patrol craft of the jet age: United States naval airships of the M and ZPG-3W classes in service from 1943 to 1956 and 1958 to 1962 respectively.

these were ordered, but only four were commissioned. Their capacity ranged from 625,000 to 647,000 feet, or 725,000 feet for a modified version in use just after the war. One of these modified M-class ships, the XM-1, set up a new endurance record in the early winter of 1946 by cruising off the East Coast of the United States and over the Caribbean for seven days on end.

In addition, seven small ships of the G class, numbered from G-2 to G-8, were completed during or immediately after the war and used as trainers. They were slightly larger than the G-1, but like her closely resembled the commercial airships built from time to time by Goodyear and used to advertise a variety of merchandise.

At the end of the war, many K-class ships were scrapped. Others were retained and used, in most cases after modification, for maritime reconnaissance during the period of tension that followed the Berlin crisis of 1948–9 and the Communist invasion of South Korea in 1950. At least one M-class ship remained in service until 1956. Meanwhile Goodyear introduced, with the N-1 of 1951, a new generation of relatively large pressure-airships capable of remaining on patrol for ten days or more without refuelling. The N-1 was 324 feet long, had a capacity of 875,000 cubic feet, and carried a crew of fourteen at speeds up to ninety miles an hour. She was followed by twelve 1,011,000-cubic-foot ships of the same class, each 343 feet long, and by five similar ships with built-in radar scanners. At a time when the Soviet Union seemed to be drawing ahead in the race to be first with intercontinental ballistic missiles, these were used to extend the range of the North American early-warning system by making continuous patrols off the East Coast of the United States. Dacron, a synthetic material which needs no special treatment to make it weatherproof and rotproof, was used from 1956 for the envelopes of all Goodyear airships.

A demand for even greater endurance led in 1958 to the introduction of exceptionally large pressure-airships of the ZPG-3W class. With these 400-foot-long, million-and-a-half-cubic-foot airships, Goodyear reached what is probably the practical limit of size for non-rigid airships, since larger blimps than these would be very difficult to handle on the ground. Four ships of the ZPG-ZW class were built, but one was lost when she collapsed in the air in 1960. In the same year an N-class airship of the sub-class ZPG-2 was used to carry observers of the first launching of a Polaris missile from a submerged submarine.

Routine patrols were suspended in 1961. Two airships retained for experimental purposes remained in service until the late

The Güldenring. *A Goodyear L-class blimp used by the United States Navy for some years as a trainer. Became the* Underbeg *in 1956, the* Güldenring *in 1959 and the* Schwab *in 1961. Sold in 1967 to a Japanese buyer.*

summer of 1962, and it was not until 1964 that the United States Navy disbanded the last of its airship units after nearly half a century of continuous development.

In recent years many references have appeared in the press to attempt to 'bring back the airship'. The phrase is misleading, for there has never been a time during the past ninety years or more when airships were not in service somewhere in the world. Countries in which civil airships of recent design and manufacture have flown since the end of the Second World War include Britain, Canada, Italy, Japan, the Soviet Union, West Germany and the United States. At the time of writing it is possible to order from a German manufacturer, for reasonably prompt delivery, a pressure airship to lift either a two-ton or a nine-ton payload. Orders for ships of both sizes have been placed, and considerably larger ships with correspondingly heavier payloads are projected.

Typical examples of the post-war small commercial airship are the Goodyear *America*, completed in the United States in 1959, and the same firm's *Europa*, assembled by British labour in a corner of the shed at Cardington which once housed the R.101. Soon after her completion in 1972, the *Europa* broke from her mast as a result of faulty mooring, and astonished a farmer some miles away by coming to rest within sight of his bedroom window. With a new envelope brought from the United States, she afterwards flew to Italy, where she was stationed during the winter of 1972–3. At one time it was intended that she should provide an airborne platform for television cameras during the Olympic Games at Munich, but the project was dropped for fear that her presence might revive unpleasant memories of the Nazi-organized games of 1936, at which the *Graf Zeppelin* was present.

About a dozen pressure airships, some of them designed by Nobile, were built in the Soviet Union between 1931 and 1938 and used either as passenger aircraft or to carry equipment and supplies to meteorological stations and scientific missions in areas otherwise hard to reach. The Soviet authorities seem then to have lost interest in lighter-than-air machines until in 1957 Professor A. G. Vorobyev, a leading authority on the subject, persuaded the Geographic Society of the Union of Soviet Socialist Republics to set up a committee in Leningrad for the study of aerostatics.[5] Work was begun in 1962 on a design for a small pressure-airship intended mainly for forestry, and at least one such airship, the LL-1, has been built and used for lifting

A newer ship built to substantially the same desigh as the Güldenring*: the* Braun sixtant *(formerly the* Trumpf*).*

timber and for fire-watching and fire-fighting in densely wooded areas. Pressure airships have also been used for lifting timber in British Columbia.

The Soviet authorities are also interested in developing relatively large semi-rigid airships as freight-carriers. Calculations made as the sequel to a conference of experts from all parts of the Soviet Union, held at Novosibirsk in 1965, were said to show that such airships could carry moderate loads over long distances at one-third of the cost of transport by fixed-wing aircraft and one-twelfth or less of the cost of transport by helicopter.[6] Russian advocates of lighter-than-air projects claim that 'hundreds of millions of roubles' could be saved if airships were used for the construction of a proposed power grid linking European Russia with a hydro-electric power station in Siberia.

However, as a rule when people speak of 'bringing back the airship' they have in mind not small pressure airships of the class represented by the *America*, the *Europa*, the LL-1 and their West German counterparts, but the large rigid airships of the nineteen-thirties.

To bring back these airships in the sense of making a fresh start where the designers of the nineteen-thirties left off would, of course, be pointless. The *Graf Zeppelin* and the *Hindenburg* would be as much out of place in the world of today as any of the heavier-than-air bombers, fighters and transport aircraft of their era.

Moreover, these prejet-age airships belong not only to a stage of development that has passed but also to a class of aircraft for which there is, at the moment, no demand so pressing that it cries out for attention. It is true that large rigid airships could be produced today which would carry passengers to their destinations more cheaply, in greater comfort and with far less deleterious effects on the environment than contemporary airliners are capable of doing, and that their lower speed would be offset to some extent by greater freedom in the choice of sites for arrival and departure. But no urgent need of an alternative to the heavier-than-air machine as a passenger-carrying aircraft has yet declared itself in the capitalist world. What the capitalist world does need, according to experts who have studied problems of transportation in the light of first principles, is a more efficient and more expeditious method of carrying manufactured and partly-manufactured goods from producer to distributor than the present complex of surface systems can provide. It is this need which, in the opinion of some of them, makes it imperative not that the large passenger-carrying airships of the nineteen-thirties should be brought back, but that the large rigid airship should be re-invented as a cargo-carrier.

So far as the experts are concerned, this opinion does not reflect a mere sentimental attachment to the airships of the past, or to airships in general. It stems from their awareness that, so far as can be seen at present, the airship is the only form of transport that can meet tomorrow's needs. Trains are confined to railways, lorries to roads and ferries. Fixed-wing aeroplanes can operate only between airports, ocean-going ships between seaports or ports linked with the sea by deep-water canals. Helicopters, if they could be made large enough to carry heavy loads, would be grossly inefficient and their running costs would be prohibitive. Airships designed to hover and to dispense with mooring masts would be comparatively cheap to run, could go anywhere except across high mountain ranges, and could move goods without transhipment between virtually any point on the surface of the earth and virtually any other point. They could carry homogeneous or miscellaneous cargoes in containers from, say, Birmingham to Milan in six to eight hours, from the United Kingdom to Australia in four days. They could also lift large indivisible loads, thus greatly simplifying the manufacture of certain electrical and engineering products which have at present to be made in several pieces and assembled on site.

Some of these considerations have occurred to men who are not transportation experts. As long ago as 1958 an American Presbyterian minister with naval connections, Monroe Drew, conceived the idea of building a 'Faith Fleet' of large airships for the twofold purpose of carrying food, bibles and trade goods to undeveloped countries and of earning large sums of money which could be used to finance further evangelistic enterprises. In the following year Drew met John Fitzpatrick, a naval officer and former naval rating with a considerable experience of blimps. He raised substantial sums of money from members of his flock and other sympathizers, formed a company called the Aereon Corporation, and persuaded Fitzpatrick to

The Cardington-built Europa *of 1972.*

join him on his retirement from the navy. The company's name was taken from that of an unpowered but allegedly dirigible balloon devised in the eighteen-sixties by Solomon Andrews, a medical practitioner and gifted inventor who was mayor of Perth Amboy, New Jersey, during and after the Civil War.[7]

Fitzpatrick designed for the Aereon Corporation an airship which resembled the original Aereon in being eighty feet long and of trilobe configuration, but differed from her in being powered by a cheap four-cylinder engine. He calculated that the hull, because of its flattened elliptical cross-section, would act as a primitive aerofoil. The ship would take off under power and would not, therefore, have to be lighter than air in order to fly. This would make her, in Fitzpatrick's judgement, easier to handle on the ground than a conventional airship. At the same time, the 50,000 cubic feet of helium in her gas-bags would provide additional lift, and for this reason the new Aereon would be far cheaper to run than an aeroplane of comparable payload. Furthermore, only a short runway would be needed.

The ship, intended as a scaled-down prototype of much larger Aereons with payloads of the order of 200 tons, was built to Fitzpatrick's design by a retired airship rigger named Everett Linkenhoker. She took a long time to complete, but never flew. While moving along a runway on 15 April 1966 she failed to respond to her controls and was abandoned by her crew and wrecked.

Drew and Fitzpatrick than asked the General Electric Space Center's computer at Valley Forge, Pennsylvania, to work out the optimum configuration for an aircraft intended to combine the virtues of an airship with some of the more desirable qualities of an aeroplane. In effect, the computer's answer was that such an aircraft should resemble a delta-wing or dart-shaped aeroplane in plan and an airship of sorts in elevation. This answer was, however, based on the assumption that aircraft of substantial size, endurance and payload would be required. When calculation showed that an aircraft of the shape proposed by the computer would derive no significant advantage from carrying helium unless it was fairly large the company decided, with what seems an odd lack of logic, to build a number of models which would contain no helium and would not, therefore, be airships in any sense, but merely aeroplanes of a rather awkward and inefficient kind.

Soon afterwards Drew fell out with Fitzpatrick and lost control of the company to William Miller, a God-fearing capitalist who held the degree of Master of

GOODYEAR
GOODYEAR
SCANIA

Theology but was not a practising clergyman. After a series of four-foot-long models had been tested without success at Lakehurst, Miller ordered from a well-known builder of model aeroplanes a model less than two feet long, propelled by a single hank of twisted rubber. This made a successful flight towards the end of 1967 in a hangar at Mercer County Airport, New Jersey.

Finally, tests were made in 1970 and 1971 with a seven-foot-long remotely-controlled model and a piloted version nominally twenty-six feet long but in fact somewhat longer. These showed that an aircraft of the configuration worked out by the computer but with no helium to give aerostatic lift could be coaxed to fly at moderate heights and speeds. Whether the much larger, helium-filled 'aerobodies' the Aereon Corporation would like to build would be successful remains an open question.

Less controversial projects which have attracted substantial support in a number of countries envisage rigid airships of orthodox appearance with capacities ranging from 10,000,000 to 40,000,000 cubic feet. New methods of calculation and construction and the use of synthetic materials would make such airships easier and relatively much cheaper to build than the large rigid airships of the past. Since the world's output of helium has risen by some 1,600 per cent in the past twenty years and could be expanded at a still greater rate with a corresponding reduction in cost, the supply of gas to fill the airships of the future should present no problem.

Nuclear propulsion for airships has been proposed by the American Professor A. N. Morse and by some European experts, but its adoption seems likely to be delayed for some years by disadvantages which include the weight of nuclear reactors and their shields, their high initial cost, and the difficulty of convincing the ordinary citizen that they could be used without undue risk in an aircraft which might crash. Despite the millions of passenger-miles flown since 1909, no fare-paying passenger apart from the thirteen killed when the hydrogen-filled *Hindenburg* was destroyed has ever lost his life in an accident to a commercial airship. The nervousness of the general public in face of many mishaps to naval and military airships is none the less a factor that has to be borne in mind when the future of lighter-than-air machines is discussed.

The widely held though mistaken belief that airships are inherently more dangerous than aeroplanes has not prevented proposals for the revival of passenger services from being ventilated in Germany and Soviet Russia. A German proposal in 1958 for a 9,300,000-cubic-foot airship

'Lifting Body Airship' or 'Dynairship', proposed in 1967 by the Aereon Corporation, of New Jersey. Since that date the Corporation's ideas have been modified to some extent in the light of experiments with the Aereon 26 of 1970–1.

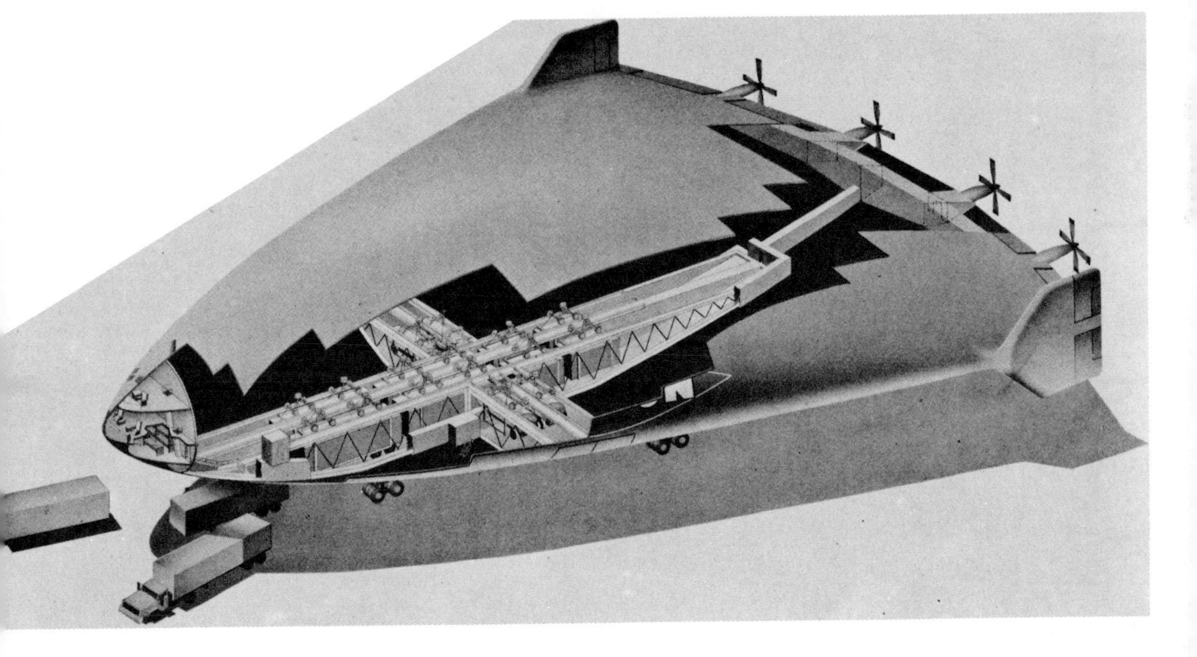

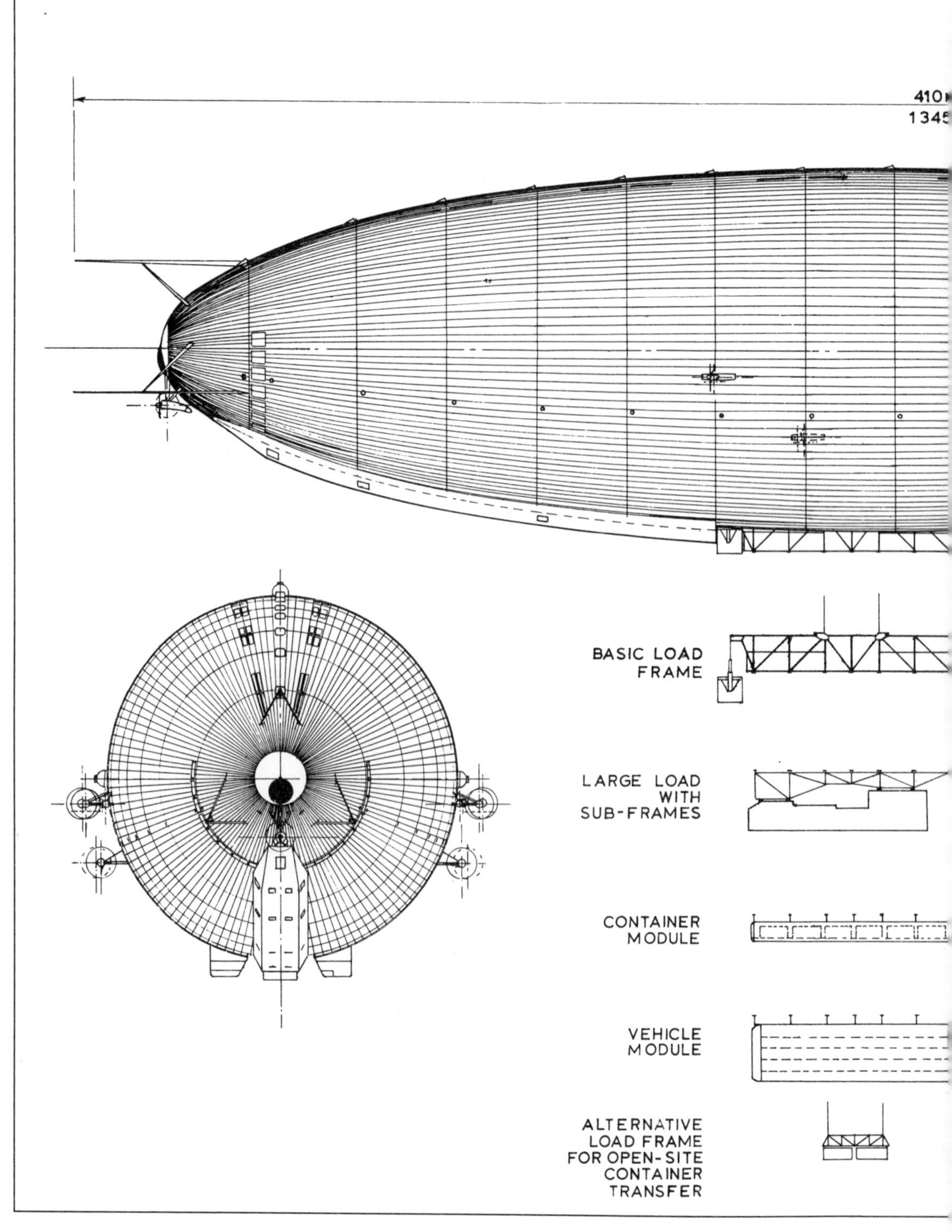

Scale drawings of large freight-carrying airship designed by Dr E. Mowforth for Airfloat Transport Limited.

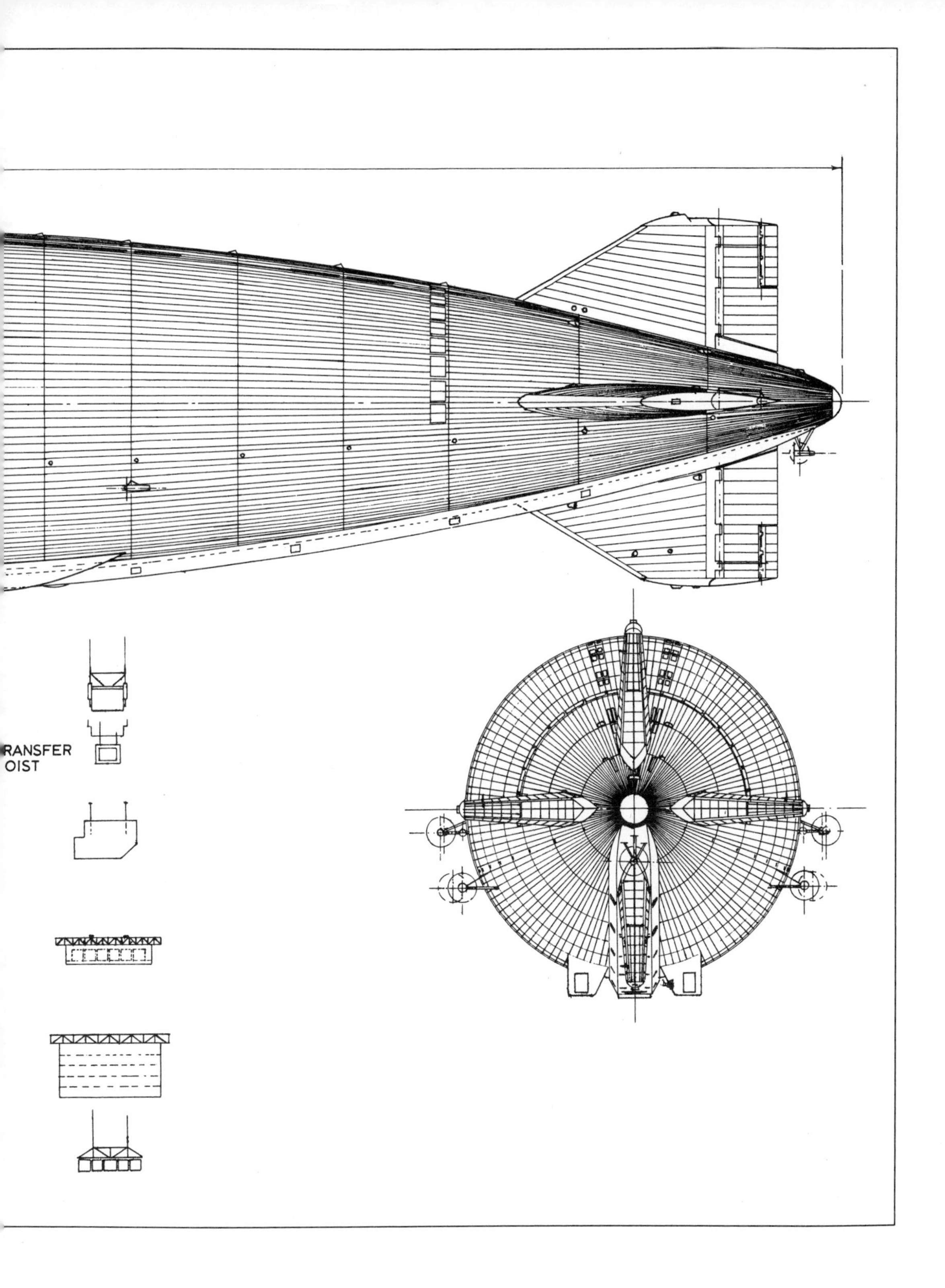
RANSFER
OIST

Model of large airship proposed by Aerospace Developments for possible use by Shell International to move natural gas from one part of the world to another.

'suitable for the tourist trade' failed to find a backer, but more recently at least two West German shipbuilding firms have shown interest in building rigid airships suitable for carrying both goods and passengers between European cities. According to a report from Moscow, work began in the Soviet Union towards the end of 1970 on an 18,000,000-cubic-foot 'super-airship' intended to carry up to 500 passengers, as well as mail and freight, at speeds in the region of 150 miles an hour on transcontinental and intercontinental routes.[8] Although confirmation of this report is hard to find, the construction of such an airship would be in line with the known trend of Soviet thinking during the years when the project is said to have been under consideration. Airships with accommodation for hundreds of passengers or an equivalent number of troops would, of course, be particularly useful to the Russians in view of the sparseness of their surface communications and the vast distances separating the maritime provinces from European Russia.

Since Britain's past prosperity was founded largely on the development of her merchant navy, it is natural that the usefulness of the airships of the future as cargo-carriers should outweigh all other considerations in the eyes of British experts. The same is broadly true of the Netherlands, whose mercantile marine was the basis of her Far Eastern trade and made her a world power. In two articles in *Holland Shipbuilding* Robert Harthoorn has described the technical characteristics of an imaginary 24,000,000-cubic-foot airship intended to compete as a freight-carrier with the Boeing 747 F Jumbo Jet on the Amsterdam–New York route. Propulsion would be by seven diesel engines, each of some 2,000 horse-power. Harthoorn's hypothetical airship would take about four and a half times as long to complete the voyage as the freighter version of the Boeing, but her payload would be three or four times as great and her operating costs on a ton–mile basis, including interest on an estimated initial cost of 20,000,000 United States dollars, would be some thirty per cent lower.[9] Doubling the gas capacity of the ship by increasing her length from 315 to 385 metres and her maximum diameter from seventy to eighty-six metres would multiply her payload by a factor of 2·2 to 2·5 and should result in a considerable saving even when the higher cost of the larger airship is taken into account.

British transportation experts envisage airships with gas capacities of the order of 30,000,000 to 40,000,000 cubic feet. Some of them see little advantage in building merely one or two airships of that size, believing that the aim should be to create a new transportation system with its own means of transport in the shape of a whole fleet of cargo-carrying airships ready to operate on scheduled routes. They claim that the existence of such a system would itself create a demand for its services and thus go far to ensure the maximum utilization which seems essential if airships are to be made to pay. Others point out that, since airships of the size proposed would be capable of shifting loads which cannot be carried by any means of transport now available, even a single airship of that kind could be a valuable possession.

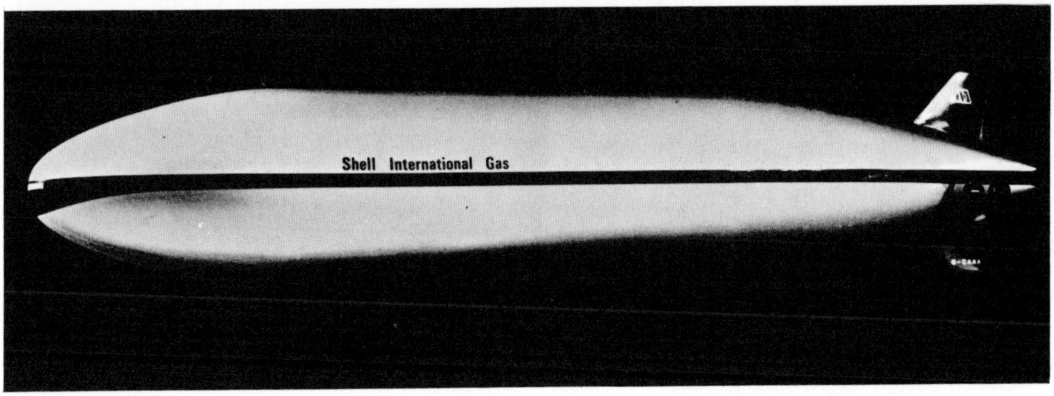

In recent years two British firms, Airfloat Transport Limited and Cargo Airships Limited, have studied these problems in depth. Both recognize that, should a new system of transportation be created, it would stand or fall largely by its ability to provide direct delivery of goods which have at present to be shuttled from one system to another, with the result that costs pile up and time is lost. The system would have to be independent of existing terminals, and methods of loading and unloading would be crucial. On the other hand, exceptionally high speeds would not be needed. An airship engaged on such a task as the shifting of an electrical transformer too heavy and bulky to be delivered by road or rail would have no competitors. Where airships did enter into competition with other means of transport, Harthoorn's comparison with the Boeing 747 F would seldom apply. On most routes the cargo airship would be competing not with jet-propelled heavier-than-air machines but with relatively slow surface vessels, or with a combination of air and surface systems whose overall average speed is at present fairly low, and is likely to become lower still as congestion of surface systems increases. Airships capable of maintaining an average speed of 100 miles an hour in all weathers and of providing a door-to-door service would compete on favourable terms with existing systems on most routes where an alternative means of transport was available. Diesel, diesel-electric or gas-turbine engines would provide this performance without difficulty, but might eventually be replaced by nuclear reactors since these would be virtually silent and would give almost unlimited range without refuelling.

A team headed by Dr E. Mowforth, of the Department of Mechanical Engineering in the University of Surrey, has designed for Airfloat Transport Limited, of which company Dr Mowforth is a director, a rigid airship of orthodox appearance with a gas capacity of approximately 40,000,000 cubic feet. Ships built to this design would be assembled on a turntable and would live in the open air.[10] Cargo would be loaded and unloaded by built-in winches. Mr B. R. V. Hughes, Managing Director of Airfloat Transport Limited, estimates that the first airships could be ready within thirty to thirty-six months of his receiving the order to go ahead.

An obvious advantage of this method of loading and unloading is that it renders the airship independent of external aids such as cranes or lighters. An objection sometimes made to it is that the weight of the winches encroaches unduly on the payload. However, with a theoretical payload of 500 tons for short hauls of 600 miles or less, Dr Mowforth's airship should be a respectable performer even at intercontinental ranges. For example, if we take the distance between suitable points of departure and arrival in the United Kingdom and North America to be 3,400 miles, multiply by a factor of two in the interests of safety and deduct one ton from the short-haul payload for every twenty-five miles of additional distance flown, we are left with the not unimpressive figure of 252 tons as the payload which the ship could carry on transatlantic flights without refuelling. On longer hauls, or where a bigger payload was essential, the airship could be refuelled in flight.

Cargo Airships Limited is an offshoot of Manchester Liners Limited, a company which operates in association with Furness, Withy and Company Limited a fast container service by ocean liner between the United Kingdom and Canada. As pioneers in their particular field, the directors of Manchester Liners Limited read with considerable interest one of a series of articles in which a writer named M. J. Rynish expressed the opinion that the principle of containerization was 'utterly right and absolutely logical', but added that the mistake that was being made lay in trying to impose it upon 'the jumbled mixture of surface systems which we have inherited from our forefathers'.[11] They asked Mr Rynish to call on them. At the end of a long talk he agreed to supervise an inquiry into the problem of developing airships suitable for a container service. Cargo Airships Limited was formed for the purpose as a subsidiary of Manchester Liners Limited, with Mr Rynish as Managing Director. Mr Peter White, formerly Chief Aerodynamicist of Handley Page Limited, joined the organization on the technical side.

Max Rynish believes that it is essential to create a system, not merely to build a few airships. At the same time he recognizes that a comprehensive system must evolve gradually. He suggests starting with daily services on one route, say from

Ulster to Munich by way of Birmingham and the Ruhr. As more airships became available, further routes would be opened and services would become more frequent. Mr Rynish has outlined a network linking Britain with all parts of Europe, and also linking all parts of Europe, through Britain, with North and South America, the Far East and Australasia. For Europeans the development of such a system would have the advantage of making Europe once again the centre of a world-wide carrying trade – a state of affairs likely to be particularly beneficial to the British. At the same time it would confer on other nations, and especially on undeveloped countries at present hampered by poor internal communications, benefits comparable in some respects with those which followed the opening of British ports and markets to the whole world after the Napoleonic Wars.

To meet the needs of a world-wide air-oriented cargo system, the staff of Cargo Airships Limited have designed a family of airships to be constructed with stressed metal skins, on the principle of the ZMC-2 of more than forty years ago, and with the flattened elliptical cross-section proposed by Commander Burney in 1929 to facilitate hovering flight. Hovering flight would also be assisted by shrouded airscrews mounted on swivelling axes which could be turned through 180 degrees. The largest of these ships would be capable of carrying up to fifty ten-ton containers at a time, and her range would be virtually unlimited since she would be refuelled in flight. Essentially she would consist of two helium-filled, sausage-shaped cells, or 'pontoons', connected by girders. Additional helium would be contained in nose and tail fairings.

The company does not propose, however, that ships large enough to carry a 500-ton payload should be built immediately. The proposal is that a start should be made with a scaled-down prototype which would provide experimental data and also bring in revenue. The construction of a fairly large number of these small ships might be followed by the introduction of an intermediate version with a payload of, approximately 100 to 200 tons. Only when experience had been gained with these ships would construction of the 500-tonner be undertaken.

Until recently, Cargo Airships Limited proposed that loading and unloading should be done by straddle helicopters. These would be expensive, and dorsal hatches would have to be provided so that loading and unloading could be done from above. It is now proposed that the ships should be loaded and unloaded from below by small airships similar in appearance and general character to the mother ship.

These aerial lighters would not need to be very large, since only one container would have to be lifted at a time.

Another possibility is that specially-designed large airships might be used to carry natural gas from one part of the world to another. A firm of consultants, Aerospace Developments, has investigated this possibility on behalf of Shell International Gas Limited. The project seems technically feasible; whether it will be judged economically viable is, of course, a different matter.

Hitherto most British champions of the large rigid airship have been so keenly aware of a prejudice against lighter-than-air machines in English-speaking countries that they have been careful to disclaim any intention of recommending airships as passenger aircraft. Nevertheless it is only to be expected that, if airships with big payloads are reintroduced as cargo-carriers and prove successful, their usefulness for other purposes will become apparent. The large rigid airship is not likely to *supersede* the passenger-carrying heavier-than-air machine in the foreseeable future. Nor, for that matter, will it replace the surface vessel as a carrier of bulk cargoes such as oil and grain. But it might well provide an alternative means of transport for travellers who cannot spare the time for long sea voyages but who find – as many do – that covering thousands of miles in a few hours unsettles them so much as to render them unfit to transact business for some hours after their arrival. An up-to-date transatlantic airship service would enable a man with business interests on both sides of the Atlantic to do a full week's work in London, spend most of Saturday at home, and arrive in New York, refreshed and relaxed by a comfortable journey and a good night's rest, in ample time to keep an appointment on Monday morning. During the journey he would be able to walk about the ship, eat, sleep, read and write or dictate letters with the same ease as if he were at home or staying at a first-class hotel.

Airships could also be a boon for short journeys of a few hundred miles. There is no reason why helium-filled airships, once they were accepted as a safe and reliable means of transport, should not be allowed to embark and disembark passengers in built-up areas. Instead of motoring to Heathrow or taking a train to Gatwick, a traveller bound from London to Paris would then be able to step into an airship from the roof of a high building in the centre of London at, say, 6.30 p.m., drink a duty-free whisky and soda over the Channel, and step out of the airship within sight of the Place de la Concorde in ample time for dinner. Many European capitals

External view of new design for simple-technology freighter airship, codename the Transporter, *developed by Cargo Airships Limited, London. Payload: 500 tons carried in fifty ten-ton standard ISO containers. Airspeed: around 100 mph. Range: virtually unlimited when refuelled air-to-air. Cargo, fuel, crew, etc. ferried up to transporter by smaller airship of same basic proportions.*

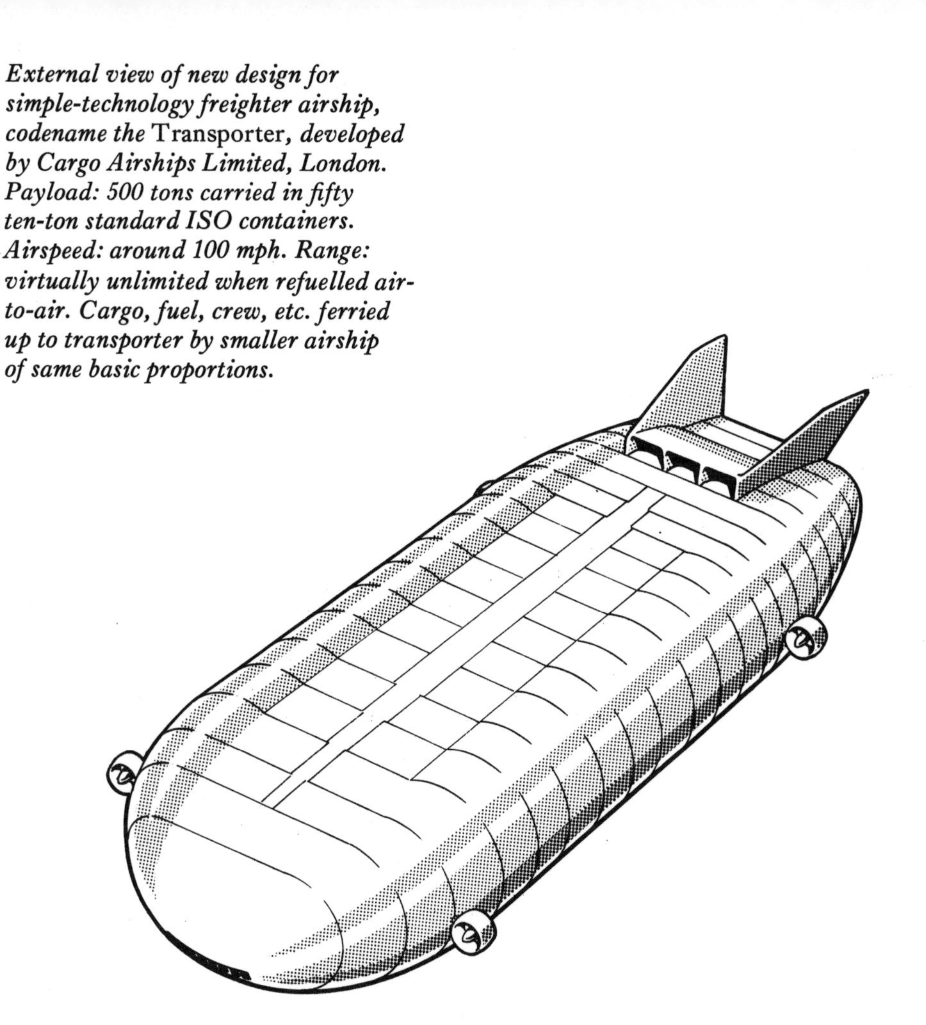

could be reached by fast airship from the centre of London in little more time than is spent at present in travelling from city centre to airport and from airport to city centre.

Again, airships with accommodation for large numbers of passengers could be extremely useful to the British Army, not as weapons of war but merely as a means of transport. Britain is under an obligation to maintain troops on the mainland of Europe for many years to come, and these troops have to be relieved from time to time. Troops have also to be shuttled between their depots and trouble-spots such as Northern Ireland. To carry out troop movements the army relies at present on an assortment of vehicles which includes aircraft chartered from commercial airlines and trains moving on a foreign rail system over which the British government has no control and which could be paralysed at a moment of crisis for the North Atlantic Treaty Powers by industrial unrest. A single large airship owned by the Ministry of Defence, or available on charter, could move a whole brigade from its assembly area in the United Kingdom to its ultimate destination in North-West Germany in one lift.

Appendix 1

German rigid airships completed before the First World War

LZ.1 Completed 1900. Capacity 399,000 cubic feet, length 420 feet, two fifteen-hp. Daimler engines. Speed sixteen mph. Broken up in 1901 after three flights.

LZ.2 Completed 1905. Similar to LZ.1, but two seventy-five-hp. Daimler engines. Speed unknown. Wrecked by storm in 1906 when incorrectly moored after second flight.

LZ.3 Completed 1906, rebuilt 1909. Similar to LZ.1 and LZ.2, but two eighty-five-hp. Daimler engines. Speed twenty-seven mph. Bought by German Army and became Z.1. Broken up in 1913.

LZ.4 Completed 1908. Capacity 529,800 cubic feet, length 446 feet, two 105-hp. Daimler engines. Speed thirty mph. Intended for German Army, but wrecked during acceptance flight in 1908.

LZ.5 Completed 1909. Similar to LZ.4. Bought by German Army and became Z.2. Wrecked in 1910.

LZ.6 Completed 1909. Similar to LZ.5. Intended for German Army but not accepted. Accidentally burnt in 1910.

LZ.7 Completed 1910. Similar to LZ.6 but Maybach engines. Acquired by DELAG and became *Deutschland.* Wrecked in 1910.

LZ.8 Completed 1911. Similar to LZ.7. Acquired by DELAG and became *Ersatz Deutschland.* Seriously damaged in 1911 by collision with shed.

LZ.9 Completed 1911. Capacity 628,700 cubic feet, length 459 feet, three 150-hp. Maybach engines. Speed forty-seven mph. Bought by German Army and became *Ersatz Z.2.* Broken up in 1914.

LZ.10 Completed 1911. Similar to LZ.9. Acquired by DELAG and became *Schwaben.* Wrecked by gale and fire in 1912.

LZ.11 Completed 1912. Capacity 659,700 cubic feet, length 485 feet, three 105-hp. Maybach engines. Speed forty-seven mph. Acquired by DELAG and became *Viktoria-Luise.* Requisitioned by German Army and afterwards transferred to German Navy. Used as trainer. Wrecked in 1915.

LZ.12 Completed 1912. Capacity 628,700 cubic feet, length 459 feet, three 150-hp. Maybach engines. Speed forty-seven mph. Bought by German Army and became Z.3. Broken up in summer of 1914.

LZ.13 Completed 1912. Capacity 659,700 cubic feet, length 485 feet, three 180-hp. Maybach engines. Speed fifty mph. Acquired by DELAG and became *Hansa.* Requisitioned by German Army. Broken up in 1916.

LZ.14 Completed 1912. Capacity 793,600 cubic feet, length 518 feet, three 170-hp. Maybach engines. Speed twenty-nine mph. Bought by German Navy and became L.1. Lost at sea during naval manoeuvres in 1913.

LZ.15 Completed 1913. Capacity 690,500 cubic feet, length 459 feet, three 180-hp. Maybach engines. Speed forty-eight mph. Bought by German Army and became *Ersatz Z.1.* Wrecked in summer of 1914.

LZ.16 Completed 1913. Similar to LZ.15. Bought by German Army and became Z.4. Broken up by 1917.

LZ.17 Completed 1913. Capacity 688,000 cubic feet, length 462 feet, three 180-hp. Maybach engines. Speed forty-seven mph. Acquired by DELAG and became *Sachsen*. Requisitioned by German Army and afterwards transferred to German Navy. Used as trainer. Broken up in 1916.

LZ.18 Completed 1913. Capacity 953,600 feet, length 518 feet, four 180-hp. Maybach engines. Speed forty-seven mph. Bought by German Navy and became L.2. Wrecked by explosion in 1913.

LZ.19 Completed 1913. Similar to LZ.15. Bought by German Army and became second *Ersatz Z.1*. Wrecked in summer of 1914.

LZ.20 Completed 1913. Similar to LZ.15. Bought by German Army and became Z.5. Landed behind Russian lines in 1914 after being damaged by gunfire.

LZ.21 Completed 1913. Capacity 737,100 cubic feet, length 485 feet, three 180-hp. Maybach engines. Speed forty-six mph. Bought by German Army and became Z.6. Crashed in Germany after being damaged by gunfire over Liège on 6 August 1914.

LZ.22 Completed January 1914. Capacity 782,000 cubic feet, length 512 feet, three 180-hp. Maybach engines. Speed forty-five mph. Bought by German Army and became Z.7. Crashed behind French lines in 1914 after being damaged by gunfire.

LZ.23 Completed February 1914. Similar to LZ.22. Bought by German Army and became Z.8. Brought down by gunfire in France in 1914.

LZ.24 Completed May 1914. Capacity 793,600 cubic feet, length 518 feet, three 210-hp. Maybach engines. Speed fifty-three mph. Bought by German Navy and became L.3. Wrecked in 1915 by forced landing in Danish territorial waters.

LZ.25 Completed July 1914. Similar to LZ.22. Bought by German Army and became Z.9. Destroyed in shed at Düsseldorf by British aircraft in October 1914.

SL.1 Completed 1911. Capacity 750,000 cubic feet, length 420 feet, three 180-hp. Maybach engines. Speed thirty-eight mph. Bought by German Army and retained manufacturer's designation. Broken up in summer of 1914.

SL.2 Completed 1914. Capacity 882,750 cubic feet, length 472 feet, four 180-hp. Maybach engines. Speed fifty-four mph. Bought by German Army and retained manufacturer's designation. Wrecked in 1916.

Appendix 2

German naval airships, 1914-1918

Rigid Airships (*Zeppelin*)

L.3 Class (capacity 793,600–879,500 cubic feet, length 518–29 feet, speed fifty-three mph, ceiling 9,300–10,200 feet):
L.3, L.4, L.5, L.6, L.7, L.8, L.9

L.10 Class (capacity 1,126,700 cubic feet, length 536 feet, speed sixty-one mph, ceiling 12,800 feet):
L.10, L.11, L.12, L.13, L.14, L.15, L.16, L.17, L.18, L.19

L.20 Class (capacity 1,264,400 cubic feet, length 586 feet, speed fifty-nine mph, ceiling 13,800 feet):
L.20, L.21, L.22, L.23, L.24

L.25 Class (capacity 1,126,700 feet, length 536 feet, speed sixty-one mph, ceiling 12,800 feet):
L.25 (a rebuilt version of the army airship LZ.88)

L.30 Class (capacity 1,949,600 cubic feet, length 649 feet, speed sixty-four mph, ceiling 17,700 feet):
L.30, L.31, L.32, L.33, L.34, L.35, L.36, L.37, L.38, L.39, L.40, L.41

L.42 Class (capacity 1,960,000–1,977,900 cubic feet, length 645–649 feet, speed sixty-two–seventy-one mph, ceiling 17,000–24,000 feet):
L.42, L.43, L.44, L.45, L.46, L.47, L.48, L.49, L.50, L.51, L.52, L.53, L.54, L.55, L.56, L.58, L.60, L.61, L.62, L.63, L.64, L.65

L.57 Class (capacity 2,419,400 cubic feet, length 743 feet, speed sixty-seven mph, ceiling 26,900 feet):
L.57, L.59

L.70 Class (capacity 2,196,900 cubic feet, length 694 feet, speed eighty-one mph, ceiling 23,000 feet):
L.70, L.71 (L.72)

Rigid Airships (*Schütte-Lanz*)

SL.3 Class (capacity 1,147,575 cubic feet, length 513 feet, speed fifty mph, ceiling 7,900 feet):
SL.3, SL.4

SL.6 Class (capacity 1,239,380 cubic feet, length 534 feet, speed fifty-eight mph, ceiling 8,500 feet):
SL.6

SL.8 Class (capacity 1,370,000 cubic feet, length 571 feet, speed fifty-eight mph, ceiling 11,500 feet):
SL.8, SL.9, SL.12, SL.14

SL.20 Class (capacity 1,989,700 cubic feet, length 651 feet, speed sixty-three mph, ceiling 16,400 feet):
SL.20, SL.22

Non-rigid Airships (*Parseval*)

PL.6 (capacity 282,500 cubic feet, speed thirty-three mph)

PL. 19 (capacity 363,700 cubic feet, speed forty-eight mph)

PL.25 (capacity 473,150 cubic feet, speed forty-four mph)

Non-rigid Airship (*Gross-Basenach*)

M.IV (taken over from army, November 1914) (capacity 688,550 cubic feet, speed fifty mph)

Appendix 3

German military airships, 1914-1918

Rigid Airships (Zeppelin)

Z.4 Class (capacity 690,500 cubic feet, length 459 feet, speed forty-eight mph, ceiling 5,900 feet):
Z.4, Z.5

Z.6 Class (capacity 737,100 cubic feet, length 485 feet, speed forty-six mph, ceiling 9,200 feet):
Z.6

Z.7 Class (capacity 782,000 cubic feet, length 512 feet, speed forty-five mph, ceiling 9,200 feet):
Z.7, Z.8

Z.9 Class (capacity 793,600 cubic feet, length 518 feet, speed fifty-three mph, ceiling 9,300 feet):
Z.9, Z.10, Z.11, LZ.34, LZ.35, LZ.37

Z.12 Class (capacity 883,000 cubic feet, length 529 feet, speed fifty mph, ceiling 11,800 feet):
Z.12

LZ.38 Class (capacity 1,126,700 cubic feet, length 536 feet, speed sixty-one mph, ceiling 12,800 feet):
LZ.38

LZ.39 Class (capacity 879,500 cubic feet, length 529 feet, speed fifty-three mph, ceiling 10,200 feet):
LZ.39

LZ.72 Class (capacity 1,126,700 cubic feet, length 536 feet, speed sixty-one mph, ceiling 12,800 feet):
LZ.72, LZ.74, LZ.77, LZ.79, LZ.81, LZ.85, LZ.86, LZ.87, LZ.88, LZ.90, LZ.93

LZ.95 Class (capacity 1,264,400 cubic feet, length 586 feet, speed fifty-nine mph, ceiling 13,800 feet):
LZ.95, LZ.97, LZ.98, LZ.101, LZ.103, LZ.107, LZ.111

LZ.113 Class (capacity 1,949,600 cubic feet, length 649 feet, speed sixty-four mph, ceiling 17,700 feet):
LZ.113, LZ.120

Rigid Airships (Schütte-Lanz)

SL.2 Class (capacity 882,750 cubic feet, length 472 feet, speed fifty-four mph, ceiling 6,200 feet):
SL.2

SL.5 Class (capacity 1,147,575 cubic feet, length 513 feet, speed fifty mph, ceiling 7,900 feet):
SL.5

SL.7 Class (capacity 1,239,380 cubic feet, length 534 feet, speed fifty-eight mph, ceiling 8,500 feet):
SL.7

SL.10 Class (capacity 1,370,000 cubic feet, length 571 feet, speed fifty-eight mph, ceiling 11,500 feet):
SL.10, SL.11, SL.13, SL.15, SL.16, SL.17

SL.21 Class (capacity 1,989,700 cubic feet, length 651 feet, speed sixty-three mph, ceiling 16,400 feet):
SL.21

Non-Rigid Airship (Parseval)

P.IV (capacity 388,100 cubic feet, speed forty-six mph)

Non-Rigid Airship (Gross-Basenach)

M.IV (handed to navy, November 1914) (capacity 688,550 cubic feet, speed fifty mph)

Appendix 4

United States naval airships, 1916-1964

Rigid Airships

ZR-1 (Shenandoah) Capacity 2,115,000 cubic feet, length 680 feet, speed sixty mph. Built to a design based by the Bureau of Aeronautics on drawings and descriptions of the German L.49. Assembled at the Naval Air Station, Lakehurst, New Jersey, from parts constructed by the Naval Aircraft Factory at the Philadelphia Navy Yard. Completed in 1923. Used chiefly for research and training, but took part in one naval exercise with the Scouting Fleet and two minor operations with the battleship *Texas*. Broke up in a storm over Ohio in 1925.

ZR-2 (R.38) Capacity 997,500 cubic feet, length 535 feet, speed about sixty-two mph. Construction at Cardington, Bedfordshire, England, begun by Short Brothers and completed by Royal Airship Works. Broke up during a trial flight over the Humber, England, in 1921.

ZR-3 (LZ.126, Los Angeles) Capacity 2,472,000 cubic feet, length 658 feet, speed seventy-six mph. Built by Luftschiffbau-Zeppelin in Germany and flown to the United States in 1924. Use for warlike purposes forbidden by international agreement, but took part occasionally in naval exercises and made many demonstration flights. Taken out of service in 1932. Recommissioning as trainer proposed in June 1933, but countermanded in July. Thereafter used from time to time for mooring trials. Scrapped in 1940.

ZRS-4 (Akron) Capacity 6,500,000 cubic feet, length 785 feet. Contract speed eighty-four mph, maximum attained on trial about eighty-one mph. Built in the United States by the Goodyear-Zeppelin Corporation, an offshoot of the Goodyear Tire and Rubber Company and Luftschiffbau-Zeppelin. Completed in 1931. Took part in two naval exercises and made many demonstration flights. Wrecked off the East Coast of the United States during a storm in 1933.

ZRS-5 (Macon) Identical with the ZRS-4 except for minor modifications which made her about three and a half tons lighter and some four miles an hour faster. Completed in 1933. Took part in many naval exercises. Wrecked off the West Coast of the United States during a storm in 1935.

Pressure Airships

Between 1916 and 1958 the United States Navy acquired well over 250 American-built pressure airships, but the figure is reduced to 220 or so if ships recommissioned after modification are counted only once. In addition twenty-one foreign-built pressure airships were acquired during or shortly after the First World War, but only seven of these were shipped to the United States. The American-built ships are grouped below in classes or categories listed as far as possible in the order of their appearance. Ships delivered after 1919 can be assumed to have been built by the Goodyear Tire and Rubber Company or the Goodyear Aerospace Corporation unless the contrary is stated.

DN-1 Capacity 150,000 cubic feet, length 175 feet, speed not known. Built by the Connecticut Aircraft Company and delivered in 1916. Scrapped in 1917.

B Class Capacity 75,000 to 84,000 cubic feet, length 156 to 167 feet, speed about fifty mph. Sixteen ships of this class, numbered from B-1 to B-16, were delivered in 1917 and 1918. Three of them were rebuilt and numbered from B-17 to B-19, and a new ship, the B-20, was afterwards completed. The builders were Goodyear, Goodrich, and the Connecticut Aircraft Company. Used for anti-submarine patrols and convoy escort.

C Class Capacity 181,000 cubic feet, length 192 feet, speed sixty mph. About ten airships of this class, some built by Goodyear and others by Goodrich, were delivered in or after 1918. They were intended for anti-submarine patrols and convoy escort, but two were transferred to the United States Army when the army became responsible in 1921 for off-shore coast-defence patrols.

D Class (D-6 excluded) Capacity 189,000 cubic feet, length 198 feet, speed fifty-six mph. Five ships of this class were delivered in 1919. Three were built by Goodyear, two by Goodrich. One was destroyed by fire in 1919; the others were transferred to the United States Army in 1921.

E Class Capacity 95,000 cubic feet, length 162 feet, speed fifty-six mph. The sole representative of this class was the E-1. She was built by Goodyear in 1919 for commercial use but afterwards bought by the navy.

F Class Capacity 95,000 cubic feet, length 162 feet, speed fifty-two mph. The F-1, again the sole representative of her class, resembled the E-1 in all respects save that her engine was less powerful. She, too, was built by Goodyear in 1919 for commercial use but bought by the navy.

D-6 Capacity 181,000 cubic feet, length 192 feet, speed not known. A 'one-off' airship which combined a C-class envelope with a car built by the Naval Aircraft Factory. Completed in 1920 and destroyed by fire in 1921.

H Class Capacity 35,000 cubic feet, length ninety-five feet, speed not known. Only one ship of this class was built. She was delivered in 1921 and destroyed by fire in the same year.

J Class Capacity 210,000 cubic feet, length 196 feet, speed sixty mph. Three ships of this class were acquired by the navy between 1922 and 1927. One was lost at sea in 1933 during a search for survivors from the *Akron*. Another was used for a time by the United States Army but afterwards reverted to the navy. She was scrapped in 1940.

G-1 Capacity 178,000 cubic feet, length 184 feet, speed sixty-two mph. This ship differed considerably from the G-class ships mentioned below. She was built by Goodyear in 1929 for commercial use and acquired by the navy in 1935.

ZMC-2 Capacity 200,000 cubic feet, length 149 feet, speed sixty-two mph. This remarkable craft was unique among pressure airships in having a thin but strong and gas-tight metal envelope with riveted seams. Intended as the prototype of a new generation of metal airships with capacities up to 10,000,000 cubic feet, she was designed by Ralph H. Upson (assisted by V. H. Pavlecka and others) for the Airship Development Corporation (afterwards the Metalclad Airship Corporation) of Detroit, Michigan. She was completed in 1929, when she made a trouble-free delivery flight from Detroit to Lakehurst. Although formally removed from the active list in 1939, she continued to give good service until 1942, when she was dismantled to make room for larger ships. Notwithstanding her excellent record, she was so much in advance of her time that attempts by her manufacturers to obtain further orders from the navy were unsuccessful.

K-1 Capacity 319,000 cubic feet, length 218 feet, speed sixty-five mph. Built by Goodyear and the Naval Aircraft Factory in 1931 as an experimental craft and scrapped in 1941.

L Class Capacity 123,000 cubic feet, length 149 feet, speed sixty mph. Based on a type developed by Goodyear for commercial use. Twenty-two ships of this class, including some taken over from commercial users with their crews, were acquired by the navy between 1937 and 1942 and used as trainers.

TC-13, TC-14 Capacity 360,000 cubic feet, length 233 feet, speed not known. The TC-13 was built by Goodyear for the United States Army in 1933, transferred to the navy in 1937, and commissioned as a naval airship in 1940. The TC-14 was similar in design and performance, but her envelope was made by Air Cruisers Incorporated and her car by the Mercury Corporation. She, too, was built for the army and transferred to the navy in 1937. She was commissioned as a naval airship in 1938. Both ships were scrapped in 1943. Two other ships, the TC-10 and the TC-11, were transferred from the army to the navy in 1937, but they were not put into commission.

K-2 Capacity 404,000 cubic feet, length about 250 feet, speed not known. Built by Goodyear and the Naval Aircraft Factory as an experimental craft in 1938.

K Class (K-1 and K-2 excluded) Capacity 416,000 to 456,000 cubic feet but usually 425,000 cubic feet, length about 250 feet, speed seventy-five mph. Developed from the K-2 but distinct from her. More than 130 ships of this class, numbered from K-3 to K-135, were built during the Second World War and used for convoy escort and anti-submarine patrols.

G Class (G-1 excluded) Capacity 196,000 cubic feet, length 192 feet, speed sixty mph. Seven ships of this class, numbered from G-2 to G-8, were ordered in 1942 and delivered during the next three years or so. Some were still in service as late as 1959.

M Class Capacity 625,000 to 725,000 cubic feet, length about 310 feet, speed seventy-five mph. Four ships of this class were in service between 1943 and 1956.

N Class (Sub-Classes ZPN-1 and ZP2N)

Sub-Class ZPN-1 (afterwards ZPG-1) Capacity 875,000 cubic feet, length 324 feet, speed ninety mph. The sole representative of this sub-class was delivered in 1951.

Sub-Class ZP2N (afterwards ZPG-2) Capacity 1,011,000 cubic feet, length 343 feet, speed eighty mph. Enlarged version of the ZPN-1, capable of remaining on patrol for ten days or more without refuelling. Twelve ships of this sub-class were completed, the first appearing in 1953.

ZP4K Class (afterwards ZSG-4) Capacity 527,000 cubic feet, length 266 feet, speed eighty mph. Post-war development of K Class, equipped to replenish and change crews without landing. Fifteen ships of this class were completed, the first appearing in 1953.

ZP5K Class (afterwards ZS2G-1) Capacity 650,000 cubic feet, length 285 feet, speed about eighty-five mph. Enlarged version of the ZP4K with more powerful engines. Nineteen ships of this class were built, the first appearing in 1954.

N Class (Sub-Classes ZP2N-1W and ZPG-3W)

Sub-Class ZP2N-1W (afterwards ZPG-2W) Capacity 1,011,000 cubic feet, length 343 feet, speed eighty mph. Early-warning version of the ZP2N, with built-in radar scanner. Five ships completed, the first appearing in 1957.

Sub-Class ZPG-3W Capacity 1,516,000 cubic feet, length 403 feet, speed ninety mph. Enlarged version of the ZP2N-1W, again with built-in radar scanner, and with more powerful engines. Four ships completed, the first appearing in 1958. One collapsed in the air in 1960. Early-warning patrols were discontinued in 1961, but two ships continued to make experimental flights until 1962, and the last airship unit was not formally disbanded until 1964.

Bibliography

Books

ALLEN, John E., and BRUCE, Joan (Editors). *The Future of Aeronautics*. London, 1970. (Devoted almost entirely to heavier-than-air machines.)

ANDREWS, C. F. *Vickers Aircraft since 1908*. London, 1969. (Mostly about heavier-than-air machines, but includes a chapter on airships.)

BARKER, Ralph. *Great Mysteries of the Air*. London, 1966.

BLAKEMORE, Thomas D., and PAGON, W. W. *Pressure Airships*. New York, 1927.

BOUCHÉ, H. *See* Dollfus, C.

BOWERS, Peter M. *See* Swanborough, Gordon.

BRUCE, Joan. *See* Allen, John E.

BURGESS, Charles P. *Airship Design*. New York, 1927. (A textbook on the design of rigid airships.)

BURNEY, Commander Sir Charles Dennistoun. *The World, the Air and the Future*. London, 1929. (A thought-provoking book which still repays study.)

BUTTLAR-BRANDENFELS. Horst Freiherr Teusch von. *Zeppelins over England*. New York, 1932. (First-hand account by a German airship pilot whose navigation was not impeccable.)

CLARKE, Basil. *The History of Airships*. London, 1961. (A standard work.)

—— *Polar Flight*. Shepperton, Middlesex, 1964.

DOLLFUS, C., and BOUCHÉ, H. *Histoire de l'Aéronautique*. Paris, 1942. (Definitive work by a veteran aeronaut and his collaborator.)

DÜRR, Ludwig. *25 Jahre Zeppelin-Luftschiffbau*. Berlin, 1924. (Dr Dürr was the company's Chief Constructor.)

ECKENER, H. *My Zeppelins*. (Translated D. Robinson.) London, 1968.

GAMBLE, C. F. Snowden. *The Story of a North Sea Air Station*. London, 1928. (Edition consulted, London, 1967.) (Scholarly work which covers a wider field than the title suggests.)

GIBBS-SMITH, C. H. *Aviation: An historical survey from its origins to the end of World War II*. London, 1970. (By a leading authority on heavier-than-air machines. Supersedes the author's *A History of Flying*. London, 1953.)

HARDWICK, Michael. *The World's Greatest Air Mysteries*. London, 1970.

HIGHAM, Robin. *The British Rigid Airship, 1908–1931: A Study in Weapons Policy*. London, 1961. (Scholarly, authoritative work.)

—— *Britain's Imperial Air Routes, 1918–1939*. London, 1960.

HILDEBRANDT, A. *Airships Past and Present*. (Translated W. H. Story.) London, 1908.

HODGSON, J. E. *The History of Aeronautics in Great Britain*. Oxford, 1924.

HOEHLING, A. A. *Who Destroyed the Hindenburg?* Boston, 1962. (The author believes the *Hindenburg* was sabotaged by a named member of the crew.)

HOGG, Garry. *Airship over the Pole*. London, 1969.

HOOD, J. F. *The Story of Airships*. London, 1968.

JACKSON, Robert. *Airships in Peace and War*. London, 1971.

JONES, H. A. *The War in the Air*. Volumes 2–5. Oxford, 1928–35. (Contains authoritative account of German airship raids on Britain, based on British and German documents.)

KIRSCHENER, Edwin J. *The Zeppelin in the Atomic Age.* Urbana, Illinois, 1957.

LAUNAY, A. *Historic Air Disasters.* Shepperton, Middlesex, 1967.

LEASOR, James. *The Millionth Chance.* London, 1957. (A dramatic, well-written account of the R.101 disaster.)

LEWIS, Peter. *Squadron Histories, RFC, RNAS and RAF, 1952–1959.* London, 1959.

LEWITT, E. H. *The Rigid Airship.* London, 1925.

MEAGER, Captain George. *My Airship Flights, 1915–1930.* London, 1970. (Throws valuable light on behaviour of R.101 before lengthening but after gasbag wiring was let out.)

MILBANK, Jeremiah, Jnr. *The First Century of Flight in America.* Princeton, 1943.

MILLER, Ronald, and SAWERS, David. *The Technical Development of Modern Aviation.* London, 1968. (Consulted for material about development of heavier-than-air transport aircraft.)

MOONEY, Michael M. *The Hindenburg.* London, 1972. (Deals with the *Hindenburg*'s last voyage.)

MORPURGO, J. E. *Barnes Wallis: A Biography.* London, 1972. (Throws an interesting light on relations between Wallis and Burney.)

MORRIS, Joseph. *The German Air Raids on Great Britain.* London, no date. (Interesting, but less authoritative than Jones and Robinson.)

NOBILE, U. *My Polar Flights.* (Translated F. Fleetwood.) London, 1961.

NORWAY, N. S. *See* Shute, Nevil.

O'BRIEN, T. H. *Civil Defence.* London, 1955. (Throws useful light on civil defence aspect of German airship raids during First World War.)

PAGON, W. W. *See* Blakemore, Thomas L.

RALEIGH, Sir Walter. *The War in the Air.* Volume 1. Oxford, 1922. (Edition consulted, London, 1969.) (Some useful facts about early airships.)

ROLT, L. T. C. *The Aeronauts: A History of Ballooning, 1783–1903.* London, 1966. (Mostly about balloons, but deals also with early airships. Extremely interesting and well written.)

ROBINSON, Douglas H. *The Zeppelin in Combat: A History of the German Naval Airship Division, 1912–1918.* London, 1962. (An invaluable source which supplements the account in Jones. Contains a wealth of technical data.)

—— *See also* Eckener, H.

ROSENDAHL, Charles E. *Up Ship!* New York, 1931.

—— *What About the Airship?* New York, 1938.

(Two books by an experienced commander of airships who also commanded the Naval Air Station at Lakehurst, N.J.)

SANTOS-DUMONT, Alberto. *My Airships.* London, 1904. (Interesting book by a pioneer.)

SAWERS. David. *See* Miller, Ronald.

SHUTE, Nevil (Nevil Shute Norway). *Slide Rule.* London, 1954. (Invaluable account of the creation of the R.100. Before becoming a world-famous novelist the author worked as an aircraft designer. He was employed by the Airship Guarantee Company as Chief Calculator. Written long after the events described and contains some minor inaccuracies.)

SMITH, Richard K. *The Airships Akron and Macon, Flying Aircraft Carriers of the United States Navy.* Annapolis, Maryland, 1965. (Scholarly, thoughtful monograph with a useful bibliography.)

SPANNER, E. F. *This Airship Business.* London, 1927.

—— *The Tragedy of 'R.101'.* 2 vols, London, 1931.

(An able engineer, but prejudiced, the author was a relentless critic of the Air Ministry's airship programme.)

SPRIGG, Christopher. *The Airship.* London, 1932.

SWANBOROUGH, Gordon, and BOWERS, Peter M. *United States Navy Aircraft since 1911.* London, 1968. (Deals with both heavier-than-air and lighter-than-air machines.)

TEMPLEWOOD, Viscount. *Empire of the Air.* London, 1957. (The author, then Sir Samuel Hoare, was Secretary of State for Air in the Conservative governments which preceded and followed Ramsay MacDonald's Labour government of 1924.)

TOLAND, John. *Ships in the Sky*. London, 1957.

VAETH, J. GORDON. *Graf Zeppelin*. London, 1959. (Deals mainly with the voyages of the *Graf Zeppelin* and the career of Hugo Eckener, but includes accounts of Zeppelin's early experiments and the *Hindenburg* disaster.)

WYKEHAM, Peter. *Santos-Dumont: A Study in Obsession*. London, 1962. (Interesting account of Santos-Dumont and his airship ventures by an experienced airman.)

Periodicals

Valuable lists of articles dealing with the airships of the past, and cognate topics, will be found in *The British Rigid Airship*, by Robin Higham, and *The Airships Akron and Macon*, by Richard K. Smith. (See above.) The following is a brief list of some recent articles on the airships of the present and the future:

DAFTER, Ray. 'Airship is now more plausible.' *Financial Times*, 24 February 1971.

DROESMAR, Fred. 'Zurück zum Zeppelin.' *Deutsches Allgemeines Sonntagsblatt*, 14 February 1971.

FERGUSSON, Adam. 'Return of the airships?' *The Times* (London), 15 May 1971.

GREEN, Peter. 'UK's freight airship could provide work for shipyards.' *Journal of Commerce*, 6 August 1971.

HARTHOORN, R. 'The airship, the missing link in the transport chain?' *Holland Shipbuilding*, March–April 1971.

JEFFRIES, Michael. 'Airships could be back in business.' *Evening Standard*, 6 December 1968.

MCPHEE, John. 'The Deltoid Pumpkin Seed.' *New Yorker*, 10, 17, 24 February 1973.

MUTSCHALL, Vladimir. 'Status of the Airship in the USSR.' *Foreign Science Bulletin*, Volume 1, Number Ten, October 1965.

RYNISH, Max. 'Nuclear power and airships get together'. *Guardian*, 7 June 1969.

—— 'Airship Argosies are the Answer.' *Illustrated London News*, 11 July 1970.

—— 'Cargo airships – a plan for the future.' *Engineering*, June 1971.

STINTON, Darroll. *A New Look at Airships*. Flight International, 19 November 1970.

WREN, Major M. W. 'The Airship – A new form of transport.' *British Army Review*, April 1972.

Notes

1 Beginnings

1 Rolt, *The Aeronauts*, 27.
2 For a detailed and lively account of these and other early experiments with free balloons, see Rolt, *op. cit.*, 29 ff.
3 Clarke, *History of Airships*, 22; Rolt, *op. cit.*, 204.
4 Sixteen water-colour drawings of Meusnier's design are preserved in the Musée de l'Air at Chalais-Meudon.

2 The Airship Flies

1 Clarke, *History of Airships*, 29; Rolt, *The Aeronauts*, 208; Jackson, *Airships*, 30.
2 For a detailed account of Santos-Dumont's aeronautical career, see Wykeham, *Santos-Dumont: A Study in Obsession.*
3 Jackson, *op. cit.*, 47.
4 Raleigh, *The War in the Air*, i, 82.
5 Jackson, *op. cit.*, 48; Rolt, *op. cit.*, 230.
6 Dr Barton's son, D. W. A. Barton, joined the Royal Naval Air Service and became a successful balloonist and airship pilot.
7 Jackson, *op. cit.*, 75.
8 *ibid.*, 77–79; Raleigh, *op. cit.*, 157.
9 Raleigh, *loc. cit.*; Higham, *The British Rigid Airship*, 13.
10 Jackson, *op. cit.*, 81; Higham, *op. cit.*, 16.
11 Jackson, *op. cit.*, 82.
12 *ibid.*, 83.
13 Andrews, *Vickers Aircraft*, 27.
14 *ibid.*, 28.
15 Jackson, *op. cit.*, 87; Clarke, *op. cit.*, 72–3.
16 Clarke, *op. cit.*, 73; Jackson, *op. cit.*, 87.
17 Jackson, *op. cit.*, 89.

3 The Rigid Airship: 1895–1914

1 Jackson, *Airships*, 41; Rolt, *The Aeronauts*, 222.
2 Vaeth, *Graf Zeppelin*, 33. There is some conflict of evidence as to the duration of the LZ.1's flights, but the following figures are believed to be reliable:

1st flight, July 2	18 minutes
2nd flight, October 17	80 minutes
3rd flight, October 24	23 minutes
Total flying time	121 minutes

3 Although controlled by Zeppelin, the Maybach company sold engines to other manufacturers of airships, including the Schütte-Lanz company.
4 Jackson, *op. cit.*, 62; Vaeth, *op. cit.*, 39.
5 Evidence of contemporary photograph in Luftschiffbau-Zeppelin collection.
6 The LZ.18 was designed in consultation with the staff of the Zeppelin company by Felix Pitzker, a naval architect chosen for the task by the Ministry of Marine. Some of Pitzker's innovations were hotly criticized, both before and after the accident, by his collaborators. Windscreens on which he insisted were held to have contributed to the accident by preventing gas sucked into the forward gondola from escaping. (Jackson, *op. cit.*, 67; Robinson, *The Zeppelin in Combat*, 23, 27–8.)

7 Andrews, *Vickers Aircraft*, 19. Raleigh, *The War in the Air*, i, 173, gives a different figure.
8 Andrews, *op. cit.*, 21. See also Higham, *The British Rigid Airship.*
9 Not to be confused with a photograph taken after the nose of the airship was pushed back into the shed.
10 Andrews, *op. cit.*, 20–1.
11 *ibid.*, 21–2.

4 Airships in World War I: 1914–15

1 Jones, *The War in the Air*, iii, 77; Robinson, *The Zeppelin in Combat*, 34.
2 Jackson, *Airships*, 119.
3 *ibid.*, 125.
4 Raleigh, *The War in the Air*, i, 171, 219.
5 *ibid.*, 357; Gamble, *The Story of a North Sea Air Station*, 82.
6 Raleigh, *op. cit.*, 463.
7 Jackson, *op. cit.*, 114; Meager, *My Airship Flights*, 28 and *passim.*
8 Robinson, *op. cit.*, 34–5, 382–6.
9 Jones, *op. cit.*, Appendices I and II; Gamble, *op. cit.*, 341–2; Robinson, *op. cit.*, 382–6; Jackson, *op. cit.*, 227–34.
10 Robinson, *op. cit.*, 49–56; Jackson, *op. cit.*, 95–7; Gamble, *op. cit.*, 121.
11 Jones, *op. cit.*, 76; Gamble, *op. cit.*, 118.
12 Jones, *op. cit.*, 91; Gamble, *op. cit.*, 122.
13 Robinson, *op. cit.*, 67; Jones, *op. cit.*, 94.
14 Robinson, 68; Jones, 94.
15 Robinson, 67; Jackson, 100; Jones, 95.
16 Gamble, *op. cit.*, 126.
17 Jones, 103; O'Brien, *Civil Defence*, 7; Robinson, 77.
18 O'Brien, *op. cit.*, 8.
19 Gamble, 131–2.
20 *ibid.*, *loc. cit.*; Robinson, 95–6.
21 Robinson, 109.
22 *ibid.*, 404. Jones, Appendix III, omits some abortive sorties.
23 Robinson, 81–2.

5 Airships in World War I: 1916

1 Jones, *The War in the Air*, iii, Appendix I; Robinson, *The Zeppelin in Combat*, 382 ff.
2 Robinson, *op. cit.*, 120.
3 Jones, iii, 135–41; Robinson, 121–6.
4 The L.16, L.17, L.19 and L.20. Jones, iii, 137, omits the L.19, but see 142 fn. and Robinson, 127–8.
5 Jones, iii, 141.
6 Robinson, 378–9.
7 Jones, iii, 142 fn.
8 *ibid.*, 141; Robinson, 127.
9 Jones, *loc. cit.*
10 *ibid.*, 141–2.
11 *ibid.*, 142 fn.
12 *ibid.*, *loc. cit.*
13 *ibid.*, *loc. cit.*
14 *ibid.*, 183.
15 *ibid.*, 147, Appendix iii.
16 *ibid.*, 169.
17 *ibid.*, 144–5; O'Brien, *Civil Defence*, 8.
18 Jones, iii, 146, 171.
19 *ibid.*, 171.
20 *ibid.*, 181.
21 *ibid.*, 182; Jones, v, 45–51, 106–7; O'Brien, *op. cit.*, 9–10.
22 Jones, iii, 184.
23 Robinson, 129–30.
24 Jones, iii, 184; Robinson, 130, 132.
25 Jones, iii, 184, 188.
26 *ibid.*, 187; iii, Maps, Map 20.
27 *ibid.*, iii, 187.
28 *ibid.*, 189.
29 *ibid.*, 190.
30 *ibid.*, 193.
31 *ibid.*, 192. Robinson, 136, gives a slightly different account.
32 Jones, iii, 195.
33 *ibid.*, 198.
34 *ibid.*, *loc. cit.*
35 *ibid.*, *loc. cit.*
36 Jones, iii, 194–5, points out that, even after the war, these reports were still regarded in Germany as reliable.
37 Jones, iii, 202.
38 *ibid.*, 209.
39 *ibid.*, 211–12.
40 *ibid.*, 212–13; Robinson, 142–4.
41 Robinson, 145.

42 Jones, iii, 402–3; Robinson, 146.
43 Robinson, 145–6.
44 Jones, ii, 408.
45 *ibid.*, 415; Robinson, 152, 157.
46 Robinson, 159; Jones, ii, 417.
47 Robinson, 159.
48 *ibid.*, 161; Jones, ii, 417.
49 Robinson, 165–6.
50 Jones, iii, 225.
51 Robinson, 174.
52 Robinson, 183, 180 (Table); Jones, iii, 227, and iii, Maps, Map 39.
53 Jones, iii, 229.
54 *ibid.*, 231, 245.
55 Robinson, 190.
56 Quoted by Jones, iii, 237.
57 Robinson, 196.
58 *ibid.*, 197.
59 Jones, iii, 240, and iii, Maps, Map 42; Robinson, 200.

6 *Airships in World War I: 1917–18*

1 Jones, *The War in the Air*, iv, 40–1.
2 Andrews, *Vickers Aircraft*, 22–3; Higham, *The British Rigid Airship*, 348–50.
3 Lloyd George, *War Memoirs*, i, 702.
4 Jones, iv, 47.
5 Lloyd George, *op. cit.*, i, 690.
6 *ibid.*, 702.
7 Jackson, *Airships*, 121–2.
8 Jones, v, 20.
9 Robinson, *The Zeppelin in Combat*, 205–8.
10 *ibid.*, 208.
11 *ibid.*, 216.
12 Jones, v, 10.
13 Robinson, 220–1.
14 Jones, iv, 16.
15 Robinson, 224–5.
16 *ibid.*, 224.
17 *ibid.*, 226.
18 *ibid.*, *loc. cit.*
19 Jones, v, 34. Ellerkamm afterwards gave a slightly different account of the rescue.
20 Robinson, 233.
21 *ibid.*, 262–3.
22 Jones, v, 55–6.
23 Robinson, 264.
24 *ibid.*, 266.
25 Jones, v, 95–6.
26 Robinson, 282.
27 Jones, iii, 67.
28 Robinson, 284.
29 *ibid.*, 287.
30 Jones, iii, 67.
31 Robinson, 304.
32 *ibid.*, 302, quoting evidence of Seaman Lamotte.
33 Jones, v, 122.
34 Robinson, 308.
35 *ibid.*, 316–18.
36 *ibid.*, 322.
37 Jones, vi, 370.
38 Robinson, 329.
39 Jones, v, Appendix I; Robinson, 404.
40 Robinson, 341.

7 *The Post-war Years*

1 Jackson, *Airships*, 127.
2 *ibid.*, *loc. cit.*; Higham, *The British Rigid Airship*, 233.
3 Jackson, *op. cit.*, 128–9; Vaeth, *Graf Zeppelin*, 43.
4 Jackson, *op. cit.*, 118.
5 *ibid.*, 131.
6 *ibid.*, 133.
7 Andrews, *Vickers Aircraft*, 27.
8 *ibid.*, 29.
9 Jackson, *op. cit.*, 135.
10 Higham, *The British Rigid Airship*, 224.
11 Meager, *My Airship Flights*, 82–3, 96.
12 *ibid.*, 107–18.
13 Jackson, *op. cit.*, 140.
14 *ibid.*, 180.
15 Vaeth, *Graf Zeppelin*, 45.
16 Jackson, *op. cit.*, 182.

8 *New Horizons*

1 Higham, *The British Rigid Airship*, 232–3.
2 *ibid.*, 234–5.
3 *ibid.*, 237.
4 *ibid.*, 244.
5 *ibid.*, 243; Andrews, *Vickers Aircraft*, 31.
6 Higham, *op. cit.*, 287, 294.
7 Meager, *My Airship Flights*, 134–5.
8 *ibid.*, 135–6; Higham, *op. cit.*, 266–7.

9 Higham, *op. cit.*, 315; Andrews, *op. cit.*, 27.
10 Higham, *op. cit.*, 281.
11 Jackson, *Airships*, 141.
12 Nobile, *My Polar Flights*, gives a first-hand account of his adventures.
13 Communications from General Nobile dated 25 May 1973. General Nobile points out that the figure of fifty-four miles given in the English translation of his book is incorrect. For a detailed account of the *Italia*'s polar flights see Hogg, *Airship over the Pole.* Hardwick, *The World's Greatest Air Mysteries*, also refers; but see Nobile, *op. cit.*
14 Communication from General Nobile.

9 The Intercontinental Airship: 1928–30

1 Vaeth, *Graf Zeppelin*, gives detailed accounts of some of the *Graf Zeppelin*'s most important flights.
2 Vaeth, *op. cit.*, 65.
3 *ibid.*, 75.
4 *ibid.*, 78–9.
5 The number of passengers aboard the *Graf Zeppelin* on 15 August is variously given as 20 and 22. Which figure is right depends on whether one counts as passengers or crew the two American naval officers, who travelled as guests of the Zeppelin company and helped with the handling of the ship. The nationalities of the twenty whose status as passengers is not in doubt were: German seven, Japanese six, British two, American one, French one, Italian one, Spanish one, Swiss one.
6 The statement in Vaeth, *op. cit.*, 100, that Eckener left Yakutsk 'on a north-east heading' is evidently a slip. Ayan lies south-east of Yakutsk and almost due north of Yokohama.
7 Vaeth, *op. cit.*, 110.
8 Higham, *The British Rigid Airship*, 299.
9 Meager, *My Airship Flights*, 151.
10 Higham, *op. cit.*, 299.
11 Meager, *op. cit.*, 180, 225.
12 *ibid.*, 189.
13 *ibid.*, 190.
14 *ibid.*, *loc. cit.*
15 Higham, *op. cit.*, 304.

10 The Intercontinental Airship: 1930–7

1 Meager, *My Airship Flights*, 211, 230. Other accounts give different mileages; Meager, who was First Officer, says the ship covered 3,364 nautical miles (i.e. nearly 4,000 statute miles).
2 *ibid.*, 224. The distance covered, according to Meager, was 2,955 nautical miles.
3 The best sources for the facts relating to the loss of the R.101 and the events leading up to it are the report and minutes of evidence of the Court of Inquiry. Higham, *The British Rigid Airship*, reviews this material and takes into account a number of alternative interpretations of the evidence. Leasor, *The Millionth Chance*, gives a dramatic account of the R.101's last flight and Spanner, *The Tragedy of 'R.101'*, develops in forthright terms the theory that the ship broke up in the air.
4 Communicated to the author by Lord Dowding, *c.* 1957.
5 Many accounts describe the certificate as having been 'issued' on 2 October and handed over on 4 October. It was dated 2 October, but whether it can be said to have been issued before it was handed over is debatable.
6 Conversations with the author on various dates between 1957 and 1959.
7 This paragraph is based on Sir Sefton Brancker's papers and on material communicated by people who knew him.
8 *The Aeroplane*, 17 September 1930.
9 Higham, *op. cit.*, 305.
10 *ibid.*, 305, 318.
11 *ibid.*, 305.

12 *ibid.*, 317.
13 Communicated to the author by Atherstone's niece.
14 Higham, *op. cit.*, 308.
15 *ibid.*, 315–16; Meager, *op. cit.*, 166.
16 Higham, *op. cit.*, 315.
17 Written and oral communications to the author.
18 Jackson, *Airships*, 255.
19 Hoehling, *Who Destroyed the Hindenburg?*, 24–5.
20 *ibid.*, 98.
21 *ibid.*, 133.

11 *Yesterday and Tomorrow*

1 Smith, *The Airships Akron and Macon*, 45.
2 *ibid.*, 97–151.
3 *ibid.*, 163–5.
4 Swanborough and Bowers, *United States Navy Aircraft Since 1911*, give useful information about the navy's airships.
5 *Foreign Science Bulletin Volume I, Number 10* (Art. Vladimir Mutschall).
6 *ibid.*
7 *New Yorker*, 10, 17, 24 February (Art. John McPhee).
8 *Deutsches Allgemeines Sonntagsblatt*, 14 February 1971 (Art. Fred Droesmar).
9 *Holland Shipbuilding*, March–April 1971 (Art. R. Harthoorn).
10 Communicated by Airfloat Transport Limited.
11 *Engineering*, June 1971 (Art. M. J. Rynish).

Tables

TABLE 1
German airship raids on Britain, 1915: Phase One

Date	*Airships despatched*	*Remarks*
Jan. 19–20	L.3, L.4, L.6	20 people killed or injured in East Anglia
Feb. 26	L.8	Attempt by L.8 to reach London unsuccessful. No casualties
March 4	L.8	L.8 attempted on initiative of commander to fly to London. Crashed after coming under fire from Belgian troops
April 14–15	L.9	2 people injured in Northumberland
April 15–16	L.5, L.6, L.7	1 woman injured in East Anglia
April 29–30	LZ.38	Bombs but no casualties in East Anglia
May 10	LZ.38	3 people killed or injured at Southend in early morning
May 17	LZ.38	3 people killed or injured at Ramsgate in early morning
May 26–7	LZ.38	6 people killed or injured at Southend
May 31–June 1	LZ.38	42 people killed or injured in eastern suburbs of London
June 4–5	L.10, SL.3	8 people injured in Kent
June 6–7	L.9, LZ.37, LZ.38, LZ.39	64 people killed or injured at Hull. LZ.37 destroyed on way home by Sub-Lt R. A. J. Warneford
June 15–16	L.10, L.11	L.10 attacked Tyneside. 90 people killed or injured

Summary
Number of raids *13*
Number of sorties *22*

British casualties:
Killed *59*
Injured *180*

Table 2
German airship raids on Britain, 1915: Phase Two

Date	*Airships despatched*	*Remarks*
Aug. 9–10	L.9, L.10, L.11, L.12, L.13, L.14, SL.3, SL.4	Attempted raid on London unsuccessful. 38 people killed or injured elsewhere. L.12 damaged by Dover guns and aircraft from Dunkirk
Aug. 12–13	L.9, L.10, L.11, L.13	Attempted attacks on London and Hartlepool unsuccessful. 30 people killed or injured in East Anglia and Essex
Aug. 17–18	L.10, L.11, L.13, L.14	L.10 first naval airship to reach London. 58 people killed or injured. No damage elsewhere
Sept. 7–8	LZ.74, LZ.77, SL.2	SL.2 and LZ.74 reached London. 56 people killed or injured
Sept. 8–9	L.9, L.11, L.13, L.14	Bombs from L.13 started big fire in City of London. 109 people killed or injured in London, 11 elsewhere
Sept. 11–12	LZ.77	Bombs in Essex failed to explode
Sept. 12–13	LZ.74	Bombs in East Anglia and Essex caused minor damage and no casualties
Sept. 13–14	L.11, L.13, L.14	Bombs in East Anglia caused minor damage and no casualties. L.13 hit by anti-aircraft fire
Oct. 13–14	L.11, L.13, L.14, L.15, L.16	3 ships reached London. 149 people killed or injured there and 50 elsewhere

Summary
Number of raids *9*
Number of sorties *33*

British casualties:
Killed *149*
Injured *352*

TABLE 3

German airship raids on Britain, 1916: Phase One

Date	*Airships despatched*	*Remarks*
Jan. 31–Feb. 1	L.11, L.13, L.14, L.15, L.16, L.17, L.19, L.20, L.21	First airship raid on Midlands. Most bombs wide of objectives, but 183 people killed or injured. L.19 foundered in North Sea
March 5–6	L.11, L.13, L.14	Attempted raids on Forth, Tyne and Tees unsuccessful. 70 people killed or injured elsewhere
March 31–April 1	L.9, L.11, L.13, L.14, L.15, L.16, L.22, LZ.88, LZ.90, LZ.93	Most bombs wide of objectives, but 112 people killed or injured. L.13 and L.15 hit by anti-aircraft fire. L.15 down in sea
April 1–2	L.11, L.17	L.11 reached Sunderland. 152 people killed or injured
April 2–3	L.13, L.14, L.16, L.22, LZ.88, LZ.90	Attempted raids on Forth Bridge and Rosyth unsuccessful, but L.14 and L.22 reached Edinburgh. 37 people killed or injured
April 3–4	L.11, L.17	No casualties or damage
April 5–6	L.11, L.13, L.16	10 people killed or injured in northern counties
April 24–5	L.11, L.13, L.16, L.17, L.20, L.21, L.23	Attempted raid on London unsuccessful. 2 casualties
April 25–6	LZ.87, LZ.88, LZ.93, LZ.97, one unidentified	LZ.97 reached outskirts of London. 1 person injured
April 26–7	LZ.93	No bombs on land
May 2–3	L.11, L.13, L.14, L.16, L.17, L.20, L.21, L.23, LZ.98	Attempted raid on Forth unsuccessful. 39 people killed or injured in northern counties. L.20 made forced descent near Stavanger

Summary
Number of raids *11*
Number of sorties *57*

British casualties:
Killed *182*
Injured *424*

TABLE 4
German airship raids on Britain, 1916: Phase Two

Date	*Airships despatched*	*Remarks*
July 28–9	L.11, L.13, L.16, L.17, L.24, L.31 and 4 others	4 ships turned back, 6 flew over northern and eastern Britain. No casualties
July 31–Aug. 1	L.11, L.13, L.14, L.16, L.17, L.21, L.22, L.23, L.30, L.31	8 ships over eastern counties. No casualties
Aug. 2–3	L.11, L.13, L.16, L.17, L.21, L.31	6 ships over eastern counties. 1 boy injured. L.17 hit by anti-aircraft fire
Aug. 8–9	L.11, L.13, L.14, L.16, L.17, L.21, L.22, L.23, L.24, L.30, L.31	9 ships over north and east. 21 casualties at Hull and 5 elsewhere
Aug. 23–4	LZ.97	1 ship over Essex. No casualties
Aug. 24–5	L.11, L.13, L.14, L.16, L.17, L.21, L.23, L.24, L.30, L.31, L.32, SL.8, SL.9	L31 first airship to reach London since October 1915. 49 people killed or injured, all in London area. L.13 hit by anti-aircraft fire
Sept. 2–3	L.11, L.13, L.14, L.16, L.17, L.21, L.22, L.23, L.24, L.30, L.32, SL.8, LZ.90, LZ.97, LZ.98, SL.11	14 ships over north and east. 16 people killed or injured. SL.11 shot down by Lt W. Leefe Robinson
Sept. 23–4	L.13, L.14, L.16, L.17, L.21, L.22, L.23, L.24, L.30, L.31, L.32, L.33	9 ships over Britain. 151 casualties in London area, 19 elsewhere. L.32 and L.33 shot down
Sept. 25–6	L.13, L.14, L.16, L.21, L.22, L.23, L.30, L.31 and 1 other	6 ships over England. 47 people killed or injured at Sheffield, 27 elsewhere
Oct. 1–2	L.13, L.14, L.16, L.17, L.21, L.22, L.23, L.24, L.30, L.31, L.34	7 ships over England. 2 people killed or injured. L.31 (Mathy) shot down
Nov. 27–8	L.13, L.14, L.16, L.21, L.22, L.24, L.30, L.34, L.35, L.36	7 ships over north and Midlands. 41 casualties. L.21 and L.34 shot down

Summary
Number of raids *11*
Number of sorties *109*

British casualties:
Killed *111*
Injured *268*

TABLE 5

German airship raids on Britain, 1917

Date	*Airships despatched*	*Remarks*
Feb. 16–17	LZ.107	LZ.107 flew over Deal after dropping bombs near Calais
March 16–17	L.35, L.39, L.40, L.41, L.42	Attempted raid on London unsuccessful. No casualties. L.39 destroyed over France
May 23–4	L.40, L.42, L.43, L.44, L.45, L.47	Attempted raid on London unsuccessful. 1 person killed
June 16–17	L.42, L.44, L.45, L.48	2 ships over eastern counties. 19 people killed or injured. L.48 shot down
Aug. 21–2	L.35, L.41, L.42, L.44, L.45, L.46, L.47, L.51	Attempted raid on Midlands unsuccessful. 1 person injured
Sept. 24–5	L.35, L.41, L.42. L.44, L.45, L.46, L.47, L.51, L.52, L.53, L.55	5 or more ships over northern and eastern counties. 3 people injured
Oct. 19–20	L.41, L.44, L.45, L.46, L.47, L.49, L.50, L.52, L.53, L.54, L.55	All ships except L.54 blown far astray. 91 people killed or injured, mostly by bombs from ship carried unexpectedly over London. L.55 wrecked by rough landing in Germany, L.44, L.45, L.49, L.50 failed to return

Summary
Number of raids *7*
Number of sorties *46*

British casualties:
Killed *40*
Injured *75*

Table 6
German airship raids on Britain, 1918

Date	*Airships despatched*	*Remarks*
March 12–13	L.53, L.54, L.61, L.62, L.63	Attempted raid on Midlands unsuccessful. 1 woman died of shock
March 13–14	L.42, L.52, L.56	All ships recalled, but L.42 continued against orders to West Hartlepool. 47 people killed or injured
April 12–13	L.60, L.61, L.62, L.63, L.64	Attempted raid on Midlands, with southern England as alternative, not successful. 27 people killed or injured by bombs dropped mostly by L.61
Aug. 5–6	L.53, L.56, L.63, L.65, L.70	No bombs on land. L.70 shot down by Major Egbert Cadbury

Summary
Number of raids *4*
Number of sorties *18*

British casualties:
Killed *16*
Injured *59*

TABLE 7
Ship's company of Airship *Italia*, 23 May 1928

Captain, General Umberto Nobile
Navigators, Commander Filipo Zappi, Commander Adalberto Mariano
Duties unspecified, Lieutenant-Commander Alfredo Viglieri
Wireless Operator, Petty Officer Giuseppe Biagi
Chief Motor Engineer, Ettore Arduino
Chief Technician, Natale Cecioni
Foreman Motor Mechanic, Vincenzo Pomella
Motor Mechanics, Attilio Caratti, Calisto Ciocca
Engineer, Felice Trojani
Foreman Rigger, Renato Alessandrini

Scientific Observers:
Physicist, Professor Aldo Pontremoli
Meteorologist, Professor Finn Malmgren (Swedish)
Telecommunications Expert, Professor Francis Behounek (Czechoslavakian)

Press Observer, Ugo Lago

Supernumerary, Titina (Nobile's terrier)

Note
One member of the crew and one passenger remained at King's Bay. They were Petty Officer Ettore Pedretti (Wireless Operator) and Francesco Tomaselli (Press Observer).

Index

Note
Page numbers in bold refer to illustrations

Admiralty (British):
orders Parseval airships *47;* and *Mayfly 64–7;* and HMA No 9 *67;* takes over army's airships *70;* and air defence *74, 88–9, 93;* and convoy system *117;* and R.38 *152–3;* and passenger airships *163*
Aereon Corporation *227–30;* design for 'lifting body airship' **231**
aerial steamer, Henri Giffard's **24**, *28*, **29**
Aeronautical Inspection Department *198, 199*
Aeroplane, The 203
Aerospace Developments *238;* design for airship to move natural gas **235**
Ahlhorn, German airship base *110, 124, 134, 139–41, 143, 146*
air defences, British (First World War) *74–7, 87, 88–91, 110, 131, 133, 135*
Air Ministry (British):
and R.38 *153–5;* and R.101 *162–8, 190–5, 197–208;* and R.100 *165, 168, 195, 196, 197, 208;* and R.102 *208*
aircraft carriers *103, 104, 105, 142, 146;* airships as *10, 166, 209, 219, 220*
Airfloat Transport Limited *235–6;* design for large freight-carrier **232–3**
Airship Guarantee Company *164, 165, 166, 168, 196*
airships:
American: Ritchel's aerial bicycle *32,* **32**; Wellman's French-built *America* (1906) *49,* **50**; *Akron* (1911–12) **50**, *51;* Goodyear's early Sea Scout derivatives *118,* **130**; ZR-I (*Shenandoah*) *156–7,* **157**, *158, 159–60;* ZR-II (R.38) *153–5,* **155**; ZR-III (LZ.126, *Los Angeles*) *149, 157–60,* **158**; ZRS-4 (*Akron*) *169, 209–10,* **209**, *219, 244;* ZRS-5 (*Macon*) *169, 210–11,* **210**, *219, 244;* J-4 and J-Class *220, 245;* G-1 and G-Class *220, 223, 245, 246;* K-1 and K-Class *220, 221, 245, 246;* ZMC-2 *220,* **220**, *237, 245;* TC-13 *221, 246;* TC-14 *221, 246;* M-Class *221–3,* **222**; N-Class and sub-classes **222**, *223–4, 246; America* (1959) *224, 226,* **226**; *Europa 224, 226,* **229**; *Aereon* (1966) *228;* Aereon Corporation's models *230; Aereon* **26**, *230;* lifting body airship **231**
Austrian: Haenlein's gas-driven airship **30**, *31;* Schwartz's rigid airship *52*
British: Bell's dirigible balloon *26,* **27**; Green's model *26;* Monck Mason's model *26;* Stanley Spencer's airships *41;* Barton's airship *41–2,* **42**; Willows I *42;* Willows II (*City of Cardiff*) *42–3,* **43**, *47; Nulli Secundus 44–5,* **44**; *Nulli Secundus II 45; Baby* (*Beta*) *45,* **45**, *70; Gamma 45, 70; Delta 45,* **46**, *70; Eta 70;* Clément-Bayard (A. du Cros) **46**, *47;* Lebaudy (*Morning Post*) *47;* Parsevals *47–8,* **47**; *Mayfly 64–7,* **66–7**; HMA No. 9 *67, 114,* **120–1**; Sea Scouts *70,* **70**; Sea Scout Twin *70;* Coastal *70, 114,* **132**; North Sea *114,* **138**; HMA No. 23 *114,* **115**, *116,* **116**, **124**; No. 24 *114;* No. 25 *114;* R.26 *114–16,* **119**, **127**; R.27 *116;* R.29 *116,* **128**; R.31 *116, 149–50;* R.32 *116, 150;* R.33 *116, 150, 166,* **167**; R.34 *116,* **149**, *150–1;* R.35 *152;* R.36 *152, 166;* R.37 *152;* R.38 *152–5,* **154**; R.80 *116, 151,* **153**, *166;* R.100 *168,* **169**, *181,* **189**, *190–2,* **191**, *192–3, 194, 195,* **195**, *196–7,* **197**, *203;* R.101 *166,* **166**, *168, 181, 189–90, 192, 193–5, 197, 198–208,* **205**, **206**; R.102 *208; Europa* (Goodyear) *224, 226,* **229**
French: Meusnier's design *21–2,* **21**; *Eagle* **23**, *26;* Le Berrier's model *26;* Pierre Jullien's model *27, 28,* **29**; Dupuy de Lôme's man-powered airship *32,* **33**; *La France 32–3,* **34**; Santos-Dumont's airships *38–40,* **39**; *Pax 40;* Bradsky's rotor airship *40;* Lebaudy I *40–1;* Lebaudy II *41;* other Lebaudy airships **41**, *47;* Astra and Astra-Torres airships *41, 69,* **69**, *118;* Clément-Bayard airships *41,* **46**, *47, 69;* Zodiac airships *41, 69, 118;* Wellman's French-built *America* (1906) *49,* **50**; Sea Scouts *117;* L.72 (*Dixmude*) *147, 155; Nordstern* (*Méditerranée*) *147, 155*
German: Karl Wölfert's Daimler-powered airships *35–8,* **35**, **37**; August von Parseval's airships *47–8,* **47**, *68, 85, 242, 243;* Gross-Basenach airships *48,* **48**, **49**, *61, 68, 85, 242, 243;* Ferdinand von Zeppelin's and the Zeppelin Company's LZ.1 *54–5, 240;* LZ.2 *55, 56, 240;* LZ.3 (Z.1) *56,* **59**, *60, 63, 240;* LZ.4 *56–8, 63, 240;* LZ.5 (Z.2) *60, 240;* LZ.6 *60–1, 240;* LZ.7 (*Deutschland*) *61, 240;* LZ.8 (*Ersatz Deutschland*) *61, 240;* LZ.9 *240:* compared with SL.1 *62;* LZ.10 (*Schwaben*) *61, 62,* **66**, *240;* LZ.11 (*Viktoria-Luise*) *61, 240;* LZ.12 (Z.3) *240;* LZ.13

(*Hansa*) *61*, **63**, *240;* LZ.14 (L.1) *61–2, 240;* LZ.15 (*Ersatz Z.1*) *240;* LZ.16 (Z.4) *68, 240, 243;* LZ.17 (*Sachsen*) *61, 240–1;* LZ.18 (L.2) *62, 241;* LZ.19 *241;* LZ.20 (Z.5) *68–9, 241, 243;* LZ.21 (Z.6) *68, 241, 243;* LZ.22 (Z.7) *68, 241, 243;* LZ.23 (Z.8) *68, 241, 243;* LZ.24 (L.3) *68, 72, 74–5, 84, 241, 242, 255;* LZ.25 (Z.9) *68, 69, 241, 243;* LZ.33 *77 fn.;* LZ.34 *243;* LZ.35 *243;* LZ.37 *78, 243, 255;* LZ.38 *77, 243, 255;* LZ.39 *78, 243, 255;* LZ.42 (LZ.72) *77 fn., 243;* LZ.74 *80, 243, 256;* LZ.77 *80, 243, 256;* LZ.79 *243;* LZ.81 *243;* LZ.85 *243;* LZ.86 *243;* LZ.87 *243, 257;* LZ.88 *97, 243, 257;* LZ.90 *95, 97, 243, 258;* LZ.93 *100, 243, 257;* LZ.95 *243;* LZ.97 *100, 107, 243, 257, 258;* LZ.98 *243, 257, 258;* LZ.101 *243;* LZ.103 *243;* LZ.107 *243, 259;* LZ.111 *243;* LZ.113 **145**, *146, 147, 243;* LZ.120 *146, 147;* LZ.126 (ZR-III, *Los Angeles*) *149, 157–9*, **158**, *244;* LZ.127 (*Graf Zeppelin*) *168–9, 181–9*, **183**, **184**, **185**, *192*, **193**, **194**, *211–12;* LZ.128 *212;* LZ.129 (*Hindenburg*) *212–16*, **212**, **214**, **215**, **216**, **217**; LZ.130 *217;* LZ.131 *217;* Z.1 *see* LZ.3; *Ersatz Z.1 see* LZ.15; Z.2 *see* LZ.5; Z.3 *see* LZ.12; Z.4 *see* LZ.16; Z.5 *see* LZ.20; Z.6 *see* LZ.21; Z.7 *see* LZ.22; Z.8 *see* LZ.23; Z.9 *see* LZ.25; Z.10 *243;* Z.11 *243;* Z.12 *77 fn., 243;* L.1 *see* LZ.14; L.2 *see* LZ.18; L.3 *see* LZ.24; L.4 *72, 74–5, 84, 242, 255;* L.5 *74, 76, 77, 83, 84, 242, 255;* L.6 *74–5*, **75**, *76*, **76**, *77, 84, 99, 242, 255;* L.7 *76–7, 84, 99, 100, 101, 242, 255;* L.8 *75, 76, 242, 255;* L.9 *72, 76, 78, 82, 84, 93, 99, 100, 103, 242, 255, 256, 257;* L.10 *72, 77, 78, 79, 80, 85 fn., 242, 255, 256;* L.11 **75**, *79, 80–2, 85 fn., 92, 93, 96–7, 97, 99, 103, 104, 242, 255, 256, 257, 258;* L.12 *79, 80, 85 fn., 242, 256;* L.13 *79–82, 85 fn., 86, 92, 93–4, 96, 99, 103, 104, 105, 106, 107, 112, 113, 242, 256, 257, 258;* L.14 *79–82, 85 fn., 92, 94, 96–7, 101, 103, 112, 113, 146, 147, 242, 256, 257, 258;* L.15 *82, 85 fn., 86, 92, 94–5, 242, 256, 257;* L.16 *85 fn., 86, 92, 95, 96, 98, 99, 103, 107, 112, 113, 242, 256, 257, 258;* L.17 *85 fn., 92, 95–6, 97, 99, 103, 110, 242, 257, 258;* L.18 *85 fn., 242;* L.19 *72, 85 fn., 86–8, 91, 242, 257;* L.20 *72 fn., 85, 92, 99, 100, 101*, **103**, *242, 257;* L.21 *86, 92, 99, 103, 104, 107, 109, 112, 113, 242, 257, 258;* L.22 *95, 96, 103, 104, 110, 112, 113, 242, 257, 258;* L.23 *99, 103, 107, 124, 242, 257, 258;* L.24 *103, 104, 107, 111, 112, 242, 258;* L.25 *242;* L.30 *99*, **99**, *104, 109, 110, 112, 242, 258;* L.31 *104, 105, 107, 109, 110, 111*, **112**, *242, 258;* L.32 *104, 107, 108, 109–10, 242, 258;* L.33 *109, 110, 116, 147, 242, 258;* L.34 *112, 113, 242, 258;* L.35 *112, 113, 121 fn., 122, 123–4, 133, 242, 258, 259;* L.36 *112, 113, 121 fn., 129 fn., 242, 258;* L.37 *147, 242;* L.38 *242;* L.39 *121 fn., 122, 124, 242, 259;* L.40 *121 fn., 122, 124, 125, 242, 259;* L.41 *121 fn., 122, 124, 130, 133, 134, 242, 259;* L.42 *119, 121 & fn., 122, 125, 127, 129, 142, 147, 242, 259, 260;* L.43 *121 fn., 124–5, 242, 259;* L.44 *125, 126, 127, 134, 242, 259;* L.45 *121 fn., 125, 127, 134, 135, 242, 259;* L.46 *127, 130, 131–2, 133–4, 139, 242, 259;* L.47 *121 fn., 125, 127, 133–4, 139, 140, 242, 259;* L.48 *121 fn., 127–9 & fn., 130, 242, 259;* L.49 **123**, *134–5, 242, 259;* L.50 *134, 242, 259;* L.51 *140, 141, 242, 259;* L.52 *134, 147, 242, 259;* L.53 *133, 134, 141–2, 143, 144, 146, 242, 259, 260;* L.54 *133, 141–2*, **141**, *142–3, 242, 259, 260;* L.55 *133, 134, 242, 259;* L.56 *142, 143, 144, 147, 242, 260;* L.57 *136–7, 242;* L.58 *139, 140, 242;* L.59 *137–9, 242;* L.60 *142–3, 242, 260;* L.61 *141, 142, 147, 242, 260;* L.62 *141, 142, 143, 242, 260;* L.63 *141, 143, 144, 146, 147, 242, 260;* L.64 *147, 242, 260;* L.65 *143, 144, 146, 147*, **147**, *242, 260;* L.70 *143–4, 242, 260;* L.71 *146, 147, 242;* L.72 *146, 147, 242:* as *Dixmude 147, 155;* L.73 *146, 148;* L.74 *146;* L.100 *143, 146; Bodensee 147, 148:* as *Esperia 147, 167; Nordstern 147, 148:* as *Méditerranée 147, 155;* Schütte-Lanz SL.1 *62, 241;* SL.2 *62–3, 68, 76, 80, 241, 243;* SL.3 *78, 79, 82, 242, 255, 256;* SL.4 *79, 242, 256;* SL.5 *243;* SL.6 *242;* SL.7 *243;* SL.8 *107, 242, 258;* SL.9 *107, 242, 258;* SL.10 *243;* SL.11 *108, 109, 116, 243, 258;* SL.12 *242;* SL.13 *243;* SL.14 *242;* SL.15 *243;* SL.16 *243;* SL.17 *243;* SL.20 *140, 242;* SL.21 *243;* SL.22 *147, 242;* West German post-1945 commercial airships *224*, **225**, *226;* projected *224, 230–4*

Italian: Forlanini's airships *48*, **48**, *69;* L.61 *147;* LZ.120 *147; Bodensee* (*Esperia*) *147, 169;* SR.1 *156; Roma 156;* N.1 (*Norge*) *169–73*, **170**; *Italia 173–6, 261*

airship stations (First World War): American *118;* British *70, 114;* French *118;* German *see* Allhorn,

airship stations (First World War) (*cont.*)
Cologne, Düsseldorf, Evère, Fuhlsbüttel, Ghent, Hage, Jamboli, Jüterbog, Nordholz, Seddin, Staaken, Tondern, Wittmundhaven; (Second World War) *221*
Airworthiness of Airships Panel *197–8, 207*
Akron (ZRS-4) *10,* **50**, *51, 169,* **200–1**, **209**, *209–10, 214, 219, 244*
Alcock, Sir John *150*
Alessandrini, Renato *175, 176, 261*
aluminium, first used as material for airships *52*
Ameland, L.19 flies over *87*
America (1906) *49,* **50**; (1959) *224, 226,* **226**
Amundsen, Roald *171–3, 178*
Andrews, Solomon *228*
animals, first in flight *18*
Annonay, experiments at *15–16*
Arduino, Ettore *175, 176, 261*
Arlandes, Marquis d' *18*
Armistice (1918) *146*
Armstrong, Whitworth, Sir W. G., and Company Limited *114, 116*
Ashbolt, A. H. *161*
Astra, Société des Constructions Aéronautiques *41;* Astra and Astra-Torres airships *41,* **69**, *70, 118*
Atherstone, Lieutenant-Commander Noël *206*

Baby (*Beta*) **44**, *45, 70*
Bacon, Captain R. H. S., R.N. *64,* **65**
Bacon, Roger *15*
Bairstow, Professor L. *197, 199*
Baldwin, Rt. Hon. Stanley *163*
Ballantyne (airman) *151*
ballonnet 22–3, 36, 40
balloons, hot air *15–20;* hydrogen *16–17, 20, 21, 22, 23*
Barton, D. W. A. *250*
Barton, Dr F. A. *41–2;* his airship **42**
Basenach, Nikolas *48, 61;* his airships **48**, **49**
Beardmore, William and Company Limited *114, 116, 152*
Beatty, Vice-Admiral Sir David *103*
Beauvais, R.101 crashes near *201*
Beelitz, Kapitänleutnant Helmut *75*
Behounek, Professor Francis *176–8, 179, 261*
Bell, Dr Hugh *26;* his dirigible balloon **27**
Bennett, Floyd *171*
Berlin Aeronautical Society *35*
Berlin Trade Fair (1896) *36*
Berwick-on-Tweed, bombed *96*
Beta, see Baby
Bethmann-Hollweg, Theobald von *79*
Biagi, Petty Officer Giuseppe *176, 177–8, 179, 261*
bicycle, aerial *32,* **32**
Birmingham, bombed *86, 134;* L.62 attacked near *142*
Bishop Auckland, bombed *98*
Blanchard, Jean-Pierre *20–1*
Blücher (cruiser) *83*
Böcker, Kapitänleutnant Alois *76, 92, 94, 96–7, 101, 109*
Bockholt, Kapitänleutnant Ludwig *124, 136–9*
Bodensee (*Esperia*) *147, 148, 167*
Boeing 747 **25**, *234, 235*
Boemack, Kapitänleutnant Fritz *78*
Booth, Squadron Leader R. S. *166, 196–7, 203*
Borkum *87*
Bradsky, Ottokar de *40*
Braintree, bombed *94*
Brancker, Sir Sefton *202–4, 253*
Brandon, Second-Lieutenant A. de B. *109*
Braun Sixtant (*Trumpf*) **225**
Breithaupt, Kapitänleutnant Joachim *82, 94–5, 98*
Britain *see* United Kingdom
Brown, Sir Arthur Whitten *150*
Brno (Brunn), airship tested at **30**, *31*
Bulgaria, German airship base at Jamboli in (First World War) *136–9, 144*
Burgess, Charles P. *220*
Burney, Commander Sir Charles Dennistoun *161–5, 168, 181, 237*
Bury St Edmunds, bombed *77, 95*
Buttlar-Brandenfels, Oberleutnant Horst Freiherr Teusch von *74–5, 76, 110, 111, 133, 247*
Byrd, Commander Richard, U.S.N. *171*

Cadbury, Major Egbert *144*
Calais, LZ.107 drops bombs near *259*
Campania, HMS *103, 104, 105*
Campbell, Instructor-Commander C. I. R. *152–3, 154–5*
Canada, flight of R.100 to *168,* **189**, *194, 195, 196–7,* **197**
Capper, Colonel John, R.E. *44*

Index

Cardington, R.38 built at *152–3;* becomes Royal Airship Works *152;* reduced to care-and-maintenance basis *155;* future discussed in Parliament *164–5;* R.101 built and modified at *166, 189–90, 193–5, 197–204;* R.100 at **169**, *190, 194, 196, 197;* incident of the dog in the night at *206; Europa* built at *224,* **229**
Cargo Airships Limited *235, 236–8;* design for large freight-carrier **239**
cargo-carriers, case for lighter-than-air *227, 234–7*
Casement, Sir Roger *99*
Catterick, British air base *89*
Cavendish, Henry *15*
Cayley, Sir George: his design for a navigable balloon **8**
Cecioni, Natale *176, 177, 178–9, 180, 264*
Chalais-Meudon, French airship factory at *69, 118*
Channel, English, crossed by balloon *20;* by Clément-Bayard, Lebaudy and Willows airships *43, 47*
Charles, Jacques *16–17, 18–20, 21, 22*
Chatham, commander and crew of L.15 taken as prisoners-of-war to *95*
Chelmsford, bombed *80;* L.33 intercepted near *109*
Cheshunt, L.31 makes fateful turn near *111*
Chicago Exhibition (1933) *212*
Chukhnovsky, Boris *179, 181*
Churchill, Rt. Hon. Winston S. *65–7*
Città di Milano 173, 177, 178
City of Cardiff 42–3, **43**, *47*
Civil Aviation, Department of *199, 202*
Clément-Bayard airships *41,* **46**, *47*
Cody, Samuel F. *44*
Colmore, Wing Commander R. B. B. *190, 192, 195, 196, 198–9, 202, 203*
Committee of Imperial Defence *163*
Compiègne, L.39 brought down at *124*
convoy system (First World War) *117,* **132**; (Second World War) *221*
Cros, Sir Arthur du *47*
Cuers-Pierrefeu, French airship base *185, 203*
Cuffley, SL.11 brought down at *108*
Culley, Lieutenant S. D., R.N. *146*

Daimler, Gottlieb *35–6, 38;* Daimler engines *35–8, 212*
Danby High Moor, bombed *101*
Deal, LZ.107 flies over *259*
DELAG *60–2, 68, 240, 241*
Delta 45–7, **46**, *70*
Deutsch, Henri de la Meurthe *40*
Deutschland (LZ.7) *61, 240*
Dietrich, Kapitänleutnant Martin **94**, *95, 96, 110–11, 122, 123, 125, 127, 129–30, 142*
Dietrich, Kapitänleutnant Max *86, 101, 112*
Dilham (Norfolk), bombed *100*
Dixmude (L.72) *146, 147, 148, 155, 160*
Dogger Bank, Battle of the *83–4*
Dolphin 23, 26
Dover, L.12 hit by gunfire over *80, 256*
Dowding, Air Chief Marshal the Lord *14, 198–9, 202, 208*
Dressel, Commander H., U.S.N. *210–11*
Drew, Monroe *227–8*
Drummond-Hay, Lady *186*
Dublin, HMS *125*
Dungeness, as landmark for German airship commanders *109, 110, 111*
Dürr, Dr Ludwig *168*
Düsseldorf, German airship base *69, 75, 241*
Dynairship (lifting body airship) **231**

Eagle **23**, *26, 27*
early-warning system, British (First World War) *90–1*
Eckener, Dr Hugo, writes article on LZ.1 *54;* on LZ.2 *55;* meets Zeppelin *55;* on loss of LZ.4 *58;* joins Zeppelin Company *60;* becomes airship pilot *61;* in 1916 **105**; advises against proposed transatlantic flight by L.72 *148;* takes LZ.126 to Lakehurst *158;* negotiations with Burney *161–3;* in middle age **162**; plans LZ.127 *168–9;* commands LZ.127 *181–9, 192, 211–12;* on *Hindenburg* disaster *216*
Edinburgh, bombed *96, 97, 257*
Edward VII, King *44*
Egg, Durs *23, 26*
Ehrlich, Kapitänleutnant Herbert *113, 123–4, 133, 138, 142*
Eichler, Kapitänleutnant Franz *127, 129*
electrically-propelled airships *32–3*
Ellerkamm, Heinrich *129*
Ellsworth, Lincoln *171*
Engadine, HMS *103*
Ersatz Deutschland (LZ.8) *61, 240*

Ersatz Z.1 see LZ.15, LZ.19
Ersatz Z.2 see LZ.9
Esperia (*Bodensee*) *147, 148, 167*
Eta 70
Europa 224, **229**
Evère (Brussels), German airship base *73*

'Faith Fleet', proposed *227*
Farnborough, British Army Balloon Factory *43–4, 45, 47, 70*
Fitzpatrick, John *227–8*
Flemming, Kapitänleutnant Hans *133, 134*
forestry, airships used in *224–6*
France:
early experiments with hot-air balloons *15–18,* **19***;* with hydrogen balloons *16–20;* early airships and designs for airships *21–3,* **21, 23, 24,** *26–34,* **29, 30, 31, 33, 34,** *38–41,* **39, 41, 46,** *47, 49,* **50,** *63;* airships in First World War *69, 117–18,* **136***;* naval airship service formed *117;* army airship service disbanded *118;* surrendered German airships acquired *147, 148;* L.72 (*Dixmude*) lost *147, 155;* passenger services to Algeria and Brazil contemplated *155; Nordstern* (*Méditerranée*) taken out of commission *155;* naval air service disbanded *155–6. See also* airships: **French**
France, La 32–3, **34**
Frankenberg, Oberleutnant Kurt *109, 113*
Frankfurt, airship terminal *213*
Frankfurter Zeitung 54, 55
French, Field Marshal the Viscount *89, 90, 110*
Freudenreich, Kapitänleutnant M. von *133–4, 141*
Friedrichshafen *119, 137, 143, 157, 158, 181, 182, 183, 185, 186, 189, 192, 211–12, 213*
Friemel, Oberleutnant Kurt *134*
Fritz, Kapitänleutnant Hans *74–5, 84*
Fuhlsbüttel, German airship base *68, 74*
Furious, HMS *142–3*

Galatea, HMS *101*
Gambetta, Léon *32*
Gamma 45, 70
gas engine, first used in airship *31*
gas, natural, proposed use of airships to move **235,** *238*
German East Africa, and airships (First World War) *84, 135–9*
Germany:
early pressure airships *35–8,* **35, 37,** *47–8,* **47, 48,** *49,* **49,** *61, 69, 85, 242, 243;* early rigid airships *54–63,* **59, 63, 66,** *240–1;* airships in First World War *68–147, passim., 240–1, 242, 243, 255–60;* early post-war airships, *see* L.72, *Bodensee, Nordstern,* LZ.126 (*Shenandoah*)*;* intercontinental airships, *see* LZ.127 *128, 129, 130, 131;* post-1945 airships *224,* **225,** *226;* recent projects *224, 230–4. See also* airships: **German**
Giffard, Henri *9, 26–7, 28–30, 36;* his airships **24,** *27, 28–30,* **29,** *36*
goldbeater's skin, used for airships *23, 43*
Gonesse, balloon lands at *17*
Goodyear Tire and Rubber Company and associated companies *10, 49–51, 118, 156, 163, 169, 218, 221, 223, 224, 229, 244, 245, 246;* Goodyear airships (photographs) **50, 130, 209, 210, 222, 225, 226, 229***;* (drawing) *200–1*
Goole, bombed *80*
Graf Zeppelin (LZ.127) *10, 12,* **25,** *181–9,* **183, 184, 185,** *186–9, 192,* **193, 194,** *211–12, 213, 214, 216, 217, 253*
Gravesend, bombed *78*
Great Yarmouth, as target for German airships *74–5;* British air base *77, 80, 144;* as target for German warships *99–100;* L.21 intercepted near *113*
Green, Charles *21, 26*
Grimsby, bombed *79, 95*
Gross, Major von *48, 61;* his airships **48, 49,** *85, 242, 243*
Guldenring (*Underberg, Schwab*) **225**

Haenlein, Paul *31;* his airship **30**
Hage, German airship base *92, 96, 97*
Hall, C. M. *52*
Hansa (LZ.13) *61,* **63,** *240*
Hartford, Connecticut, test made at *32,* **32**
Harthoorn, Robert *234, 235*
Harwich, British naval base *87, 93;* Harwich Force *105, 106, 143, 146;* L.48 intercepted near *129*
Hearst, William Randolph *182*

helium *9, 10, 12, 156, 158, 159, 160, 208, 209, 212, 216–17, 228, 230, 237*
Hempel, Kapitänleutnant Karl *101*
Hendon, RAF Display at *193, 203*
Héroult, Paul *52*
Higgins, Air Vice-Marshal Sir John *194–5, 198*
high-altitude airships *10, 119–23, 125–6, 131–2*
Hindenburg (LZ.129) *12, 212–13,* **213**, *213–16,* **214**, **215**, **216**, **217**, *230;* catches fire *216,* **217**
Hipper, Admiral Franz von *83, 102*
Hirsch, Kapitänleutnant Klaus *78, 83*
Hitchin, bombed *111*
Hitler, Adolf *209, 212*
Hoare, Sir Samuel *163–4, 248–9*
Hobby (whaler) *173*
Holland Shipbuilding 234
Hollander, Kapitänleutnant Heinrich *132, 133*
hot-air balloons, early experiments with *15–16, 17–18,* **19**
Howden, British airship base *114 & fn., 149–50, 151, 154;* sold for demolition but afterwards bought by Airship Guarantee Company *164, 168;* R.100 built at *168,* **191**
Hughes, Mr B. R. V. *13, 236*
Hull, bombed *78–9, 92, 97–8, 107, 133, 141, 255, 258;* riots at *79;* airships engaged by AA guns at *97, 130*

Imperial Conference (London, 1921) *161*
India, projected airship service to *161, 162–4, 168, 181, 190;* R.100 not to fly to *168;* R.101 prepares for and attempts flight to *190, 192, 193–5, 197, 198–203, 204–6*
internal combustion engine, first use in airships *35–8*
Ipswich, bombed *77, 80*
Irwin, Flight-Lieutenant H. C. *204, 206*
Italia 173–80; flies over estimated position of North Pole *175;* crashes on return flight *176;* ship's company on polar flight *261*
Italo-Turkish War *48*
Italy:
early airships *48,* **48**; airships in First World War *69, 118;* acquires surrendered German airships *147; Esperia 147, 169;* SR.1 *156; Roma 156;* N.1 (*Norge*) *169,* **170**, *171–3; Italia 173–80, 261. See also* airships: **Italian**

Jamboli (Bulgaria), German airship base *136, 137, 138, 139, 144*
Japan:
acquires surrendered German airship *147;* LZ.127 (*Graf Zeppelin*) visits *187–8;* interest in post-1945 commercial airships *224,* **225**
Jeffries, Dr John *20*
Jellicoe, Admiral Sir John *103, 105, 106, 117*
Johnson, Amy *204*
Jowett, Sir William **206**
Jullien, Pierre *27;* his model airship **29**
Julliot, Henri *40;* his airships, *see* Lebaudy
Jumbo-jet aircraft (Boeing 747 and 747-F) **25**, *234, 235*
Jüterbog, German airship base *137*
Jutland, Battle of *102–4*

Kasumigaura Japanese airship base *187, 188*
kerosene-hydrogen engines *118*
King Stephen (trawler) *88*
King's Bay (Spitzbergen) *171, 173, 175, 176, 178, 180*
King's Lynn, bombed *75*
Kingston-upon-Hull *see* Hull
Kleve, German DF station *139*
Knorr, Ludwig *214, 216*
Kober, Theodore *54*
Koch, Kapitänleutnant Robert *103, 107, 111, 124*
Kolle, Kapitänleutnant Waldemar *134, 135*
Krassin (icebreaker) *179*
Kraushaar, Kapitänleutnant Hermann *125*
Krebs, Arthur *32–3;* airship designed jointly with Charles Renard **34**

Lakehurst, United States airship base *156–7, 158, 159, 182, 186, 188, 189, 192, 209, 213, 214, 219, 230*
Lana di Terzi, Francesco *15;* his design for an airship **17**
Langley Field, United States air base *156*
Lansdowne, Commander Zachary, U.S.N. *157, 159*
Lanz, Heinrich *62;* Schütte-Lanz airships, *see* Schütte
Larsen, H. Riiser- *171–3*
Lavoisier, Antoine *15*
Law, Rt. Hon. Andrew Bonar *163*
Le Berrier, Dr *26–7*
Lebaudy airships *40–1,* **41**, *47*

Lecke, Captain R. *144*
Leefe Robinson, Lieutenant W. *108*
Lehmann, Ernst *189, 212, 213–14, 216*
Leith, bombed *96–7*
Lmena Tail light vessel *144*
Leningrad, *Norge* visits *171*
Lennox, Comte de *26, 27; Eagle 23*
Lenoir, Etienne *31*
Leyton, bombed *80*
Leytonstone, bombed *80*
Liege, attacked by Z.6 *68*
Linkenhoker, Everett *228*
Linnarz, Hauptmann Erich *77, 100*
Lion, HMS *83*
Little Wigborough, L.33 descends at *109, 116*
Liverpool, as target for German airships *85–6*
LL-1 *224–6*
Lloyd George, Rt. Hon. David *163*
Locarno treaties *158, 168*
Loewe, Kapitänleutnant Odo *82, 86–8*
Lôme, Stanislas Dupuy de *31–2;* his airship **30**, **31**
Los Angeles, LZ.127 (*Graf Zeppelin*) visits *188*
Los Angeles (ZR-III, LZ.126) *157–9,* **158**, *186, 211, 219, 220, 244*
Lossnitzer, Kapitänleutnant Johann von *143*
Louis XVI, King *17, 18, 20*
Lowestoft, L.5 drops bombs near *76;* fishing smacks sunk off *92;* bombed *95;* bombarded by warships *99–100*
Luftschiffbau-Zeppelin, *see* Zeppelin
Lundborg, Lieutenant Einar-Paal *179, 180*

MacDonald, Rt. Hon. Ramsay *164, 165*
Macon (ZRS-5) *10,* **210**, *210–11, 219, 220, 244*
Maddalena, Major Umberto *178*
Mahenge, flight to, projected *135–8;* attempted *138–9;* airship recalled *138, 139*
Maldon (Essex), bombed *76*
Malmgren, Professor Finn *176, 177, 179, 261*
Malygin (icebreaker) *211*
Manchester Liners Limited *236*
Manger, Hauptmann Kuno *124, 130–1, 133, 134, 141, 142*
Marconi Company, and R.34 **150**
Mariano, Commander Adalberto *176, 177, 179, 261*
Marie-Antoinette, Queen *18*
Marquise, French airship base *118*
Mason, Monck *26*
Mathy, Kapitänleutnant Heinrich *76, 78, 79, 82, 86, 92–3, 93–4, 96, 105–6, 107, 110;* death of *111*
Maud, Lieutenant-Colonel Philip *30*
Maybach, Carl *58, 250;* Maybach engines and Maybach factory *58, 86, 92, 99, 122, 139, 250*
Mayfly **56**, *64–7,* **67**
McCord, Commander F. C., U.S.N. *209–10*
McCrary, Commander F. R., U.S.N. *157*
Meager, Captain George *156, 193–4*
Méditerranée (*Nordstern*) *147, 148, 155*
Mellow, Prosper, design by **59**
Mercer County Airport (New Jersey) *230*
Meusnier, Captain (afterwards General) Jean-Baptiste *21–2, 23;* his design for an airship **21**
Michael (pilot of Wölfert's airship) *35*
Mieth, Leutnant zur See *129*
Mills, Flight Sub-Lieutenant J. S. *78*
Moffett, Admiral William A., U.S.N. *209*
Montgolfier, Etienne and Joseph *15–16, 17–18, 21;* Montgolfier balloon **19**
Montreal, R.100 flies to *196–7;* moored at **189**, **197**
mooring masts *99, 150, 152,* **152**, *157,* **158**, **164**, *166,* **167**, **169**, **170**, *173, 188, 189,* **189**, *190, 193, 194, 196–7,* **197**, *199, 203, 204, 214–16, 219,* **222**, *224;* not needed for loading and unloading of projected cargo airships *227, 236, 237–8*
Morin (Bradsky's engineer) *40*
Morning Post 47
Morse, Professor A. N. *230*
Mowforth, Dr E. *235–6;* his design **232–3**
Munday, Captain A. H. *142*

Newmarket, bombed *100*
Nobile, General Umberto *14, 168–80,* **170**, *224*
Noble-Campbell, Lieutenant C. H. *142*
Nordholz, German airship base *68, 74, 85, 88, 92, 96, 97, 107, 113, 122, 134, 139, 143–4, 146–7*
Nordstern (*Méditerranée*) *147, 148, 155*
Norge (N.1) *169–73,* **170**
North British Rubber Company Limited *49–51*

Index

North Sea airships *114,* **138**
North Weald Basset, British air base *89, 111*
Norway, N. S. (Nevil Shute) *168, 248*
Norwich, bombed *82*
Nottingham, bombed *110*
Novosibirsk Conference (1965) *226*
nuclear propulsion, proposed for airships *230, 235*
Nulli Secundus (*British Army Dirigible No. 1*) *44–5,* **44**; *Nulli Scundus II 45*

oars, as means of propulsion for airships *21,* **23**, *26*
Olympia, Wellman's airship shown at **50**
Olympic Games *224*
Ostend, L.12 towed to *80;* as U-boat base *114*
Otto Dr H. A. *33*

paravane *161*
Paris Exhibition (1881), model airship shown at *32, 38–40,* **39**
Parseval, Major August von *47, 48;* his airships *47–8,* **47**, *68, 85, 242, 243*
passenger services, proposed by Comte de Lennox **23**, *26;* organized by DELAG *60, 61–2,* **63**; resumed after First World War but cut short by seizure of airships *148;* intercontinental, proposed by British *151, 161–8, 181, 189–208;* by French *155;* organized by Zeppelin Company and continued by National Socialist government *181–9, 192,* **192**, **194**, *211–16,* **213**, **214**, **215**, **216**; internal, international and intercontinental, possible future *226, 234, 238–9*
Pattison, Captain T. H. *142*
Pauly, John *23*
Pax 40
Pearl Harbor *218, 219*
Pernambuco, Brazilian airship station *192,* **193**, *211, 212, 213*
Peterson, Oberleutnant Werner *76–7, 86, 95, 96, 98, 108, 109–10*
petrol, first used in airships *35, 38*
Phaeton, HMS *101*
Pierce, Lieutenant-Commander M. R., U.S.N. *157*
Pilatre de Rozier, Jean *18*
Pippard, Professor A. J. S. *197, 199*
Pitzker, Felix *250*
Platen-Hallermund, Kapitänleutnant Magnus Graf von *74–5, 84*
Pohl, Admiral Hugo von *85*
Polaris missile, airship used to observe trial of *223*
Polignac, Duchesse de *18*
Pomella, Vincenzo *176, 261*
Portsmouth, L.31 flies over *111*
postage stamps, special issues *192*
Potters Bar, L.31 shot down near *111*
Pratt, H. B. *64–5, 67, 155, 161–2*
Priestley, Joseph *15*
Pritchard, Flight-Lieutenant J. E. M. *153–4, 155*
Pritchard, Second-Lieutenant T. B. *135*
Prölss, Kapitänleutnant Eduard *105, 106, 133, 134, 146*
Pruss, Max *213, 214, 216*
Prussian Balloon Corps *36, 52*
Pulham, British airship base *114fn., 150, 151, 152, 154, 166,* **167**, *171*
Pulling, Flight Sub-Lieutenant E. L. *113*
Purfleet, L.15 hit by gunfire over *95*
Pyott, Second-Lieutenant I. V. *112*

Quevedo, Torres *41*; Astra-Torres airships. *See also* airships: **French**

Ramsgate, bombed *77, 137, 255*
Recife *see* Pernambuco
Renard, Charles *32–3;* airship designed jointly with Arthur Krebs **34**
Richmond, Lieutenant-Colonel V. C. *166, 199, 207*
Riiser-Larsen, H. *see* Larsen
Rio de Janeiro *212, 213*
Ritchel, Charles F. *32;* his airship **32**
Robert brothers, the *16–17, 20, 22–3*
Roma 156
Rosendahl, Commander (afterwards Rear-Admiral) Charles E., U.S.N. *159–60, 186, 214, 248*
Rosyth, British naval base *92, 96, 102*
Rotherham, L.35 aims bombs at objective near *133*
Royal Airship Works *see* Cardington
Russia:
buys French airships *69. See also* Union of Soviet Socialist Republics
Rynish, Mr M. J. *236–7*

Sachsen (LZ.17) *61, 240–1*
St Hubert, Canadian air station **189**, *196–7*, **197**
Santos-Dumont, Alberto *38–40;* his airships *38–40*, **39**
Saundby, Captain R. H. *129*
Scapa Flow, British naval base *104, 147*
Scheer, Vice-Admiral Reinhard *85, 88, 100, 101, 102, 103, 104–6, 107, 130*
Schramm, Hauptmann Wilhelm *100, 108*
Schubert, Kapitänleutnant Otto von *101*
Schütte, Dr Johann *62;* Schütte-Lanz airships *62–3, 68, 76, 78, 79, 80, 82, 107, 108, 109, 116, 140, 147, 241, 242, 243, 256, 258*
Schütze, Kapitänleutnant Arnold *140*
Schütze, Korvettenkapitän Viktor *92, 96, 97, 98, 101, 103, 113, 122, 127, 130;* death of *129*
Schwaben (LZ.10) *61, 62*, **66**, *240*
Schwonder, Kapitänleutnant Roderich *134*
Scott (eighteenth-century designer) *23*
Scott, Major G. H. *151, 196, 204, 206*
Scunthorpe, bombed *86*
Sea Scout airships *70–2*, **71**, *114;* bought by French *117–18;* Sea Scout Twin *70;* Zero *70*, **71**
Seaton Carew, British air base *112*
Seddin, German airship station *92*
Severnaya Zemlya *174, 211*
Severo, Augusto *40*
Seydlitz (battlecruiser) *102*
Sheerness, L.13 met by gunfire over *93*
Sheffield, bombed *86, 110, 258*
Sheldon, John *20*
Shell International Gas Limited *238;* airship designed for **235**
Shell Petroleum Company Limited *161*
Shenandoah (ZR-I) *135, 156–7*, **157**, *158, 159–60, 244*
Short Brothers Limited *116, 149, 152;* Short S.23 flying boat **24**
Shute, Nevil (N. S. Norway) *168, 248*
Siberia, LZ.127 flies over *186–7;* hydro-electric power-station *226*
'Silent Raid', the *132–5*
Simon, Sir John **206**
Sims, Admiral William R., U.S.N. *117*
Skinningrove, bombed *82, 98, 133*
Sommerfeldt, Kapitänleutnant Erich *124*
Sora, Captain Gennaro *178, 179*
Southend, bombed *77, 255*
Southwold, bombed *76*
Soviet Union, *see* Union of Soviet Socialist Republics
Sowrey, Second-Lieutenant F. *109–10*
Spanner, E. F. *207, 248*
Spencer, Stanley *41*
Staaken, German airship base *137, 138*
Stabbert, Kapitänleutnant Franz *101, 125, 126, 131*
Stavanger, L.20 makes forced landing at *101*
Stowmarket, bombed *93–4*
Strasser, Korvettenkapitän Peter *74, 75, 76, 77, 79, 80, 82, 84, 85, 91–2, 93, 94, 98, 99, 100, 101, 102, 104, 107, 109, 110, 111, 119–22, 124, 125, 126–7, 129, 130, 131–2, 133, 135, 136, 137, 139, 140, 141, 142, 143–4, 145, 147;* death of *143–5*
Sudbury, bombed *94*
Sueter, Captain Murray, R.N. *64*, **65**
Sunderland, bombed *96, 257;* projected bombardment *102, 104, 106*
Sussex (Channel steamer) *102*
Swaffham, bombed *86*

Tay, Firth of, bombed *101*
Teed, P. L. *161–2*
Teller (Alaska) *172–3*
Tempelhof, Wölfert's airship crashes at *36*, **37**; Schwartz's airship crashes at *52*
Tempest, Second-Lieutenant W. J. *111*
Temple, J. E. *161*
Templer, Colonel J. L. B., R.E. *43, 44*
Thameshaven, bombed *94*
Thomson of Cardington, the Lord *164–5, 190, 195, 199, 202, 203, 204*
Timmy (dog) *206*
Tissandier, Albert and Gaston *32;* car of their airship **33**
Titina (dog) *176, 177, 179, 261*
Tondern, German airship base *87, 101, 139, 142–3*
transatlantic flights by airships: *America* (unsuccessful) *49;* R.34 *150–1;* LZ.127 (*Graf Zeppelin*) *181–6, 189, 192, 211–12, 213;* R.100 *196–7;* LZ.129 (*Hindenburg*) *212–16;* Blimp Squadron Fourteen *221*
Trumpf 225

Tyneside, bombed *79, 255, 257*
Tyrwhitt, Commander R. Y. *105, 106, 143*

U-boat offensive (First World War) *114, 117;* British counter-measures *70, 114–17*
U.19, carries Sir Roger Casement to Ireland *99*
Uecker, Wilhelm *129*
Union of Soviet Socialist Republics:
use of airships since 1931 *224–6;* development for forestry *224–6;* LL-1 *224, 226;* proposed development as freight-carriers *226, 234;* as passenger aircraft *230, 234*
United Kingdom:
early airships *41–7,* **42, 43, 44, 45, 46, 47, 56–7,** *63–7,* **66–7;** First World War *69–72,* **70, 71,** *114–17,* **115, 116, 119, 120–1;** airship bases (First World War) *70, 114;* German airship raids on (First World War); 1915 *79–83, 256;* 1916 (*Jan–May*) *85–6, 88, 91–101, 257;* 1916 (*July–Nov*) *106–13, 258;* 1917 *122–4, 125, 126–9, 130–1, 132–5, 259;* 1918 *141–2, 143–5, 260;* developments from 1918 *149–55,* **149, 150, 152, 153, 154,** *161–8,* **162, 164, 166, 167, 168,** *169, 181, 189–208,* **189, 191, 195, 197, 205, 206;** *Europa* built in *224,* **229;** proposed development of airships as Freight carriers **232–3,** *234–8,* **235, 239;** as passenger aircraft *238–9;* as troop transports *239*
United States:
early airships *32,* **32,** *49–51,* **50;** navy orders airships similar to British Sea Scout *118,* **130,** *244;* airships in First World War *118,* **130;** US naval airship ZR-I (*Shenandoah*) *156–7,* **157,** *158, 159–60, 244;* ZR-II (R.38) *152–5,* **154,** *244;* ZR-III (LZ.126 or *Los Angeles*) *148–9, 157–9,* **158,** *186, 220, 244;* ZRS-4 (*Akron*) *169,* **200–1,** *209–10,* **209,** *219, 244;* ZRS-5 (*Macon*) *210–11, 210, 219, 244;* ZMC-2 *220,* **220,** *237, 245;* US naval and military airships in 1935 and 1937 *220, 221;* US naval airships in Second World War and later *221–4,* **222,** *245–6*

Vaniman, Melvin *49–51*
Versailles
hot-air balloons demonstrated at *17–18, 19;* Tuatz. F (1919) *146, 148*
Vickers, Sons and Maxim Ltd and Vickers Ltd *47–8, 64, 67, 114, 116, 151, 161, 164, 168. See also* Airship Guarantee Company
Viktoria-Luisa 61, 240
Vossbyer, Professor A. G. *224*

Wainwright (Alaska) *172*
Wallis, Dr (afterwards Sir) Barnes *67, 116, 155, 161–2, 168,* **168**
Waltham Abbey, bombed *97*
Wann, Flight-Lieutenant A. H. *154*
Warneford, Flight Sub-Lieutenant R. A. J. *78*
Watkins, Lieutenant H. H. P. *129*
Wellman, Walter *49;* his airship **50**
Wenke, Oberleutnant F. *80*
Werther, Kapitänleutnant Paul *145*
West Hartlepool, bombed *112, 142, 260*
Westerham, bombed *109*
White, Mr Peter *236*
Wigan, bombed *142*
Wiley, Commander, U.S.N. *211*
Wilhelm II, Emperor *36, 44, 74, 75, 76, 79, 82–3, 126, 130*
Wilkins, Sir Hubert *186, 211*
Willows, E. T. (firm) *42–3, 70;* Willows airship (photograph) **43**
Wilson, Flight Sub-Lieutenant J. P. *78*
Wingfoot Lake, United States airship school *118*
Wittmundhaven, German airship base *143, 146–7*
Wobeser, Hauptmann von *80*
Wölfert, Karl *35–8;* his last airship **35, 37**
Wood, Flight Sub-Lieutenant C. E. *80*
Wright, Orville and Wilbur *9*

Yakutsk, *Graf Zeppelin* visits *186–7*
Yarmouth, *see* Great Yarmouth
York, bombed *101*

Zaeschmar, Kapitänleutnant Walter *142*
Zappi, Commander Filipo *175, 176–7, 179, 261*
Zeppelin, Ferdinand Graf von *52–63,* **53, 105,** *148*
Zeppelin Company, formed *54;* its airships. *See also* airships: **German**
Zeppelin Foundation, established *58*
Zodiac, Société *41, 118;* Zodiac airships *41, 69*